D0579927

THE ESSENTIAL BOOK OF GARDEN DESIGN TECHNIQUES

THE ESSENTIAL BOOK OF GARDEN DESIGN TECHNIQUES

*Your guide to basic design
ideas, essential skills and
garden improvement*

LIZ DOBBS   SARAH WOOD

MARSHALL PUBLISHING • LONDON

A Marshall Edition
Conceived, edited and designed by
Marshall Editions
The Orangery
161 New Bond Street
London, W1S 2UF

First published in the UK in 2001 by Marshall Publishing Ltd

Copyright © 2001 Marshall Editions Developments Ltd

All rights reserved. No part of this book may be reproduced
in any form or by any electronic or mechanical means,
including information storage and retrieval devices or systems,
without prior written permission from the publisher, except
that brief passages may be quoted for reviews.

Originated in Singapore by ChromaGraphics
Printed and bound in Germany by Mohndrock Gmbh

ISBN 1-84028-421-8

Produced for Marshall Editions by PageOne and Axis Design
Creative Director Bob Gordon, Siân Keogh
Editors Charlotte Stock, Marion Dent, Kim Davies
Art Editors Melanie McDowell, Tim Stansfield, Sandra Marques
Picture Research Nadine Bazar, Liz Eddison
Commissioned Photography Steve Wooster, Steve Gorton, Chris Linton
Photography Stylist Frances de Rees
Illustrations Karen Gavin, Vanessa Luft

For Marshall Editions
Managing Editor Anne Yelland
Managing Art Editor Helen Spencer
Editoral Assistants Dan Green, Ben Horslen
Proofreader Gwen Rigby
Index Dorothy Frame
Editorial Co-ordinator Ros Highstead, Gillian Thompson
Editorial Director Ellen Dupont
Art Director Dave Goodman
Production Nikki Ingram, Anna Pauletti

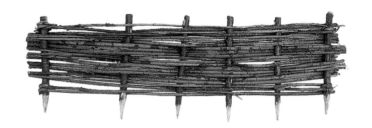

FOREWORD

Few of us have a "perfect" garden and, in any case, one person's idea of perfection in a garden is probably another's nightmarish tangle, and a third's sterile plot. Even if you begin with a totally blank canvas – perhaps you have bought a newly built house with simply a bare expanse of earth for a garden – you may be unsure what to do with it.

Most of us, however, neither want nor can afford to have our gardens designed, built and maintained by professional gardeners. Instead, we work with what we have, trying to fashion from the constraints of plot size, climatic and growing conditions, a garden that suits our personalities, interests and needs. What was appropriate for a young working couple is unlikely to function when they have to accommodate small children whose idea of a garden is a play space, or the ambitions of the middle-aged who are happy to spend time working in the garden, but also want enough hours left to enjoy it at their leisure.

Gardens evolve, not only as plants grow, but as those who use them age and change. This is one of the factors that make garden design and gardening so compelling.

ABOUT THIS BOOK

This book is for everyone whose garden does not match their garden aspirations. Whether you intend to attempt a complete redesign or simply want to know how to grow a few herbs to complement your cooking, you will find lots of practical information and advice in these pages. It is a book to dip into again and again as your wants and tastes change and your garden matures. We hope it will prove to be a handy reference, answering your gardening questions and solving your gardening problems.

Liz Dobbs

Sarah Wood

CONTENTS

Chapter 1

Chapter 2

Chapter 3

Chapter 4

Chapter 5

DECORATIVE PLANTING

Chapter 6

LOOKING AFTER THE GARDEN

Chapter 7

THE EDIBLE GARDEN

INTRODUCTION

This is a workbook for your garden that guides you from the first principles of gardening through planning, layout and simple building projects to garden techniques, starting with the soil and working upwards to trees and larger plants. Vegetable, herb and fruit growing are also covered, and there is a calendar to remind you what to do in each season. And, if the thought of all this work makes you tired, there are pages of inspiration to lift your spirits, with plenty of ideas, whatever your garden preferences.

Although the book is designed in chronological order, starting with design, it can also be used as a reference; either look up the chapter heading or refer to the index if you want to solve a particular garden problem or work on a specific area.

In chapter one, the two basic approaches to gardening – organic and chemical – are outlined; these will inform your garden practice. After this, you will learn to survey and plan the garden and to consider different solutions to different site situations.

HARD AND SOFT LANDSCAPING

Most gardens need some building work, so chapter two takes you through the basic techniques needed for paving and other building projects, together with general information on the best ways to choose and use materials for garden structures and hard surfaces. The most usual soft surface is a lawn, and this is the subject of chapter three – from treating a neglected lawn to laying a new one, with regular maintenance tasks to ensure a healthy lawn. In chapter four the most important element in any garden – the soil – is discussed, and you will find out how to determine what sort of soil you have and how to ameliorate any deficiencies, using compost or suitable additives.

If you are lucky enough to have good soil and a perfect lawn is not your priority, you will probably prefer to start planting. Chapter five looks at every

INFORMAL GARDEN
This striking garden uses contrasting shapes – the spiky leaves of grasses and cabbage plants (Cordyline australis) and the globe flowers of Allium spp. are contrasted with dramatic sculptures in natural wood tones to form a fascinating and vibrant composition, ideal for those who like a sense of informality in the garden.

aspect of planting, from planning a border and buying the plants, as well as the different types of plant and how they can be used. Trees and shrubs deserve careful thought, as the longest-lived of garden plants, and they get close attention, with tips on individual treatments and appropriate plants for each position. After this, you are ready to fill in with ground cover and lower-growing plants, or perhaps you would like to plant up some containers. Now that wildlife is understood to be such a vital part of our ecosystem, you may want to include a wildlife haven in your garden.

Once you've planted, the life of your garden begins. Now is the time to make sure everything grows happily from day one. Practical techniques are outlined in chapter six. Look up how to mulch your plants, systems for watering and weather protection, pruning and maintenance – and how to prevent common problems and work for the health of the garden. Simple methods of propagation are dealt with, from seed sowing to dividing and layering existing stock. If you have a cold frame, this is where you will find basic management techniques.

Food from the garden gives enormous pleasure, while being excellent for the diet: fresh-picked produce has a far higher vitamin and mineral content than shop-bought items. In chapter seven, you will discover how to plan a vegetable plot to avoid disease build-up and use its fertility to best effect. Techniques for growing and harvesting the different categories of vegetables and herbs are discussed, and fruit growing techniques are explained.

FORMAL GARDEN
Billowing wisteria and profusely flowering roses overflow the clipped lines of box edging in this traditional garden; this contrast is echoed by the profusion of herbaceous plants in the border, seen through the straight white lines of woodwork. The layout is formal, with focal points marked by a fountain and square containers of clipped bay.

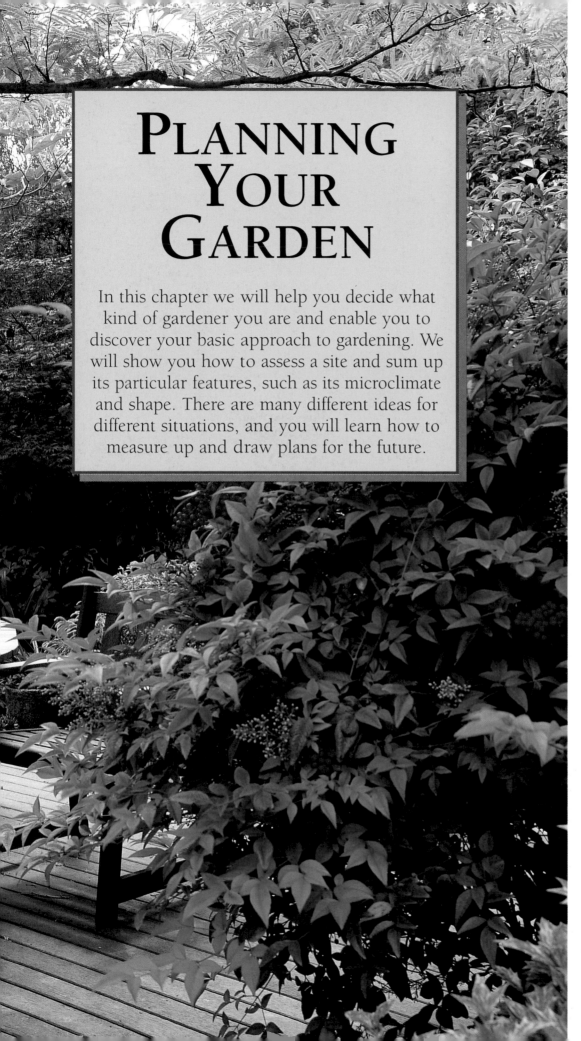

PLANNING YOUR GARDEN

In this chapter we will help you decide what kind of gardener you are and enable you to discover your basic approach to gardening. We will show you how to assess a site and sum up its particular features, such as its microclimate and shape. There are many different ideas for different situations, and you will learn how to measure up and draw plans for the future.

1

BASIC APPROACH

RIGHT PLANT, RIGHT PLACE

You will have more success with your planting if you choose:

Plants native to your area

A mixed-species lawn

In a dry garden, drought-resistant plants

To mix species roses with other plants

Try growing your vegetables mixed in with other plants, especially strong-smelling flowers like marigolds and nasturtiums. Nasturtium leaves give a sharp flavor to salads, and the bright flowers can be used as an edible decoration. A mixed planting is less likely to attract pests; different smells can confuse them.

There are several different approaches you can take to your garden, and working out your attitude will help you to decide how to plan the design (see p. 20) and the planting (see pp. 106–109) and also how you go about the work.

The aims of any gardener are to have good, healthy plants growing in the right place, flowering (or, in the case of the edible garden, fruiting or cropping) at the right time.

First of all, this requires design decisions as to where the plants are to go, and purchasing decisions on the plants or seeds themselves. After this, you will be making gardening decisions on the cultivation of the plants. Although there are two different basic approaches nowadays – organic and inorganic – the underlying principles are the same, and they are those of traditional husbandry, which was of necessity, until 50 years ago, organic.

ORGANIC GARDENING

In order to have healthy plants, you must work with nature, using the natural advantages of your plot and not trying to

force it. For instance, if you have light, chalky soil and an open site, you can grow wonderful pinks and many alpines – but will have difficulties with rhododendrons. Don't grow them.

Concentrate on keeping your soil healthy by copying nature, which never allows soil to be bare. Cover the soil's surface and build up its fertility and structure with organic mulch. Mulch will also help to keep the weeds down and moisture in.

Grow a good range of plants in conditions as near to their natural habitat as possible. To take the example of rhododendrons again – these come from wooded areas and like semi-shade, while lavenders and rock roses like hot sunshine and dry soil. Grow a range of plants together, rather than a concentrated area of one crop – a monoculture. Try companion planting in the vegetable garden, using strong-smelling plants such as onions or leeks to ward off carrot fly, for instance. Allow some daisies and buttercups in your lawn – and let your grass grow to its optimum height (see pp. 86–87).

To deal with pests, encourage the balance of wildlife by planting native varieties and plants that offer food or shelter wherever possible. Natural predators such as ladybugs can be harmed by pesticides, and poisoned slugs, for instance, may be eaten by birds or small mammals, which can then build up a dangerous level of poison themselves.

INORGANIC GARDENING

The other basic approach is inorganic, and if you have a special interest such as prize dahlias, or perfect roses alone in a rose garden, or if you want a green velvet lawn of putting-green standards, you will have to use chemicals, because all of these interests tend to work against nature. Any plant grown on its own as a monoculture will attract a disproportionate number of pests and

Roses provide a long-lasting and reliable show of flowers. However, a monocultural bed is prone to pests and diseases. If you want to grow roses on their own in a formal display, you will either have to work hard at soap-spraying aphids and removing diseased leaves, or you will have to spray intensively.

diseases, be it a perfect lawn made up of only certain selected grasses, or any other plant grown alone. In theory, it is possible to hand-weed your lawn and rake out all the moss – in practice, except on a small lawn, chemicals are the quickest and easiest answer. Similarly with roses: you can have moderate success using soapy water against the greenfly, and nipping off rust-infected leaves, but for most varieties you may have to spray chemicals.

You will have to take this approach to gardening if you are determined to have a particular garden style that, following tradition, includes plants that are not suited to your climate or soil. For example, delphiniums are grown in English cottage gardens and perennial borders. Unfortunately, they do not take well to the high heat and humidity of summers in much of the United States. To grow them in these adverse conditions requires more time and care.

Classic examples of growing plants in a soil or climate that does not suit them include planting acid-loving azaleas in alkaline soil, and growing moisture-loving plants in a dry, Mediterranean climate, or growing plants that require winter chill in frost-free areas.

REDUCING THE WORK LOAD

Whether you grow organically or not, a low-maintenance garden can save you time and effort. The key is to keep the plan simple and cover the ground with planting or mulches. Avoid fussy little beds; combine them into one. The lawn edge should be straight or a gentle curve, for easy mowing; either remove solitary trees or shrubs that need mowing around, or surround them with long grass and bulbs and mow once a year.

Grasses planted in conditions that suit them can be very low-maintenance plants. Their appearance is good throughout the year; the dry winter stems have attractive sculptural qualities. Cut back plants in spring, when the new growth has started.

MAKING THE MOST OF YOUR SITE

PLANNING TIP

When you are choosing a style for your garden design, try to visit as many gardens as possible to gather ideas and see what you like. Don't forget to consider the style of your house and landscape. The formal avenue from a country house may not translate to a suburban garden, but the plant combinations may.

This powerful formal design needs careful placing. It is appropriate for a separate enclosed garden, but will not suit a suburban or cottage-style home—even the large red-tiled house in the distance is slightly out of place. The ideal house would be starkly modern or colonnaded classical.

In order to have a garden that suits you, it is important to find out what you want from your garden, and to learn as much as possible about your site.

Think about how your garden fits into your lifestyle. Is it something to look at out of the window – a living picture – or will you spend time sitting outside? Do you have children who need a play area? Do you entertain a lot? Use a range of simple questions to ascertain your particular needs.

ASSESSING YOUR NEEDS

After this initial analysis you are ready to experiment. Together with your observations on the microclimate (see p. 16), you can work out the best place for different garden elements. If you want to have barbecue parties, you'll need a good-sized patio, access to the kitchen, and protection from wind. Use some stakes to mark out the space, and take some chairs out. Arrange them, sit in them, and see how it feels: Should it be

larger or smaller; do you need a screen here because you are overlooked; would a flower display look good?

If you want to change the shape of the lawn, and you prefer a rounded shape, a garden hose is easy to use – simply lay it out in the desired shape and, again, try it out for size. You can use a hose together with some stakes and string to mock up a length of trellis, for instance, or if you've been doing some cutting back, put some branches in at strategic points to act as shrub shapes.

FINDING THE RIGHT PLACE

The system of stakes, hose, and any other necessary props can be used over a period of time to define your new layout. Don't be in too much of a hurry – you need time to get used to the new design. Sit out where the new arbor will be and decide whether you like the view, or if it is blocked by that large forsythia bush that you've been wondering whether to take out, for instance. Is the

A patio corner takes on the appearance of a jungle by using dense, green plantings. Here, hostas and ferns grow next to a rush fence and crowd up against a wooden table that echoes the surrounding decking.

compost heap placed just too far away for convenient use? Does it need a path to it? Is the laundry line in full sun? Sit inside and look out of the window. Is the view as you've planned it, or do you need a focal point to draw your attention to it, or a framework of shrubs to enclose it?

YEAR-ROUND PLANTING

Now is also the time to take stock of your plants. The best way of studying what you have is to wait for one whole year, making notes of what flowers when, and where the gaps are. Is there a good evergreen structure in winter, for example, and what about the shape of the plants? Flowers are fairly fleeting, but the form and foliage effect will be with you all the time. If you don't have the time or patience for this tried-and-tested method, and you have knowledgeable

friends, invite them around. Ask them to identify what you have, and then look up each plant in a book.

Go to the local garden centre for advice, or ask a professional garden designer for a consultation – this could save time and money in the long run. Ask for a recommendation or a list of local designers from a professional organization of landscapers, gardeners, or landscape designers. Phone one or two and say that you would like a consultation; tell them the size of the garden and (roughly) how densely planted it is. Find out how much they charge per hour, whether expenses such as travelling time are included, and how long a consultation is likely to take. The best time to have the consultation is early summer, when deciduous plants will be in leaf, but the garden will not yet be in completely rampant growth.

This extraordinary collection of conifers was clearly planted too closely together. An inventive solution has been to chop them down to size and then to keep them clipped into various shapes and sizes. Their background colours of yellow and green are contrasted with the bright red roses.

MICROCLIMATES

POINTS TO WATCH FOR

A gap in the hedge that lets through the prevailing wind

The dry soil at the base of the house wall

The dip at the bottom of the garden where the frost collects

The waterlogged patch on the lawn

SEE ALSO

All kinds of weather
See *Gardens in different climates, pp. 18–19*

Just as one part of a country will have a climate a little different from the next – perhaps windier because it is higher, or tending to get earlier frost because of the configuration of the hills – so your garden will have different climates in different areas. These are known as microclimates, and they are caused by similar factors.

Near the house, for instance, it is warmer because of the shelter of the house walls, which reflect heat if they face the sun all day. The beds along the walls are thus warmer, but also drier, because they are overhung by the building. This microclimate is relatively warm and dry, so you can grow slightly more tender plants here than you can elsewhere in the garden, but you have to plant them away from the wall or water them regularly to keep them healthy. A north-facing wall, or one with houses close by that cast shade, will have low light levels, which is another aspect of its microclimate. Plants that thrive in woodlands, under the dry shade of trees, such as *Epimedium* or *Cyclamen hederifolia*, will be happy in this type of situation.

BUILT-UP AREAS

In towns, the microclimate is noticeably warmer than in outlying areas, due to the accumulated effect of the heat from buildings

Herbs are generally well adapted to sun and like good drainage, and these pots catch what sun there is in a shady garden. The pots allow easy drainage, but you must remember to water them regularly. Mint, in particular, likes more moisture than many herbs.

To thrive in seaside gardens, plants need to withstand strong winds, salt spray, and often harsh sunlight. Here Cordyline, Roman, and tussock grasses enjoy a coastal habitat.

and streets, but the light levels are much lower. Even if you think your town garden is sunny because it is hot when you sit outside, the chances are that it gets direct sun for only a few hours a day. This may explain, for example, why your roses don't do as well in the back garden as the front, where the wide open street gives them extra light all day.

SLOPES AND VALLEYS

If your garden is sloping, perhaps the top of the slope is drier, and the bottom collects the rain in puddles where the soil becomes sticky and hard to work in winter, especially where the sun doesn't reach it. Add to this the prevailing wind, which cuts across between a gap in the hedge and blows full on the upper level, and you have two distinct microclimates: One sheltered, damp, and shady and the other drier, exposed, possibly sunnier, but windy. The wind that dries your laundry so quickly can have a devastating effect on plants because they lose moisture from their leaves more rapidly than they can draw it up from their roots. Wind turbulence is another element in different parts of the garden. A partial windbreak such as a hedge or a trellis screen will slow the wind, but a solid barrier such as a brick wall, or even a close-woven fence, will compress the force of the wind so that it swirls over and creates a turbulent spot on the other side, flattening plants in the process.

On the other hand, if the lower part of the hill forms a valley, it may be a frost pocket that collects the frost on winter mornings as it rolls off the hill. This effect is not confined to large areas – it works on a small scale, and you can even feel the difference in temperature, particularly on a cool, still evening as you walk down the slope.

ASSESSING MICROCLIMATES

Start to notice which parts of the garden are in sun at different times of the day and year. If there is a prevailing wind, see what direction it comes from. Is it sufficiently

strong to bend the trees in one direction? Are there fences or walls to cut it, and if so is there turbulence at the base of the wall? Are there some places that are particularly exposed or sheltered? Are there some beds that dry out completely in summer, or a patch of lawn that is waterlogged in winter?

Dealing with your microclimates is a combination of enhancing the good points and minimizing the effects of the difficulties. Plant up a gap in the hedge, or if you value the view, place a trellis to cut the force of the wind and protect certain areas. Use this information as you plan your garden: You want a good breeze to dry your clothes, but not to sunbathe in. The pond will be sited at the bottom of the slope; not only would it look ridiculous and unnatural at the top, but the waterside plants will like the damp soil and the shelter in this area.

Many plants adapted to shady conditions have big, broad leaves to catch any light there is, such as the beautiful hosta species in this dark garden. However, in a mild climate, hostas can be plagued by slugs. Maple (Acer) and box (Buxus suffructicosa) are also happy in shade.

GARDENS IN DIFFERENT CLIMATES

PLANTING SUGGESTIONS

Generally, it is easier and more effective to follow the natural vegetation of your area when selecting plants (see p. 12). You don't have to restrict your choice to native species, but go for those that come from a similar climate. Mediterranean-type plants, for example, thrive in a dry, sunny climate with mild winters, and many South African species will grow happily in these conditions.

The Himalaya mountains are home to many rhododendron species – they look good when combined with bluebells in a woodland garden. The difficulty comes in trying to grow plants that need a rich, moist soil (such as hydrangeas), together with grey-foliaged plants, many of which prefer a well-drained soil. It is not possible to satisfy both plants, so one of them will suffer – probably the one that is least suited to the natural conditions in your garden. Problems can be overcome by a judicious use of tubs and pots, where the type of soil, and its irrigation, can be more easily managed.

Gardens have different functions and even different meanings in different climates. The lush, shady courtyard garden with trickling fountains will be an idyllic refuge in a hot, dry desert region, but depressingly damp in a temperate climate. Think, as always, about its practical use: do you need shade from the sun or shelter from the wind; is it too hot or cold to sit out in the open; or can you expect to eat many of your meals outside? All of these factors will help define the style of your finished garden.

◄ BLENDING IN
This is a perfect example of using an area's natural vegetation. Tussock and other grasses form the main body of this planting and blend imperceptibly into the flowing grassland behind. Other perennials are added to give a variety of form and colour, but the grasses define the garden's overall style and effect.

▲ COASTAL SITE
The brightly coloured perennials suit the sharp light of this bayside garden, and are low enough to withstand strong winds.

◄ DRY CONDITIONS
These succulent plants, such as cacti, palms and agave, fill the garden and are well suited to the dry soil and desert climate.

◀ SEASIDE
GARDEN
A strikingly crafted
wooden seat has
a strong enough
shape to balance
the breathtaking
view of this seaside
pool garden.
Nothing more is
needed than the
simplicity of the
rocks and a spiky
potted plant on
the stone paving.

▼ FOREST RETREAT
A sturdy wooden
table and benches
are appropriate for
the clearing in this
woodland garden.
A witty touch is
provided by the tiny
potted trees, echoed
by the tall stand of
forest behind them.

▲ DENSE CANOPY
The deep shade of tall trees and the moist,
humid atmosphere account for the lush
growth of these temperate rain-forest plants.

DESIGNING YOUR GARDEN

YOU WILL NEED

Pen and pencil

Coloured pencils

Ruler

Rubber

Scrap paper

Grid paper

Tape measure

SEE ALSO

The first steps
See *From design to garden, pp. 22–23*

Taking shape
See *Designs for different shapes, pp 24–25*

Sun or shade?
See *Designs for different sites, pp. 26–27*

Best use of space
See *Design solutions, pp. 28–29*

When you are planning your garden, think about the overall style you want to create. You may have started to build up an idea of this while answering the practicalities questionnaire. For example, if you want a large patio and a wide, open lawn, you are probably not keen on a wild and overgrown look. Thinking about this now will make it easier to make decisions that add up to a consistent appearance rather than a muddle of last-minute choices. Your planting and garden furniture should all complement your chosen style.

It may help to think about your taste in interior decorating. You probably already have a clear idea of this. Is your preferred look rather formal and tidy, or sharply modern, for instance? The same preferences are likely to show in your taste in gardens. If you are neat and tidy, then a wild garden may not be for you. Or perhaps you would enjoy the contrast between house and garden.

A mixture of styles can have pleasing results. Here a clean-edged formal lawn contrasts with an expressive border.

STYLE CHECKLIST

Look at the styles below to build up your own composite for your ideal garden. Add your own variations – for example, modern architectural might be meditative, entirely natural and simple, or could use new man-made materials and strong colours. Formal might be grand and impressive, or the severe lines and stonework could be overgrown with romantic climbers. And remember: the rules are there to be broken.

STYLE	HARD LANDSCAPING	OTHER FEATURES
Cottage	• Straight brick or gravel path, simple wooden arch, trellising, picket fence.	• Box edging, espaliered fruit trees, wooden furniture.
English country	• York stone paving, summerhouse.	• Herbaceous borders, yew hedges.
Modern architectural	• Decking, concrete paving, brightly stained wood trellis.	• Stainless-steel sculptures, sculptural plants, modern topiary.
Formal townhouse	• Straight lines, stone paving and steps, arbour or pergola.	• Clipped evergreen hedges, modern topiary in containers.

DRAWING UP A SITE PLAN

1 Draw a rough outline of the garden and the house on a piece of plain paper. Go into the garden and measure the full length and then the full width, jotting these down on your rough plan. Mark the house walls and any garden buildings.

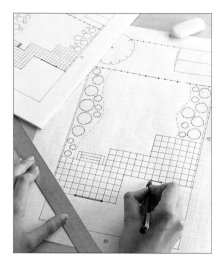

2 Use gridded paper, with one square to represent one square metre or square yard. Now draw the garden outline to scale, and then the walls of the house. Measure items such as ponds and pergolas, then the lawns and beds and any large plants. Add them to the garden plan.

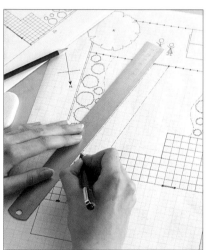

3 Mark the principal compass points. This will help to show where the sun shines in the garden. Then mark power supply points and access. Add any microclimate notes you have gathered, and note the use your family makes of the space, such as a shortcut straight across the lawn.

4 When you have worked out the changes you wish to make, you are ready to draw up the new plan. Place tracing paper over the map of the present garden and draw the outline of your new garden. Omit any unwanted items and add the new elements.

A scrapbook of colours, favourite plants and inspiring gardens will help you to formulate your individual style.

GATHERING IDEAS

The best way to get ideas is to talk to friends – visit their gardens and see what would work for you. Collect magazine pictures of gardens that appeal to you, and try to identify what it is that attracts you, whether it is the colours or layout, or perhaps it is just a pretty picture. Some of your favourite gardens may be open to the public, and this is an ideal opportunity to deepen your familiarity with a particular style. Try to see how your favourite effect is achieved – there will probably be several ingredients. The casual, almost accidental look of a cottage garden is nearly always set against simple straight lines of box edging or paths. Italianate formality is achieved with balustrading and steps – but the width of the step is what gives it the necessary scale and grandeur. Garden owners are often delighted to explain how they attained an effect, and will tell you what worked and why, saving you much time and effort.

FROM DESIGN TO GARDEN

WORK SCHEDULE

Clearing

Repairs

Marking out new design

Building structures

Lawn and bed shapes

Preparing soil

Planting

HANDY HINTS

Wear protective clothing when tackling heavy work, and cover arms and legs as a precaution against cuts and bruises.

Rent equipment for heavy work – a brushcutter with metal blades will handle brambles and rough growth, and a winch will pull out trees and roots. Always read instructions carefully before using equipment, and consider hiring an operator with the equipment – it may be quicker, safer, and more economical.

Now that you have your plan, and you've tried out various mock-ups with tape and string in the garden (see p. 14), it is time to work out how to make it a reality. These are the stages in a garden-building programme; depending on your budget and the time available, you may have to tackle things at different times, but following this order avoids damaging work already done.

CLEARING THE SITE

Before you start, you will need to do any clearance necessary to put your plan into effect. You want as clear a space as possible to do the work, which will inevitably involve a certain amount of mess. Consider what access there is to your garden. If it is through the house, then take precautions – it is unwise to have a new carpet laid just before

Sometimes it is hard to decide which shrubs to move or to keep. The brilliant pink fruits of the spindle tree (Euonymus europaeus) and bright red rose hips make a delightful fall picture. Keep them if you can in a wilder corner of the garden.

If you have a sense of fun and fantasy, you can use pieces of scrap metal and shape them into sculpture. This garden has been created with an intricate layout of wonderful shapes and curves in beds and topiary. It requires a lot of work in maintenance, including lawn edging and hedge clipping, but the effects are fantastic.

garden work, for instance. Where will you store materials? Can a delivery be made right into the garden, or will you have to wheel it through your house? Do you need to clear a bed to store topsoil from digging out the patio? Is there space for a pile of aggregate? Planning now can save extra work later.

RECYCLE GARDEN WASTE

Clearing may mean removing overgrown shrubs or trees (for a large tree you may need to employ a tree surgeon) and other unwanted plants. Always remove the roots of plants and the stump of any tree, or they will sprout and cause more work later. Put the green waste on the compost heap and rent a shredder for woody growth. This will provide useful wood chips that can be used as a mulch. Clearing away any old paths or rubble heaps will produce foundation for your patio, but probably a lot of unusable rubbish as well. For a large amount, you will need to rent a skip. Repairs to fences and garden structures are worth doing at this stage while the garden is clear.

ADDING STRUCTURE

When the site is clear, mark out the new design. Use pegs and string or bricks to mark out shapes, and bear in mind that they will have to be visible for a while if you take some time to build the garden.

Build any fences or boundary structures first, before other construction takes place. If you need to move a tool shed, or you are buying a new one, now is also the time to make the concrete base (see pp. 36–37). You can move an existing toolshed immediately; a new one can be assembled on delivery. Other permanent structures should also be tackled at this point, starting with the ground work of patio and paths (see pp. 38–39) or decking (see pp. 56–57). Garden features such as trellis screens and pergolas (see pp. 62–63) should also be done at this stage if possible, but you may need to leave them until after the lawn and bed shapes are clear,

so that you can be absolutely sure you are positioning them where you want them.

Mark out the shape of the lawn with a hose or spray paint, and cut out any new beds that jut out into it. You may be able to reuse the leftover turf if you are going to enlarge the lawn; otherwise stack the excess pieces upside down and leave them to break down into loam.

Dig over the beds and add organic matter (see pp. 94–95). Now you are ready to plant – trees (see pp. 118–119), shrubs (see pp. 138–39), ground cover (see pp. 146–147), and bulbs (see pp.152–153) in that order. After this, lay any new turf that is needed. Now you can begin gardening!

Hard landscaping is an expensive but permanent investment in your garden. It must be carefully thought out and planned, and installed before other work is undertaken. Remember that if there is no direct access to your garden, all equipment and materials will have to be brought in through the house. You will need to take care of carpets and paint work when having such work done.

DESIGNS FOR DIFFERENT SHAPES

DESIGN TIP

Decide what shapes you
would like for a garden,
and use that shape for
the lawn. Shape the
flower beds around the
lawn, not the other way
around. Build the flower
beds around an existing
shrub or tree, using it as
an anchor point.

SEE ALSO

The first steps
See *From design to
garden, pp. 22–23*

Sun or shade?
See *Designs for different
sites, pp. 26–27*

Best use of space
See *Design solutions,
pp. 28–29*

Awkward sites
See *Unusual shapes and
situations, pp. 30–31*

Gardens come in all different shapes and
sizes, and each one presents its own
unique opportunities and difficulties.

LONG AND THIN

The classic long, narrow town or suburban
garden can be dull, with its beds running
symmetrically down on either side, but this is
easy to remedy in various ways. You can
accept the straight lines and even emphasize
them in a formal style with stone paving and
straight edges to the lawns, culminating in a
focal point at the far end of the garden – a
statue, perhaps, or a fountain, framed in turn
with tall, narrow shrubs or trees. A trompe
l'oeil-mirrored doorway is effective in this
situation, though you may get tired of its
illusion after a while. For a less formal effect,
try breaking up the line of the garden, with
beds jutting out from either side, so that the
view to the end of the garden is interrupted.
The beds can be straight edged, or curved,
but avoid making them too intricate.

SLOPING SITES

Sloping gardens need different treatments,
depending on which way they slope, and
how steep the slope is. The advantage of a
garden sloping up from your house is that
it rises in front of you like a picture, whereas
with a slope down from the house, there
can be a feeling of falling away, and it is
important to anchor the house with a
substantial terrace. In either situation,
terracing will be necessary for a steep slope,
or a stepped path through the garden to the
end, with banked beds on either side, for a
less steep incline.

ADDING CURVES FOR EFFECT
*This long, narrow garden has been reshaped to add interest
and a sense of drama. The straight side beds have been
curved, bulging out around existing shrubs and a tree, and
curving right back into the side boundary, so that the garden
now flows down towards the focal point. This is positioned
at the end of the garden, half-glimpsed from the terrace
through the leaves of the tree.*

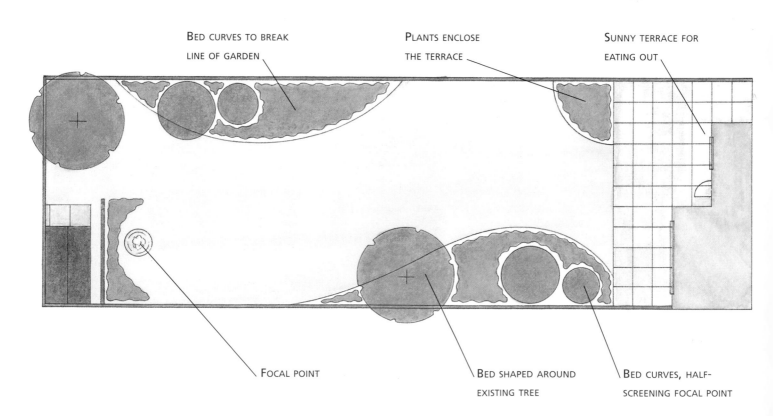

BED CURVES TO BREAK
LINE OF GARDEN

PLANTS ENCLOSE
THE TERRACE

SUNNY TERRACE FOR
EATING OUT

FOCAL POINT

BED SHAPED AROUND
EXISTING TREE

BED CURVES, HALF-
SCREENING FOCAL POINT

SHORT AND WIDE

A short, wide garden presents a flat appearance from the house and often lacks a focal point. To increase the sense of depth, give the garden as much length as possible, taking the lawn right up to the back wall in the centre, and develop the sides of the garden. You can do this two ways. Create smaller, separate gardens on either side, so that your centre garden becomes smaller but more interestingly shaped. Or, emphasize the side areas, using either a seat, a clump of trees, or even a distinctive large shrub arrangement to draw the eye away from the back of the garden.

GARDEN WITHIN A GARDEN
One solution to a square or short, wide garden, is to introduce a whole new garden shape within it. In this case, a meandering steppingstone path leads to a secluded seat enclosed by shrubs and a tree, and facing a small pond. This design has the added benefit of giving a separate, simple lawn area for children to play on, while adults can sit quietly out of range!

AWKWARD SHAPES

Think about the overall shape of your garden, and then use the shape to make it unique by turning what may be seen as a disadvantage into an advantage. Slopes can have seats at unexpected angles, or perhaps individual little gardens at different levels.

Long gardens can be mysterious when you can't see all the way down. They invite you to wander down to the end. Short gardens can have a bold centrepiece, but always remember to make the shape of the lawn attractive. Your eye will not notice the heart-shaped bed, only the place where the edge bulges out into the lawn. Shape the flower beds around the lawn, not vice versa.

MAKING THE MOST OF AN ODD SHAPE
The circular lawn is the strongest feature in this oddly shaped garden. It has the effect of "stretching" the garden to look as wide as possible by taking the lawn right up to the boundary. Shrub beds surround the lawn, while a small summerhouse is situated in one corner, with space for a tiny garden around it, making good use of an awkward spot.

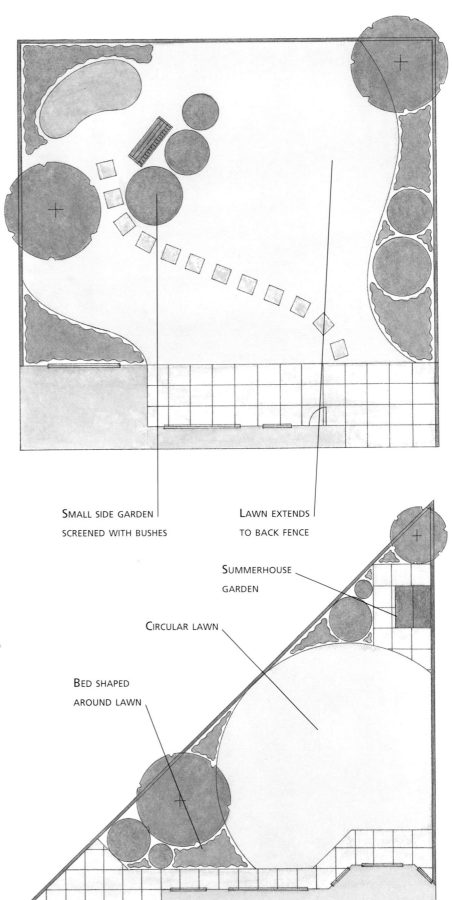

SMALL SIDE GARDEN
SCREENED WITH BUSHES

LAWN EXTENDS
TO BACK FENCE

SUMMERHOUSE
GARDEN

CIRCULAR LAWN

BED SHAPED
AROUND LAWN

DESIGNS FOR DIFFERENT SITES

MAIN POINTS

Work with the local environment, rather than trying to change it, and choose native species that will thrive in the growing conditions offered by your garden.

Remember that a tree is not only part of your garden, it also becomes part of the neighbourhood. Respect what else grows locally.

SEE ALSO

Best use of space
See *Design solutions, pp. 28–29*

Awkward sites
See *Unusual shapes and situations, pp. 30–31*

Plant sculptures
See *Creating shapes with plants, pp. 158–159*

When planning your garden, you need to take into account its environment and aspect. In a shady woodland valley, the only way you could achieve a hot, sunny Mediterranean garden would be to fell most of the trees, which is generally neither feasible nor desirable. It is far better to create a woodland garden with shrubs and flowers that are happy in these conditions. If you have acid soil, this is the ideal location for rhododendrons, which often look unhappy when people try to grow them in harsh sunlight on alkaline soil.

Think about whether you want to contradict or to blend in with your local area. If you live in a busy city, you may want a calm retreat. An enclosed courtyard garden, either formally planted with simple pots and paving, or overgrown like a jungly oasis, will give you the contrast and peace that you need.

The style of your house, too, will influence the design. A modern house can take exotic sculptural plants and abstract shapes, while a traditional farmhouse would be better suited with climbing roses and trelliswork.

BLENDING IN

If you can, it is best to accept the local environment and work with it; in this way you respect the "genius of the place", as the great 18th-century English landscapers recommended. This way your garden will seem to have grown naturally, rather than being artificially imposed on the area. In a country garden, either in a village or on its own, be careful in particular about what trees you plant. If the predominant native trees are mainly green, your striking purple plum tree or large yellow conifer hedge will be intrusive and unsuitable.

BLENDING INTO THE NEIGHBOURHOOD
The planting of white roses and green foliage blends well with the background of white boarding and trelliswork in this suburban garden. The cast-iron arbour provides support for more roses and adds a modern look.

DAMP SHADY GARDEN
This is the perfect design for a damp rain-forest garden, with a simple seat made from old logs and a backing of tree ferns and other shade-loving plants. The busy lizzies add a touch of colour, and are happy in bright shade.

VALLEY GARDEN
This valley garden tends to be damp, with less free movement of air than a hillside garden. Consequently, roses may suffer from mildew and other diseases, particularly when planted close together. The grey gravel garden is an attractive feature, but again it is not well adapted to this situation, being better suited to dry, sunny conditions.

DESIGN SOLUTIONS

MAIN POINTS

Use your site's advantages to best effect, focusing on the fabulous cityscape view from a roof garden, or disguising an ugly view of surrounding buildings in a suburban setting.

A front garden can say a lot about you – "boring" may not be the characteristic you want the world to infer.

SEE ALSO

Sun or shade?
See *Designs for different sites, pp. 26–27*

Awkward sites
See *Unusual shapes and situations, pp. 30–31*

Designing with plants
See *Styles of planting, pp. 112–113*

Hedge design
See *Styles of hedge, pp. 122–123*

All kinds of climbing plants
See *Choosing climbers and wall shrubs, pp. 126–127*

All gardens are different, but some garden situations require special thought and particular solutions.

FRONT GARDEN

Your front garden is your face to the world – do you really want to hide away behind a mysterious creeper-clad screen or hedge? You could have a winding path through overhanging bushes up to your front door, with glimpses of old statues, and groupings of magical ferns and shade-loving plants. Or say "Hello" to the neighborhood with a cheerful display of flowers. Bear in mind the style of your house – the front door to a town house is enhanced with formal bay trees in pots or urns on either side of the steps, whereas a beach house might look too formal treated this way.

ROOF GARDEN

You may have only a garden on the roof – in which case your views may be fantastic, but you will have to be careful of the weight of soil in any planting containers you use. A garden can be made with no plants at all, simply by the careful placing of stones and sculpture. Position these around the edge of the roof, never in the centre, and if in doubt, consult a structural engineer. Wind can be a problem in this situation – plan for wind screening with securely fastened trelliswork, and arrange your seating area in the most sheltered place. Generally, plants that withstand drought are suitable in this position – small leaves are best, since large floppy leaves will soon be torn to shreds. Grasses will be lovely, swaying in the wind.

WELCOMING FRONT GARDEN
This front garden is approached by short, wide tiled steps which take account of a sloping site and invite the visitor in. The clipped lines of the hedges and mass of greenery contrast well with the white walls of the house and its boundary.

SOFTENING AN UNWANTED VIEW

Distraction is often effective when your view is poor. One solution is to draw the eye away with a focal point elsewhere, such as a striking plant, a piece of sculpture, or a seat.

You could also reposition the seating area so that you don't face the view, and screen the view with planting. Partial screening of a view with a hedge or trellis may be effective. If an ugly tool shed is a problem, cover it with trellis and grow a climber over it.

Children's play equipment need not be made of bright plastic – there are many attractive wooden structures available.

ROOFS AND ROOFTOPS

This hilltop garden (left) has all the conditions of a rooftop, starting from a marvellous view and wind! The planting of narrow-leaved hebes, flax (Phormium tenax), and grasses is appropriate and blends well into the natural landscape. On an old wooden roof (below), houseleeks (sempervivum) form an evergreen cushion of lovely textures but be sure that the roof is strong enough to hold the planting.

UNUSUAL SHAPES AND SITUATIONS

PLANTING SUGGESTIONS

Take time to ensure that your garden plans are clear before you start serious work. Once you have decided how to treat your situation, follow this through to the style of garden (see p. 20), so that the garden structures, furniture and planting reinforce the picture.

In a modern city garden, for instance, you may decide to use paving and gravel – these lend themselves well to the use of contemporary garden furniture. Simple sculptures or even large rocks, carefully placed, and plants with dramatic leaf shapes will increase the effect.

If you are gardening on a slope, you can terrace it with brick walls or wooden railway sleepers – don't completely hide these with plants, but allow the structure to show through. At least a third of your plants should trail down the walls, with perhaps one or two taller plants to accentuate the dramatic effect of the slope.

Every garden has its own unusual features, and these present possibilities as well as difficulties – the solution you find will give your garden its own individual quality. In some cases you may work to disguise its shape, in others you may want to emphasize it. Work with the surrounding area as far as you can – an attempt at a rural look may be out of place in the city, but an abstract modernist design can look marvellous. Use the advantages, such as the seclusion of an enclosed garden or the splendid views from your rooftop.

▶ QUIET CORNER
The walkway to the secluded seating area, in a sheltered corner beside the house, is through a formally laid out garden, set four-square and defined by paved paths. The small acacia trees mark the center point of each of the four beds. The house's traditional style blends well with the garden's old-fashioned look.

▲ FORMAL APPROACH
This courtyard has a rather grand look, emphasized by the columns and the white cast-iron furniture. It provides an enclosed space, which then opens out on to an idyllic country view with the pool of water stretching into the distance.

◀ GARDEN SHADE
This country garden exudes peaceful tranquillity by the use of cool-coloured flowers, which contrast with the verdant lawn under the shade of a spreading tree.

▲ ROOFTOP GARDEN
With views such as this, there is no need for fussy detail. The rocks and gravel, set off by the decking, provide a feeling of calm.

◄ FRONT GARDEN
This charming and welcoming front garden catches the eye with a dazzling display of bright red geraniums, set off perfectly against the white house and picket fence.

► URBAN STYLE
The bold, modern design of this enclosed garden is well adapted to an urban setting, but would need very careful placing in the countryside. The use of straight lines and simple green planting emphasizes the starkness and simplicity of the whole.

▲ SLOPING SITE
This sloping site, with brick terracing and steps and plants trailing over the walls, incorporates white roses to accentuate the height and rhythm of the composition.

HARD LANDSCAPING TECHNIQUES

Hard landscaping, such as paving and decking, forms the basic skeleton of a garden. In this chapter we look at the different elements and their functions in the garden. We show you some basic building techniques that, once learned, can be adapted to suit your site or used as a base for more elaborate features of your plans.

BUILDING TOOLS

If you want to carry out simple landscaping construction, there is a range of tools that will be useful besides the usual garden equipment of rakes, forks, shovels, and spades.

PROTECTIVE CLOTHING

First of all, you need the correct protective clothing for whatever work you are doing. For any outdoor work, especially where stone or concrete is involved, you need heavy-duty work gloves and over-the-ankle boots fitted with steel toe caps. Protective goggles for cutting work, particularly with power tools or a bolster chisel, are essential to shield your eyes from any flying debris and clouds of dust. If you use power equipment, such as a power hammer drill, a face mask will protect you from flying splinters of concrete or brick and stop you from inhaling dust.

MARKING OUT AND CHECKING LEVELS

The first step in any job is measuring up and marking out. A 8-m (28-ft) steel tape measure is necessary for carpentry work, and a long, 30-m (100-ft) tape measure is also useful for large areas of paving. For marking out the area of paving or structure, use pegs and a string line. Flat-topped pegs are easier to use when you have to balance a piece of wood on top to check the level. You will need a long spirit level – a good all-purpose level is usually about 60 cm (24 in) long – to check the level of the site. Use this with either a straight piece of board or a string line and pegs. It will also be necessary for the uprights of fence posts or a pergola. You can now buy a spirit level that beeps when it is level. This is useful when you are working in muddy conditions.

FOUNDATIONS

You will need a spade for digging out, a shovel for lifting aggregate, and a heavy-duty builder's wheelbarrow with a pneumatic tyre. This will not collapse under the weight of building materials – do not use an ordinary garden wheelbarrow. For breaking up hardcore, a sledgehammer is vital. Get the heaviest one you can easily lift over your head to bring down and smash up old bricks and concrete. You will also need the sledgehammer for driving in the uprights of fencing and pergolas. If, on clearing the ground, you find really large pieces of concrete, or even concrete reinforced with iron, you will find it a slow, hard job to remove. At this point either rethink the project or rent industrial-strength equipment. Rent the largest tool that you can lift and manoeuvre because the larger it is, the faster and better it will be to work with. But you must be able to lift and handle it. Try it out in the store. A tamper is for consolidating your foundation. It is basically a heavy lump of metal on the base of a wooden handle, and you hold it in front of you with both hands and lift it up and down.

MIXING CONCRETE

You'll need your shovel for mixing and moving aggregate or ballast and for mixing up the sand, concrete and aggregate. You will also need a stout wooden board to mix it on.

For large amounts of concrete (more than 2–3 cu. m [3–4 cu. yd] at a time), consider renting an electric mixer, or contact a company that supplies ready-mixed concrete. You will need to move the concrete mix to its final position in a wheelbarrow – or a bucket for very small quantities.

CONCRETE BASE
FOR UPRIGHTS

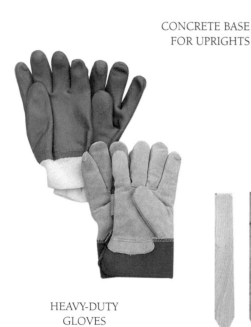

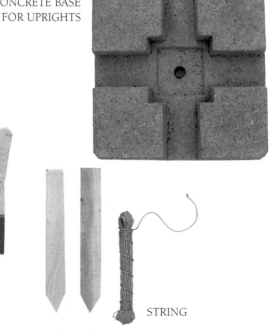

HEAVY-DUTY
GLOVES

TROWELS

BOLSTER CHISEL

POINTING TOOL

STRING

MARKING-OUT
PEGS

RUBBER
MALLET

Once the concrete is in position and roughly spread with a shovel, a wooden float is used to get an even finish.

LAYING MORTAR

For mortar for either slabs or bricks, you will need string lines to ensure that the bricks are level and true and also for laying the first line of slabs to make sure they are straight. A mortar trowel is used for placing the mortar on top of the bricks when you are laying them and also to lay mortar for slabs. There are several different sizes available, but either medium size or large is fine to use. A smaller pointing tool is available for pointing.

BRICKS AND SLABS

No matter how carefully you plan, there will always be some bricks or slabs that need to be cut to fit. Use a club hammer and a bolster chisel for this. The bolster chisel has a wide, flat blade, which gives a clean cut, rather than the shorter, narrow head of a cold chisel, which is better for knocking off the edge of a lump of concrete or old cement from a brick. A rubber mallet is useful for tapping slabs into position without damaging them.

WOODWORKING

You will need the basic tools for woodworking, such as a hammer and a saw – this should be used only for cutting wood or you will blunt it. You can use a cross-cut saw or rent a circular power saw – 23 cm (9 in) is suitable – for cutting thick, hard pieces of wood such as railway sleepers. The power saw will be quicker and easier. If you want to keep your toolbox simple, just use one type of screw and one screwdriver, either slotted or Phillips. There is no real advantage to one or the other. A carpenter's square is used for marking wood square or to a 45-degree angle. You will also need this for marking cuts on bricks or slabs. A bradawl is very useful for marking holes where screws are to go and for starting the hole, and a chisel or two are useful for cutting off corners and making joints.

You will need a power drill for making holes to put bolts through. A good all-purpose medium-size drill is a 400–600 watt multispeed hammer drill. This will get through most concrete and drill most holes. For anything more, rent a larger one. A drill is used for wood and also for drilling into concrete or brick, in order to attach pieces of wood or metal spike bases, or to fix posts and trellis to a brick wall. Together with the drill, you will need drill bits. There are two different types, one for wood and another, tipped with hardened steel, for drilling into brick or concrete.

G clamps (20 cm[8 in] is a good size) are used for holding pieces of wood together before you have drilled or fixed them. It is useful to have a pair of these, so that if you are putting up the bearers across two posts, you can use one at each end.

For any high work, such as pergola construction, you will need a stepladder. Lightweight aluminium ladders are best, 1.8–2.5 m (6–8 ft) high.

FIXING UPRIGHTS

When fixing fence posts or uprights for attaching trellis and other supports, you will need a metal spike that grips the base of the post and ensures a firm hold in the ground. Make sure you fit a purpose-made block on to the spike's metal casing so that you do not damage the casing when you hammer the spike into the ground. Interlocking concrete post bases offer a no-dig alternative, and are a good solution when working with heavily compacted ground that is difficult to dig.

SPIRIT LEVEL

SET OF INTERLOCKING CONCRETE POST BASES

PROTECTIVE SPIKE CAP

METAL POST BASE

METAL POST SPIKE

SLEDGEHAMMER

PAVING FOUNDATIONS

YOU WILL NEED

Protective clothing

Pegs, string

Spade, fork, shovel, garden rake

Long level

Boards, hammer, nails

Aggregate or rubble

Sledgehammer, tamper

Sand or ballast

SEE ALSO

Using tools
See *Building tools,*
pp. 34–35

Handling turf
See *Laying turf,*
pp. 78–79

Soil types
See *Identifying your*
soil type, pp. 90–91

A paved area is an essential for most gardens. When properly placed and laid, it is a trouble-free, all-weather surface that may be in use for most of the year. A paved area can also be one of the most expensive elements in the garden, so it is important to get the design and construction right.

The properties of different paving materials are discussed on the next few pages, but before you lay any kind of permanent paved surface you will need a good foundation. If the area is to be used for parked cars or storing heavy objects, than a stronger foundation will be needed. If your soil is sandy or gravelly, it may be possible to lay a few slabs directly on the earth, but this is not usually advisable, since it is unlikely to give you a good finish.

There are several disadvantages to laying paving directly on the earth. For example, the slabs will sink into the earth, especially after heavy rainfall and in areas of constant use. After a while, the surface becomes very uneven and tends to silt up, making the area muddy and slippery.

Drainage is an important consideration when laying foundations. The finished height of the paving must be at least 15 cm (6 in) below the top of the foundations of your house. Paving should always be laid so that it is gently sloping; the "falls" should be between 2.5 and 15 cm (1 and 6 in) to 2 m (7 ft). This ensures that that rainwater drains away from the house and is directed into the surrounding flower beds and lawns. To work out the depth that you need to dig, add together the thicknesses of a single paving unit and the base plus a minimum of 10 cm (4 in) for the foundation.

Fine rubble or stones, referred to as aggregate, are the main constituent of a good base, and allow rain to drain away freely. When it is well compacted, hard core makes a firm, strong surface that prevents any movement or sinkage. On top of this, a layer of finer material, usually sand or small pebbles (ballast) is laid and raked smoothly to fill in the spaces between the larger stones. This ensures that that the finished foundation surface is quite flat and even.

STORING TURF

Turf that has been lifted to make way for paving can be laid elsewhere to create a new lawn. It is also useful for repairing worn areas in your existing lawn and should prove to be a good "match". If there is no scope to reuse the turf, and you cannot find anyone to take it off your hands quickly – it will dry out fast, especially if the weather is warm – stack the pieces with the grass side facing downward. Large strips of turf are best rolled up, with the grass side facing inward. Cover the turf with an old blanket or carpet to keep out the light.

After about 12 months, the stacked turfs will have formed good usable loam that can be spread on your flower beds.

MAKING FOUNDATIONS

1 Using the plan that you have made for your patio, mark out the area of your paving with pegs and string, and clear away any obstructions. When the area is empty and clearly marked, stand back and look at the space to assess whether it is the right size and shape. Alter the layout as necessary.

2 Dig down to the required depth, keeping the turf, dark topsoil, and light subsoil in separate piles away from the area. Break up any large bricks or stones and remove any protruding objects. Check the slope with a level and rake out any dips and bumps or tamp the soil down.

3 Shuttering keeps the foundation in shape. Cut lengths of plywood or wooden board to fit the outside edge of the area. Drive in wooden pegs to hold the shuttering, and nail them to the boards. Remember that the foundation surface will be inside the shuttering and so will have slightly smaller dimensions.

4 Fill the area with a shallow layer of aggregate or rubble, and spread it over the area with a rake. Break up any large pieces with a sledgehammer, using it to tamp down and bed the pieces in. Repeat this process until the required depth of about 8 cm (3 in) is achieved, to allow for the sand or ballast.

5 Shovel on sand or ballast over the top of the aggregate base. This is the binding material, used to fill in the gaps and bind the foundation together. Spread the sand evenly over the area using a rake or wooden plank. Check the slope again with a level to make sure that the falls are in the correct direction and that there are no dips or bumps.

6 Tamp firmly or use a vibrating plate machine. This piece of equipment can be rented and will vibrate the foundation until all elements are settled and the surface is quite hard. Alternatively, leave the foundation for a week or two until it is rained in, or hose it down to draw the sand into gaps between the aggregate materials, then tamp firmly.

Laying large paving slabs

YOU WILL NEED

Spirit level

Protective clothing

Shovel, garden rake

Stiff broom

Mortar trowel

Rubber mallet

Plywood

Piece of hose

SEE ALSO

Using tools
See *Building tools*, pp. 34–35

Laying foundations
See *Paving foundations*, pp. 36–37

Planting in crevices
See *Planting in rocks and gravel*, pp. 148–149

Large units of paving, or paving slabs, are used to give a slightly more formal look than smaller paving materials. The classic pavement material is flagstone, but other natural stones include limestone, which has an attractive creamy appearance.

Plain concrete has a rather stark, streamlined appearance, but textured concrete is available in a wide selection of colours and sizes. Good-quality slabs that imitate stone are made from concrete and can be virtually indistinguishable from natural stone. Alternatively, you can opt for an unashamedly fake look and lay bright pink or apple-green slabs. The drawback to concrete slabs is that they are prone to frost damage and so wear away at the edges.

The traditional way to lay flagstones is on a sand base, using a keystone or small slab, around which larger slabs are laid. By repeating this process, you can achieve a pleasing pattern that avoids a continuous line of joints. Natural stone comes in many thicknesses, so you will need to increase or reduce the amount of sand beneath the slab to achieve an even surface. The stones are butted up close to each other and dry sand is brushed between the joints. This is a perfectly good method, but takes more skill than the spot-bedding mortar method shown opposite. Close-butted joints do not need to be filled with mortar, while larger gaps can be grouted with mortar or planted up with creeping plants such as thyme or pennyroyal.

Paving materials can be used to good effect in most gardens and are an ideal base for plants in containers. The regular edges can be softened by plants spilling over them.

Mixing mortar

Mortar for paving should be weak to allow for some movement. Some slight settlement is inevitable, and a strong mortar will simply crack. Use a mix of 4 parts sand to 1 part cement, and add plasticizer in the recommended amount to keep the mix flexible. Dry-mix the materials thoroughly, shaping them into a cone. Scoop out a hollow in the top and slowly add water. Mix again, gradually drawing the dry mix to the centre to make the whole mix moist. Keep adding water until the mixture is well blended – it should be slightly sticky but not runny. Make mortar in small amounts, otherwise you will be rushing to finish before the mortar sets (usually after an hour, depending on the weather). Avoid mixing mortar when the temperature is below 41°F (4°C).

LAYING SLABS USING MORTAR

1 Spread sand over your foundation surface. Use a spirit level to check the grading of the sand surface, making sure that it is sloping evenly in the direction you have determined. Add or remove sand as necessary, and rake it to a smooth surface.

2 Set the paving slabs out in alignment over the entire area. Make a chalk mark on any slabs that will need to be cut to fit exactly. If you would prefer not to cut slabs, consider a layout that allows for irregular margins or introduce occasional large gaps in the paving. These can be filled with plants.

3 When all the slabs have been set out to your satisfaction, prepare enough mortar to bed down the slabs. Take up each slab individually and place blobs of mortar on the underside: one at each corner and one in the centre. Lower the slab carefully back into position on the bed.

4 Using a rubber mallet, tap the slab gently into position to settle it on the mortar cushions. Check that it is in the correct position, aligned with its neighbours. Use a level to check that it is even with other slabs. Make sure all the slabs are sloping in the right direction and at the right angle for drainage.

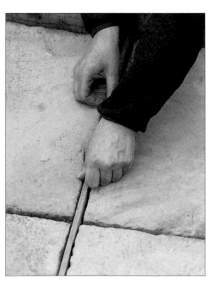

5 If you are laying square slabs that are all the same sizes, use slim lengths of plywood as spacers to keep the joints even between the slabs. Carefully adjust the slabs in line with the spacers so that the joints are even. It is important to keep the joints straight and regular because they will form part of the overall paving pattern.

6 Working on one section of paving at a time, take up some mortar on your trowel and lay it gently in the joint. Go over the mortar with a pointing tool, then repeat the process on the next section of paving. Brush off any excess with a stiff broom and wipe clean any spills.

LAYING PAVERS

YOU WILL NEED

Spirit level

Protective clothing

Shovel, garden rake

Stiff brush

Rubber mallet

SEE ALSO

Using tools
See *Building tools,*
pp. 34–35

Making shuttering
See *Paving foundations,*
pp. 36–37

Mowing edge
See *Caring for your lawn,*
pp. 84–85

Small paving units range from bricks, concrete and brick pavers, granite and concrete setts, down to differing types and sizes of cobblestone. They are ideal for use in small areas of paving or for irregular shapes, such as curving paths and rounded patios. Brick is perhaps the most versatile paving material; reclaimed stock bricks have a traditional, rustic look, while paving bricks or blue engineering bricks create a sharper,

more modern effect. Granite setts are also traditional in appearance but tend to be more uneven, which makes them uncomfortable to walk on and unsuitable for seating and dining areas. Although they are very attractive, cobbles have an uneven surface that makes tables and chairs wobble.

Where a hard surface is needed for purely visual effect, large stones are often used to deter pedestrians because they are difficult to walk across. Remember that uneven paving alongside a lawn is likely to damage mower blades, so insert a smooth edging strip between the paving and the grass to avoid this problem.

Many moulded paving systems are available, and are usually supplied with suitable edging bricks and curved elements.

Small paving units can be laid in two ways: either directly on a bed of sand spread over the prepared foundation or on a weak dry cement mix, which has the advantage of preventing weeds. Cobbles are placed upright, with the narrower end facing upward, and packed together very tightly.

Available in many colours, small, regular pavers, laid on a bed of mortar, make an attractive, hardwearing and low-maintenance surface for patios.

CUTTING BRICKS

To hand-cut bricks or slabs you will need a bolster chisel with a 5- or 8-cm (2- or 3-in) blade, and a hammer. Protect your face with goggles and a mask, and wear heavy-duty gloves. Mark the cutting line with a pencil or score the top of the brick with a nail. Place the brick or slab on a solid surface, such as an old paving slab, and tap the chisel to score a groove

along the line. Repeat the process on the other side of the brick. Place the bolster chisel in the top groove and hammer it hard several times. Work your way along the cutting line until the brick breaks in two. If you have a lot of cutting to do, consider renting an angle grinder with a stone-cutting or diamond-tipped blade. Mark the slab or brick as before and run the grinder along the cutting line.

LAYING SMALL PAVING UNITS

1 Working on an area of 5 sq m (17 sq ft) at a time, spread out the sand to a depth of 5cm (2 in). Using a spirit level, check the grading of the sand surface, making sure that it is sloping evenly in the direction you have determined. Even out the sand as necessary and rake the surface smooth.

2 Decide on the pattern (for example, basketweave or herringbone) in which you will lay out the paving, and set out the bricks. Start from the house or main wall and work outwards across the site, to avoid walking over your work. Check that the main lines are straight, and adjust the bricks as you go so that the joints are aligned and straight.

3 Use a trowel to fill the joints with sand, and brush it in carefully with a stiff brush. Tamp down the sand firmly, using a small piece of wood. You may need to add more sand if it is washed out after rain.

4 Place a wooden board across the bricks and hammer them gently but firmly with a rubber mallet. Be careful not to work too close to the edge of the paved area or you will push the bricks out of alignment. Keep a constant check with a spirit level, to ensure that the surface of the bricks is even.

5 Use wooden shuttering to hold back any edges that are not restrained by a wall. Once the paving is firmly in position, lay a concrete edging to stop the units from moving outwards. Angle the edging from just below the top surface of the paved area down to the base of the foundation.

Helpful hints

Jointing can be carried out with sand alone, or with a dry mix of sand and cement, using the proportions of 3 parts sand to 1 part cement. Make sure that the paving slabs are quite dry when using a cement mix, otherwise they will stain. Apply the mix with a stiff brush, and ease it into the joint. Leave the mix to set gradually or use a watering can with a rose to sprinkle water gently into the joints. When the mortar is dampened, run a piece of old garden hose or other piping over it to create a slightly recessed, smooth joint, which will harden.

USING CONCRETE

YOU WILL NEED

Ready-mix concrete

Concrete dye

Shovel

Wooden shuttering

Industrial grease

SEE ALSO

Using tools
See *Building tools,*
pp. 34–35

Laying foundations
See *Paving foundations,*
pp. 36–37

Concrete is one of the least expensive surface materials for a large area, although it is probably best used in utility areas rather than for decorative features. It can be poured in one block, but anything larger than 3 sq m (3 sq yd) or laid next to house foundations will need expansion joints. Concrete is easier to handle in small sections, so try to work in areas of up to

1 sq m (1 sq yd), which will give the effect of concrete paving slabs. These can be poured separately and allowed to dry before proceeding with the next square.

Concrete can be poured directly on a firm soil base, but it is wiser to lay a foundation first. If new concrete is to be poured on an old base, this must be thoroughly broken up and then treated as aggregate. For small areas, you can buy bags of dry ready mix, but this can prove expensive in large quantities. The most economical way is to buy dry ingredients in bulk and hand mix or rent a small mixer. Combine the ingredients, using a formula of 1 part cement to 5 parts ballast (sand and gravel) and 5 parts water.

For larger areas, consider having ready-mixed concrete delivered to the site. It is essential that all your preparation work is carried out before the delivery is made, and that you have sufficient help to lay the concrete within two hours. Areas larger than 3 sq m (3 sq yd) will need to be reinforced by mesh laid within the formwork.

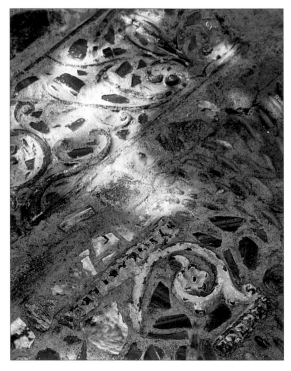

All sorts of materials can be pressed into partially set concrete to soften its potentially utilitarian appearance. They include cobblestones, pieces of broken china or ceramic tiles, and different-coloured rocks and gravel.

MIXING CONCRETE

Concrete is an extremely versatile material, and can be treated in many different ways. You can produce your own concrete "slabs" by making a wooden grid in a simple layout of four slabs. Oil the inside surfaces of the grid and pour in the concrete mixture, lifting the grid off when the blocks are partly hardened, and repeating the process until you have filled the area of your path or patio.

There is also a treatment that imprints a paving pattern on to partially hardened concrete; this is normally done by licensed contractors, but there is no reason why you should not experiment in your own garden. This technique will leave you with a complete block of concrete, since the grid does not penetrate right through; thus the potential weed problem is avoided.

For a large strip, expansion joints must be included.

The same principle of impressing into partially hardened concrete can be used for cobblestone pavings and also for patterns or mosaics. You can use attractive and different-sized stones, pieces of glass (but beware of splinters – upturned bottle-ends can be effective and safe), or fragments of brightly coloured china.

LAYING CONCRETE

1 Prepare the foundation, adding an extra 10 cm (4 in) to the dimensions so that they are slightly larger than the finished surface. Build a strong shuttering framework, using lengths of 2.5 x 7.5 cm (1 x 3 in) timber. Grease any dividers before installing them so they can be removed easily after the concrete has been poured.

2 If you are making coloured concrete, add the colour to the dry mix of sand and cement at this point. Mix up a shovelfull to test the colour, and let it dry. Make sure it is evenly mixed or you will have streaks in the finished paving. Mix in the gravel, then slowly add the water and turn the ingredients until they are well combined.

3 Pour the concrete from one end of the form, spreading it evenly with a rake or shovel. To level the concrete, rest a heavy plank on the framework and move it slowly across the surface in a zigzag motion. Any excess concrete can be removed in this way.

4 When the surface water has evaporated, drag a wooden float across the concrete in order to fill any small hollows and to smooth down high spots. Run the point of your trowel between the form and the concrete to make a clean edge to the area.

FINISHING

A ggregate combined in the concrete mix can be exposed to give a textured, pebbled finish. Once the concrete is almost set, hose it down gently and brush away the top layer of cement. The stones of the aggregate will remain in view on the surface.

Helpful hints

Cover the concrete with plastic sheeting or tarpaulins to allow it to dry slowly. This prevents the surface from powdering or flaking. Allow at least three days for the concrete to dry, or up to ten days during winter. In areas where the temperature falls below freezing, it is best to use a mix containing an air-entraining agent to minimize the cracking caused by alternate freezing and thawing. Once the concrete is dry, the new surface can be used for lightweight traffic and loads. Avoid placing any heavy loads on the surface for another two weeks.

For a non skid surface, brush the surface with a

STYLES OF PAVING

PLANTING SUGGESTIONS

Paving combined with plants looks great. Plants with strong shapes and colours or distinctive leaves work best. Spiky plants, such as *Agave* or *Cordyline*, are ideal; so too are pots filled with brightly coloured annuals. Paving can get very hot, so water potted plants regularly, moving them to a shady place if you go away. If it's difficult to remember to water, remove one or two slabs and grow the plants directly in the soil. This is easier, but less versatile, than using pots.

Gravel is an ideal medium for plant growth; a gravel path with plants growing through makes a charming picture. If you want to sit on your paving, however, you will need a solid surface. If money is scarce, use a smaller amount of hard paving, perhaps combined with gravel or railway sleepers.

A hard surface such as paving is one of the most important garden elements. It is often the most expensive, however, so it pays to get it right the first time around. If you are not quite sure what shape your paving should be in the garden, lay the foundation first, and live with it for a short while before laying the final paving. That way you can change it more easily if the area of paving needs to be larger or smaller. There is a great number of types of paving – from traditional bricks and stone to concrete – either in slab form or shaped into setts or pavers – and more unusual alternatives such as wooden blocks or railroad ties, which combine well with gravel to give a less expensive surface. Placing potted plants at strategic areas, putting plants directly into the middle of the paved area, or arranging the paving in a pattern will add variety to your garden.

▲ PAVING SETTS
This attractive, winding country path is made of concrete setts that have the appearance of real stone.

▲ RAILWAY SLEEPERS
Filled in with gravel, these sleepers create an informal setting. Self-seeding plants, such as candytuft and *Verbascum*, grow in small stones that reflect heat upwards.

◄ STEPPINGSTONES
Irregularly shaped stones, forming a path of steppingstones through the pebbles, are commonly used in Japanese gardens. They look particularly attractive after rainfall.

◄ SIMPLE PATIO
The simplicity of the tiled surface is lifted by its decorative edging of blue and red zigzags. The pots, painted with bright primary colours and filled with strangely shaped cacti and other sun-loving plants, complement this unconventional treatment. Perched above the seat is a bright blue fringed umbrella that echoes the strong colours in the rest of the garden.

▲ PAVED SPIRAL
A spiral shape, in different sizes and colours of stone, forms a centrepiece; the rest of the garden's design follows from it.

► PAVED STEPS
The wooden risers are darker in colour than the treads, so are clearly visible. The horizontal line forms part of the steps' design.

SIMPLE PAVED STEPS

YOU WILL NEED

Sledgehammer

Wooden stakes

Concrete slabs

Spade, shovel

Ballast, cement

Float

Soft sand

Bricklaying trowel

Frostproof bricks

Bolster chisel

Club hammer

Spirit level

Sharp sand

Rubber mallet

Pebbles

SEE ALSO

Mixing concrete
See *Using concrete*,
pp. 42–43

Paving designs
See *Styles of paving*,
pp. 44–45

Wooden steps
See *Simple timber steps*,
pp. 48–49

Steps can be an important design feature in the garden, and it is worth spending some time making sure that they fit in with the general look. As a rule, garden steps should be less steep than stairs in the house, and a minimum of 1 m (3 ft) wide – the shallower and wider the steps, the more leisurely the effect. An attractive impression can be made with steps that are built across the entire width of a small garden, and incorporate both planting holes and collections of pots.

Make sure that the materials used for the steps complement the house and garden – modern concrete steps look good leading from a starkly formal patio, while simple wooden steps are more in keeping with a woodland area. Metal steps are best used close to the house – for example, steep wrought-iron steps can be effective leading down from a balcony. Brick steps with stone or concrete treads are a classic combination, and blend well into many areas. The stone or brick should be repeated elsewhere in the garden if possible – perhaps forming the paving material for the path or terrace. Old stock bricks and natural stone will give a

traditional effect, while blue engineering bricks and sharp white concrete can bring a modern feel to the garden.

To create a frame for steps, line them with raised beds or a simple row of stakes, as shown here. Alternatively, a dense planting of shrubs works well, particularly if you want to screen the areas on either side of the path.

Helpful hints

When planning steps for a garden, consider carefully the proportions of the riser (height) to the tread (depth). Generally, the deeper the steps, the shorter the riser should be to facilitate easy stepping. Use the following guidelines to help you:

Tread	Riser
35 cm (14 in)	15 cm (6 in)
40 cm (16 in)	13 cm (5 in)
45 cm (18 in)	10 cm (4 in)

When calculating the total height of a step riser, allow for the height of the mortar joints and the thickness of the paving slab as well as the height of the riser unit.

LAYING AN INFORMAL STEPPED PATH

1 Mark out and clear the site. Using a sledgehammer, hammer the first stake into the ground. Insert the next, keeping it flush with the first. Continue to hammer in the stakes, adjusting their depths so that the tops follow any natural slope. Hammer in the opposite row, leaving a space large enough for three paving slabs in between the two lines of stakes.

2 Dig the foundations for the first step. Use a spade to mark a line in the soil 1 m (3 ft) from the first stake. Dig a trench, the width and depth of the spade, along the marking. Mix together 10 shovelfuls of ballast with two shovelfuls of cement, then add enough water to make a stiff mixture.

3 Pour the concrete evenly into the trench and smooth the surface with a float. Mix together 5 parts soft sand with 1 part cement and enough water to make a stiff mortar. Lay the mixture over the concrete and smooth with a trowel.

4 Place the first brick on the mortar, close to the stakes, and push down gently. Spread some mortar on the short face of the next brick and butt it up to the first. Continue laying the first course of bricks for the riser. You may need to use a half-brick to complete the course. To cut a brick, position a bolster chisel halfway along it and strike with a club hammer until it breaks.

5 Use a spirit level to check that the first course is level, then spread some mortar over the top of the bricks. Lay the second course, placing each brick over a joint below and tapping it into place with a trowel.

6 Level the soil for the first step with a spade, then smooth the surface to just below the top of the bricks. Mix some mortar using 5 parts sharp sand, 1 part cement and enough water so that it just falls off the trowel. Spread the mortar over the step, using a float to make a layer 2.5 cm (1 in) deep that gently slopes from back to front – this will allow any water to drain off.

7 Lay the paving slabs in place, setting the first row to overlap the bricks by 5 cm (2 in), and subsequent rows so that each slab is centred over a joint in the row in front. Remove the slabs. Using the indentation as a guide, spread some mortar for the first slab. Tap it into position with a rubber mallet, then lay the rest, using a spirit level to keep the slight downward slope.

8 Fill the sides and ends of each row with pebbles, pushing them gently into place. Then lay the rest of the steps. Remove any excess mortar by gently running a stick along each joint. Do not tread on the steps for at least 24 hours, to give the mortar time to set fully.

SIMPLE TIMBER STEPS

YOU WILL NEED

Pegs and string

Spade

Geo-textile membrane

Hardcore

Club hammer

Spirit level

Pressure-treated timber pegs, 5 x 5 cm (2 x 2 in)

Pressure-treated timber, 2.5 x 15 cm (1 x 6 in), sawn into lengths

Drill and screws

Tamper

Wood chippings

SEE ALSO

Concrete steps
See *Simple paved steps, pp. 46–47*

Wooden beds
See *Timber raised beds, pp. 50–51*

Building a deck
See *Decks, pp. 56–57*

Timber steps can be made in several different styles, but they usually give a casual effect. They are not, therefore, suitable for a formal stairway, or for use in combination with grander garden materials

Built to follow a natural slope, these rough wooden steps look perfectly in keeping in a woodland area. The fallen leaves add charm, but need to be cleared to prevent slipping.

such as York stone or with features such as balustrading. They blend perfectly well with modern or informal gardens, however, and are often used for the outer, "wilder" parts of larger gardens, where their roughness does not look out of place. The heavy black lines of railway sleepers make a strong design statement when used for a flight of steps; they can be laid two deep so that they form the riser and the tread, or used as a riser with a backfill of a different material such as gravel. Used in combination with brick paving, a brick tread looks very attractive.

Decking should have matching timber steps. These can be stained in many colours, from the traditional browns to bright colours like blue or green, to give a powerful and enlivening effect. Timber is usually the most appropriate material for steps for woodland or wild areas. They can be made from rough-sawn squared-off timbers or timber planks held by pegs, and the treads can be in gravel or wood chippings. Grass treads are also attractive, but are suitable only for areas of very light use because they will turn to mud if walked on regularly in wet weather. Logs placed on their sides can also be used, but again, they are only for intermittent use.

WOOD CHIPPINGS

Wood chippings are available in varying ratios of timber to bark. The best and most expensive are the high-bark content mixtures. Price also varies according to the size of the grains – the larger the grain the higher the price. The most popular use for wood chippings is as a pleasant alternative to gravel or paving for paths or stairways. It is best kept to woodland paths or other areas where neatness is not essential. This is because wood chippings tend to spill from their intended confines. They can be contained with timber lining, but this won't stop birds from pecking up and distributing them around the garden. Wood-chip paths will need maintenance in the form of regular weeding. With due care, they should last for three to five years before they need renewing.

Plants spill on to a wood-chip path winding enticingly through a natural-looking garden.

USING TIMBER FOR STEPS

1 Mark out a slope with pegs and string. Strip the turf and soil into roughly the shape of the steps. Digging into the bottom of the slope, dig out an area twice as deep (from front to back) as the eventual step depth. The first tread will be flush with the ground. You will need to allow 10 cm (4 in) for hardcore, and 7.5 cm (3 in) for the step tread.

2 Cut the geo-textile membrane to size and lay it in place on the soil. This will stop any weeds from growing through, while allowing for drainage. Lay 10 cm (4 in) hardcore and compact it thoroughly with a club hammer.

3 Check the levels with a spirit level – the treads must be set at a very slight outward fall for drainage. Using a club hammer, bang in 5 x 5-cm (2 x 2-in) timber pegs across the middle of the hardcore base to take the first riser. They should be at least 2.5 cm (1 in) deep into the ground.

4 Place the timber in front of the pegs and check the level. Screw the first timber riser to the pegs with 7.5-cm (3-in) screws. Put the sides of the step into position, and screw them to the riser.

5 Form the second tread by backfilling with 10 cm (4 in) of hardcore, and tamping down well. Continue the steps in the same way, then finish off by laying the tread surface with wood chippings.

Helpful hints

Timber steps can become slippery after rain and, apart from those made from rough logs, should be treated regularly with a wood preservative to discourage this. Cut away any overhanging branches and clear any garden debris that has fallen on the steps. The gradient of the steps detailed above should be gentle – 50 x 10 cm (20 x 4 in) is fine – and very large steps work well in this situation. They should be 1 m (3 ft) deep (from front to back) or more, and the risers no higher than 10 cm (4 in). The tread can be sloped gently up to the riser.

TIMBER RAISED BEDS

YOU WILL NEED

Railway sleepers or lengths of timber

Power or cross-cut saw

Heavy-duty power drill

Steel reinforcing rods

Sledgehammer

Compost

Garden fork

Trowel

SEE ALSO

Wooden steps
See *Simple timber steps*, pp. 48–49

Beds made of bricks
See *Brick raised beds*, pp. 52–53

Building a deck
See *Decks*, pp. 56–57

Wood is a natural choice for a raised bed and blends well into most areas of the garden. Any durable timber can be used to make a raised bed, but railway sleepers are particularly sturdy because they are intended

This low raised bed, made from railway sleepers cut to size, has been used to create a small planting area on a patio, and draws attention to a striking specimen plant.

to last for many years in extreme outdoor conditions. They make excellent low-level raised beds, which can be used either as freestanding units, in conjunction with retaining walls, or together with steps to make terracing for a steep hillside.

The deep black-brown colour, and distinctive size and shape of railway sleepers gives them a strong design element that is put to good use in paving and seating as well as in raised beds. For areas near the house, they combine well as visual dividers between areas of paving or gravel, and you can also use them to line a pathway.

The timber used for railway sleepers can be extremely rough, and needs careful sanding, especially if it is to be used for raised beds or seating where it will come into contact with hands or clothing. Sleepers are very heavy to handle. This is useful once they are in place since it gives them stability, but means that construction is more difficult and you may need help to move them. The timber is heavy and dense, which gives it durability but makes it difficult to saw and drill. You will need a power or cross-cut saw to cut it to size, and a heavy-duty power drill for drilling holes for the reinforcing rods.

WOOD TREATMENTS

Using a preservative protects wood from the rotting that occurs wherever moisture collects.

Any timber used outdoors needs to be protected from the elements. The traditional preservative is brown creosote, which creates a permanent stain and cannot be painted over. It needs to be applied with care; it is poisonous to plants if splashed on them. Modern wood preservatives come in a wide range of colours and will not damage plants. However, all preservatives are toxic and should

not be applied in a confined space. Railway sleepers are bought ready-treated, and you can also buy pressure-treated timber, where the preservative has been forced into the wood. This type is especially useful for softwoods, which are more susceptible to rot than hardwoods. Timber that will be in the ground needs extra protection, such as metal shoes or concrete footings.

MAKING A TIMBER RAISED BED

1 Choose a site that provides a firm foundation on which to build and offers the right conditions for the plants. Using a site next to the house makes good use of wall space.

2 Cut the timber to the required lengths; you need two long pieces and four short for this bed. Stack the timber into position.

3 Drill three evenly spaced holes through the front timbers, and one hole in each side. Drill the top timbers, marking the bottom ones with the drill-hole positions, then move the top timbers aside while you drill the bottom ones. Using a sledgehammer, insert steel reinforcing rods through the holes and 30 cm (1 ft) into the ground below.

4 Fill the bed with the appropriate soil or compost, incorporating a drainage layer if necessary (see Helpful hints box below). Fork through, then tread down and water well.

5 Plan out your planting scheme on paper, or place the pots on the compost so you can see how they look before planting up the bed. Leave plenty of space between plants to allow for growth. Plant out, then firm in and water the bed well.

Helpful hints

Raised beds allow you to create the right conditions for specialist plants, such as alpines, or plants that do not thrive in your soil, such as acid-lovers in a limy soil. Although woodland species prefer damp conditions, most plants do best in a well-drained soil. For drainage, add a layer of hardcore at the bottom of a raised bed, then cover with a layer of fine-mesh wire or a proprietary water-permeable membrane. This stops the hardcore from becoming blocked with soil. Fill the bed with a good-quality topsoil that meets the needs of the plants.

BRICK RAISED BEDS

YOU WILL NEED

Spade

Frostproof bricks

Shovel

Ballast

Cement

Float

Soft sand

Bricklaying trowel

Square

Spirit level

Tiles, 5 x 10 cm (2 x 4 in)

Bolster chisel

Club hammer

Gravel, compost

SEE ALSO

Mixing concrete
See *Using concrete,*
pp. 42–43

Wooden beds
See *Timber raised beds,*
pp. 50–51

Planting in crevices
See *Planting in rocks and*
gravel, pp. 148–149

Raised beds made from brick will last for many years and can be built to suit a wide variety of garden designs and purposes. They make excellent dividers or unifying features between different areas of the garden. The patio can be edged with a low raised bed, for example, to soften the harsh outline between the lawn and paving, as well as providing a useful area for displaying any plants that need extra care and attention.

In a small paved garden, raised beds may provide the only planting areas, and, since they can be used to bring plants within easy reach, they are particularly useful for disabled gardeners or those who find movement difficult. If built with a wide coping, a raised bed can also double up as additional seating.

On these pages, we show you how to make a raised herb bed, using basic bricklaying technique. This technique can be used for a freestanding wall, up to 1 m (3 ft) high. Anything higher than this will need steel reinforcements and it is advisable to consult a builder for help. Before you start to build, choose the site carefully, making sure that it meets the needs of the plants. Mark it out,

then take a few days to get used to it. Try placing a few plants in pots raised up to simulate the effect you are looking for and make sure it is what you want.

A sunny area near the kitchen makes the ideal spot for this bed. Choose herbs that thrive in free-draining soil, such as marjoram and rosemary, and plant creepers in the gaps.

MAKING A FREESTANDING RAISED BED

1 Clear an 87.5 x 87.5-cm (35 x 35-in) space for the base, and dig out the soil to a depth of 15 cm (6 in). Level the soil, then place a single layer of bricks around the edge, leaving a gap of 1.25 cm (½ in) between each one. Mark the positions of the bricks by pushing a spade into the soil on both sides.

2 Remove the bricks. Dig a 15-cm (6-in) deep trench between the markings. Mix the concrete for the foundations, using 10 parts ballast to 2 parts cement and adding enough water to make a stiff mixture. Pour the wet concrete into the trench, to a depth of 10 cm (4 in). Smooth with a float. Leave to dry before you begin to build the wall.

3 Mix up some mortar using 5 parts soft sand, 1 part cement and enough water so it just falls off a trowel. Spread mortar over the concrete. Press the first brick into position, then spread mortar on the short face of the next and butt up against the first. Use the trowel to tap it into position. Lay the first course, using a square to make sure the corners are straight.

4 Spread some mortar over the first course and continue laying the next two courses, placing each brick over a joint below. In the fourth layer – the first layer fully above ground – create some weep holes for drainage by omitting the mortar from the middle brick on each side. Leave a space between the brick and its neighbour. Use a spirit level to help you ensure the wall is level.

5 On the fifth layer, leave a planting gap on each side. To do this, first lay the corner brick, then leave a brick-sized gap before laying the next brick. Spread some mortar in the middle of the gap and lay three tiles, bringing them level with the top of the bricks. Repeat the process for each side.

6 Lay the next course in the same way, but position the gaps in a different place. Use a spirit level to check that the walls are vertical, then lay the next two courses, alternating the planting gaps so that they match the previous two courses.

7 Lay the final two courses, placing the bricks so that the edge overhangs by 2.5 cm (1 in) and positioning the final bricks to overhang each corner. You will need to cut an extra brick to do this – position a bolster chisel over the brick and strike with a club hammer to cut. Remove excess mortar from the weep holes, then run a trowel along the joints to create a diagonal face.

8 Add 5 cm (2 in) of gravel to the base, then start filling with compost until you reach the first planting holes. Push plants into some of the gaps, packing compost around them and placing tiles at the back to keep in the compost. Push tiles or pebbles into the other gaps, again placing tiles behind the holes. Continue for the next layers, then finish filling the bed and plant up.

DRY WALLS

YOU WILL NEED

Pegs and string

Spade

Spirit level

Gravel

Club hammer

Laying membrane

Large stones or bricks

Wheelbarrow for
moving stones

Reconstituted concrete
blocks

Small stones for
drainage layer

SEE ALSO

Using tools
See *Building tools,*
pp. 34–35

Planting in crevices
See *Planting in rocks and*
gravel, pp. 148–149

Stone is one of the oldest building materials, and stone walls can be found all over the world, many of them hundreds of years old. To build a dry wall – one without any, or with very little, mortar – you can use natural stone or concrete blocks that have been made to look like stone. Although most people would prefer to have a natural rather than a man-made material, concrete blocks are worth considering in areas with no natural stone or if you are on a tight budget. Whatever material you start with, choose a finish that reflects the setting; for example, smooth-cut stone will fit in better than rough-cut in an urban site, while in rural areas, rougher finishes are more in keeping.

Building a wall that is stable when using irregular shapes and sizes of stone and no, or very little mortar, is no easy task. The free-standing dry stone walls used in country areas for livestock are tapered, that is they are wider at the bottom than the top to give them stability. To build such a wall requires skill in selecting the sizes and shapes, so it is best to seek the help and advice of an experienced craftsman. A low retaining wall is easier. It gains much of its stability from the weight of the soil behind it, but needs to be built to slope into the bank, a technique known as battering. If you use uniform blocks, there is no need for battering, but an extra pair of hands to help move and place the blocks makes the task easier.

Natural stone and flat slate are used here to give a starkly modern display, emphasized by the sculptural plants.

BUILDING A RETAINING WALL

1 Mark out the line of the wall using pegs and string. Dig away the earth from the bank, sloping towards the top of the bank. You will need a space up to 15 cm (6 in) deeper (from front to back) than the stone, to give you room to work and to allow for a drainage layer.

2 Dig out the foundation trench, about 15 cm (6 in) deep and as wide as the stones. Check the level, then add a 5-cm (2-in) layer of gravel and compact firmly with the back of a club hammer.

3 Cover the back slope with laying membrane, weighting it down with bricks or large stones to secure it.

4 Lay the largest stones on top of the foundation, making sure that they are aligned with the string line and that the top surfaces are sloping backwards. Choose each stone to fit well against its neighbour, then tap into position with the handle of a club hammer.

5 Backfill behind the first layer with small stones, level to the top of the stones. Pack them down tightly – this is a drainage layer which will be built up with the wall and the air holes between them should be as small as possible or they will fill with soil.

6 When the first row is finished and backfilled, you should have a level, even surface on which to fit the next layer of large stones. Again, choose stones that fit well together, and make sure that the smaller area of each stone is towards the front, otherwise it may work loose. Backfill behind the wall with small stones, again bringing them level with the top of the wall.

7 Lay the final course, following the instructions above. Then cover the slope with soil, and plant up a few gaps in the wall with small wall plants.

CHOOSING STONES

There are various types of stone available for a dry wall, and each has its advantages. Natural hard stones, including granite, flint nodules and slate, are hardwearing but difficult to cut, so you need to work with rough stones. This means sorting through the sizes and selecting stones of a suitable shape for each part of the wall. Natural soft stones, such as limestone and sandstone, weather attractively. They can be cut, and various finishes are available from rough to smooth. Reconstituted concrete blocks have one side moulded to look like rough, semi-dressed stone. They are uniform, so you do not need to grade the different sizes; this makes them easier to lay.

DECKS

YOU WILL NEED

Wedges, string

Square

Spade, bricks

Pressure-treated timber, 10 x 10 cm (4 x 4 in), 10 x 5 cm (4 x 2 in), 10 x 2.5 cm (4 x 1 in)

Clamp, spirit level

Drill, carriage bolts

Socket wrench

Cement, sand, aggregate

Tamper

Trowel, cross-cut saw

Wood preservative

Plastic ground cover

Joist hangers, nails

Chalk, straightedge

Decking screws

SEE ALSO

Treating wood
See *Timber raised beds*, pp. 50–51

Deck designs
See *Styles of decking*, pp. 58–59

Decking provides an informal garden surface that makes an attractive alternative to paving. The effect is modern and streamlined, which makes it more suitable for use around modern houses than traditional ones, especially brick or stone-built houses that have a formal appearance. In these cases it is still possible to use decking, but it is best to site it away from the house. Decking is ideally suited to verandahs and pool sides because the wood surface is warm to the touch and pleasant to walk on in bare feet. It can also be used to create several different levels, without relying on the natural slope of the garden.

Classical decking uses 10 cm (4 in), 15 cm (6 in), or 20 cm (8 in) wooden boards laid in parallel strips on a base of bearers and joists. A simple deck is quite easy to build, but you can also buy systems that interlock to form different styles and shapes, using boards set out in diagonal lines and other patterns. Most decks use natural woods that blend into their surroundings, but a coloured deck can make a striking display, especially in a town garden or in a separate garden area.

When choosing the site for a decking platform, avoid damp areas of the garden – the timbers can easily become slippery and dangerous in damp conditions. Check how open the site is and whether there are many overhanging trees. Before building the deck shown here, you will need to clear the site and level it – you may want help for this task since it requires hard manual labour.

MEASURING UP

To work out how much timber you need, first measure the length of the site. This gives you the measurement for the bearers, which must be supplied in single lengths. Then measure the lengths for the joists, which run perpendicular to the bearers. For the finished decking, measure the total area (length by width) and divide by the board width. However, you need prepared timber for the decking, so remember that the board width will be smaller after planing – for example, allow for 9.5 cm (3⅜ in) rather than 10 cm (4 in) when using 10-cm (4-in) boards.

MAKING A DECKING PLATFORM

1 Mark out the site with wedges and string – use a square to make sure that the corners are at right angles. Dig the post holes 45 cm (18 in) deep, spacing them 120 cm (48 in) apart in rows placed 60 cm (24 in) apart, parallel to the house. Level the base of each hole, place a brick in it, then insert 10 x 10 cm (4 x 4 in) posts, 60 cm (24 in) long.

2 For the bearers, place lengths of 10 x 5 cm (4 x 2 in) along each row of posts parallel to the house. Clamp the bearers to the end posts, keeping them 2.5 cm (1 in) off the ground. Use a spirit level to make sure the posts are vertically level and the bearers are horizontally level.

3 Drill two holes through the bearers and posts. Insert a carriage bolt into each hole and tighten with a socket wrench – remove one of the clamps for easier access once the first bolt has gone in. Mix 1 part cement to 4 parts sand and 4 parts aggregate, then moisten. Fill the holes with the mixture, tamp down, then smooth with a trowel.

4 Use a cross-cut saw to trim the post level with the top of the bearers. Paint the cut ends with wood preservative. Cover the soil below the deck with a black plastic ground cover – this prevents weed growth.

5 Set 10 x 5-cm (4 x 2-in) joists between the rows, spaced 45 cm (18 in) apart. Cut to fit with a saw, then nail a pair of joist hangers to the end of each one. Making sure that the tops of the joists are level with the bearers, nail them into position with 4-cm (1½-in) galvanized nails.

6 Using a straight-edge, mark the ends of the bearers with a chalk line, trim, then coat with a wood preservative. Place the first plank so that it runs parallel to the house at the end farthest away from it, and overhangs the frame by 2.5 cm (1 in). Secure with 6-cm (2½-in) decking screws, drilling two rows of holes spaced 45 cm (18 in) apart.

7 Lay several planks, leaving 5-mm (¼-in) gaps between them. Using a straightedge, draw a guideline for the screws along the centre of the end joist and secure. Continue securing the planks a few at a time. Once they are all secured, trim with a saw to the end of the shortest one, using a straight edge as a guide. Paint cut edges with preservative.

8 Use a length of 10 x 2.5 cm (4 x 1 in) timber to cover the ends and make a neat finish. Set it on end so that it is flush with the planks, then secure it with screws.

STYLES OF DECKING

STYLE SUGGESTIONS

Simple, clean lines of wooden seating and tables are ideal for decking, as are cane chairs and loungers or canvas chairs. It is best to avoid ornate or heavily elaborate furniture, such as decorative cast-iron seating, however, which tends to look artificial in this situation.

For additional shade, use bamboo or nylon screens attached to overhead beams – these can be rolled down as necessary, or can be attached horizontally. Screens can also be used to provide privacy from a neighbour or to block an unattractive view.

Plants can be grown through decking if a large enough hole is cut for them, and a well-shaped tree can give a striking effect and useful shade in this position.

Wooden decks are ideal on steeply sloping lots because they reclaim living space that otherwise might go unused. They also provide a valuable link between the garden and the house when the ground floor of the house is several feet above the garden level. Level lots are ideal for patios, but even in that situation you might prefer a deck for a more rustic look or to save money on building materials. The best material for decks is naturally rot-resistant wood such as red cedar, redwood or cypress. Red cedar and redwood are particularly attractive, weathering to a pleasing grey. Although rot resistant in dry climates, however, both red cedar and redwood are vulnerable to rot in areas that remain warm and damp for extended periods of time. If you live in a region where summers are hot and humid and your deck will be in shade much of the day, build with pressure-treated timber.

▲ FLOORING FOR COMFORT
Roof gardens are ideal places for a decking surface, which gives a warmer effect than a more traditional concrete surface.

► A SECLUDED CORNER
Wooden steps lead up to this enclosed corner. Heavy trellis and an overhead screen, together with planting, help to provide privacy.

▲ DINING IN STYLE
The simple wood and metal fold-up furniture is minimal yet elegant in style, and entirely fitting for the deck.

▲ JAPANESE DESIGN
This decking bridge is reminiscent of a Japanese garden, with its bamboo railings and dog-leg shape.

▲ INNOVATION
A curved corner in concrete paving has been infilled in an unusual way.

► EFFECTIVE COLOUR
This area of calm is achieved using decking, furniture, and sunroom doors painted different shades of blue.

PUTTING UP A FENCE

YOU WILL NEED

String line and chalk

Hammer and nails

Spirit level

Wood preserver

Fence posts

Fence post spikes

Fencing panels

For garden boundaries and internal enclosures, wooden fencing is an economical and versatile option; if fitted and maintained properly, it can last for years. Treat the wood with preserver and reapply it every few years. Before installing a boundary fence, first agree with your neighbour whose fence it is and who is responsible for its upkeep. Also agree exactly where the fence should be; this will avoid arguments later on over a bit of garden. Once you agree on the fence's position, remove as many plants as possible from the line of fencing; if a tree is in the way, it will have to be incorporated into the fence. Survey the ground to see if there are any noticeable obstructions, such as old concrete post foundations, and remove them. Metal spikes cannot be used for supporting wooden fences. In places where the ground freezes deeply, you must sink posts into concrete at least 30 cm (12 in) below the frostline.

If the ground slopes, either build a stepped fence – this is suitable for panelled systems – or follow the contours of the ground with the positioning of the individual uprights. A quick and easy way to put up a fence is to use fence panels. The horizontal rails and their infill make one unit, which is fixed to the posts; sink the posts in concrete or use metal spikes (see opposite). Panel systems range in design from interwoven (giving a solid fence) to trellis panels (giving a lighter screen). You may have to cut the last panel to fit. Most designs are constructed with slats, which form the end of the panel. Remove these and replace at the desired end point before cutting to make a neater finish.

Fences can be made from all kinds of timber. This fence is made from large, rough pieces to give a rustic effect, creating a strong visual contrast with the brick paving.

TYPES OF FENCING

A fence can consist of a combination of upright posts and horizontal rails. These can be infilled in various ways to give a characteristic design to the fence. To decide on the type of fencing you need, consider such practical functions as height, privacy and wind protection first. Then think about visual aspects, such as modern or traditional, strong and heavy, or light and airy, and whether it will be planted. Basic ranch-style fencing is simply post-and-rail, giving an open boundary marker. Picket, or palisade, fencing has vertical palings, which may be close- or open-spaced; these often finish in a point or curve and are painted. Featherboarding is another traditional style of fencing, as is wattle (more suitable in rural sites). Both of these, and interwoven panel fencing, give complete privacy. Louvres and slats are other options; they can be infinitely varied, placed closely or wide apart depending on their function, and can give a more modern look, especially when stained in a bright wood finish.

For a front fence, think about the appearance on both sides; the "back" can be unsightly as it is less likely to be covered in plants.

PUTTING UP A PANEL FENCE

1 Set up a string line from one end to the other along the fence's length. Pull the string as tight as possible so that each end of it is anchored securely to another fence, tree, or house wall; otherwise the line can be easily pulled out of position. Mark the centre line of the fence on the ground with chalk.

2 Drive in the first metal spike at one end, using a spirit level to make sure that it is even. Do not hammer the metal spike itself, but put a piece of wood inside it and hammer that. Bang it in far enough to ensure that the metal box is resting on the ground, and leave the base of the square protruding, to take the post.

3 Insert the post into the socket and hammer it in until it is firm. Check again with a level to make sure that the post is upright in both directions. Nail on the first two metal brackets to hold the first panel.

4 Position the first panel in the brackets and mark the far end to obtain the position of the next post. (The centre of the next post will then be half the width of the post past the end of the panel.) Allow up to 2.5-cm (1-in) leeway; don't make it too tight. Make sure that the next post is aligned along the chalked line.

5 Nail a post cap to each post with two nails. If you want a more formal look you can screw in a ball-top finial, as shown here. Apply wood preserver to any timber that has an exposed cut edge.

Helpful hints

Fencing makes a good windbreak. It slows down the speed of the wind rather than blocking it like a wall, which causes turbulence on the other side. An openwork fence is best for this purpose. You can buy special windbreak fencing for large areas, but it is not as attractive as a wooden fence.

Keep your fence in good condition by repainting it regularly with wood preserver. If it has faded, consider painting it with a coloured wood stain, but remember that this will create a distinctive visual effect. Your fence must be attractive enough to complement your garden.

BUILDING A PERGOLA

YOU WILL NEED

String

Chalk or spray paint

Straightedge

Spade

4 wooden posts, 10 x 10 cm (4 x 4 in) and 2.75 m (9 ft) long

Spirit level

4 wooden beams, 5 x 15 cm (2 x 6 in) and 1.6 m (5 ft 4 in) long

3 wooden rafters, 5 x 10 cm (2 x 4 in) and 1.6 m (5 ft 4 in) long

Clamp

Drill, bolts, nails

Wood preservative

Concrete

SEE ALSO

Using tools
See *Building tools,*
pp. 34–35

Mixing concrete
See *Using concrete,*
pp. 42–43

Treating wood
See *Timber raised beds,*
pp. 50–51

A pergola or a curving arch can add another dimension to a garden. A small, hidden structure against a wall will create a secret place, or a pleasant focal point. A simple arch over a path can serve to mark the change from one area of the garden to another and provide a pleasant walkway. Attached to the house a pergola provides some welcome shade in hot weather, and if it is covered with glass or acrylic panels, will

Draped in a profusion of 'Mary Rose', this arch has been cunningly placed to make a secluded trysting place.

give some protection from rain. Both pergolas and arches can be used as structures to support climbing plants.

The beams and rafters that are placed over the top of a pergola are usually made from wood, but the uprights can also be constructed from brick, concrete, metal, or even stone columns if a grand effect is required. Allow as much space as you can, especially if you are planning to grow climbers over the structure. Although a newly completed pergola will look large and bare, it will soon become clothed in foliage.

A painted finish can look attractive on some of the more ornate pergolas that are built to stand alone so that the structure can be seen. However, if you plan to cover the pergola in climbers, repainting will be difficult. In this case, it is better to use either wood preservative or stain. Remember that a white pergola will appear larger and will dominate the area where it stands. Green or blue are less powerful colours, and will have a less imposing effect.

The pergola described opposite is a basic construction that is 1 m (3 ft) wide and 2 m (7 ft) tall. The dimensions can be increased to make a much larger pergola.

A pergola construction can be used to turn a patio into a Mediterranean-style dining area.

AN OUTDOOR ROOM

There are many different ways in which you can use a pergola construction. A wooden pergola can be filled in at the sides with trellis, if immediate and complete privacy is wanted. This gives a secluded outdoor room. It is often worth inserting archways and "windows", which will give different views of the garden. Really large constructions make splendid avenues, with a view

or seat at the end, or they can be built over a patio to form an outdoor dining area. Create a shady walkway by covering the sides of your pergola with trellis and installing rafters quite close together at the top. Curved metal structures are also very attractive here, especially when covered in greenery so as to give the impression of a green tunnel, with fruit or flowers hanging down.

MAKING A PERGOLA

1 Mark out the site, clearing any bushes that are in the way. Use two string lines to mark out the depth of the archway, making sure that they are parallel and straight. Mark the lines on the ground, using either chalk or spray paint.

2 Mark the centre points of the posts. Dig post holes 30 x 30 cm (1 x 1 ft) to a depth of 45 cm (18 in) – you need two holes, spaced 1.5 m (5 ft) apart, on each side, with 1 m (3 ft) between the two sides. Insert the first post, brace, and use a spirit level to check that it is upright. Insert the other posts, using the markings to make sure they align on each side.

3 Place the two beams on either side of the two posts on one side. Clamp to each post, keeping the tops of the beams flush with the tops of the posts. Check that the posts are upright. Drill holes for 60 x 15-cm (24 x 6-in) bolts through the beams at the top of each post, then insert the bolts to secure. Repeat the process on the other side.

4 Place the rafters on top of the beams, starting just inside the top of the posts, and ensure that both ends protrude by 30 cm (12 in). Nail to the beams, using two 10-cm (4-in) nails per joint. Alternatively, cut grooves into the rafters and slot over the beams, then nail into position for security. Coat cut ends with wood preservative.

5 Mix up some concrete, then use it to fill the post holes up to ground level. Slope the top of the concrete slightly away from the posts, so that water will run away from the wood.

Helpful hints

To ensure the pergola or archway is tall enough to walk under comfortably, the upright posts need to be at least 2.75 m (9 ft) long, with at least 45 cm (18 in) sunk into the ground and over 2 m (7 ft) above ground.

To increase the life of posts, place concrete in the bottom of the hole as well as packing it around the sides. Posts are less likely to rot if they do not come into direct contact with the soil. Some wooden arch kits have the wood sections predrilled; this stops the wood from splitting when it is nailed.

SELF-CONTAINED WATER FEATURE

Even the smallest of spaces can include a self-contained feature to bring water into the garden and extend the range of plants grown. Make a simple raised pond by lining a raised bed with a butyl liner and securing it underneath the coping layer, or use a large container, such as the half-barrel shown here, to make a mini-pond. Alternatively, install a self-contained moving-water feature. This contains a fixed volume of water, which is constantly circulated by means of a small pump submerged in a reservoir of water. The water can be pumped upwards through a hose to cascade down, or through a jet to make a fountain or create a bubbling surface.

Because the water in the reservoir can be hidden, these features are more child-friendly than traditional ponds. The reservoir can be a feature in its own right – a large urn or a wall-mounted fountain can be used or a decorative surround made to hide a pre-formed plastic structure. An alternative is to sink the reservoir into the ground, to create a pebble fountain, for example.

Self-contained water features require less maintenance than ponds. Keep an eye on the water level and replenish it when necessary – do not allow the pump to run dry – and

clean the pump filter or strainer regularly. Occasionally, you may also need to unblock or clean the fountain nozzle. Remove the pump over the winter to prolong its life, and add a water treatment to the water at the start of the season to prevent algae forming.

Water is pumped through a hose to fall from this sculpture into the bowl below, while a combination of ferns and lilies in front gives the impression of a water's edge.

Using a submersible pump enables you to create simple but imaginative water effects.

ELECTRICITY AND LIGHTING

Most submersible pumps come with 10 m (30 ft) of cable but no plug. If you position a water feature near the house or an outbuilding, you can run the cable through a hole in the wall and plug it indoors into an RCD protected socket. Alternatively, ask a qualified electrician to fit an outdoor power outlet near the water feature and a waterproof plug to the pump. Cables should be protected with

plastic conduit and buried. If you do not have an outdoor lighting system, you can use a low-voltage lighting kit for lighting features near the house. These systems use a transformer plugged indoors to reduce the main current voltage to a safe level. The light fittings may come as spikes, which are pushed into the ground, or as underwater or floating lights.

MAKING A HALF-BARREL WATER FEATURE

1 Place the barrel in position before starting work, since it will be hard to move once it is full of water. Choose a site that gets plenty of light.

2 Cut out a circle of thick polythene that is larger than the barrel. Fit it loosely into the barrel, then fold over the edge and secure it with galvanized nails.

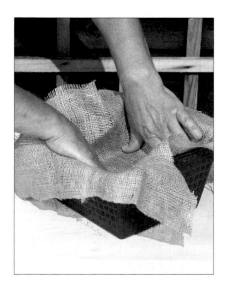

3 Line the planting baskets with hessian to keep in the soil. Fill each basket up to two-thirds full with soil, then cut the lining so that it is level with the top of the basket.

4 Plant up the pots. Top each one with a layer of gravel to stop the soil from washing away once the pot is placed in the water.

5 Half-fill the barrel with water, then gently lower the baskets into the barrel. Stack two or three bricks on the base of the barrel if planting marginal plants to keep them at the right level.

Helpful hints

Any large container can be used to make a mini-pond, but make sure it is at least 38 cm (15 in) deep or it will be difficult to control algae. Water barrels are a popular choice because they are attractive and deep enough to support an oxygenating plant, which helps to keep the water clear, as well as three or four aquatic and marginal plants. You need to choose miniature varieties or compact types of plant. Some gardeners include one or two goldfish in a mini-pond, but the container is restrictive, so it is best reserved for plants.

FLEXIBLE LINER POND

YOU WILL NEED

Hosepipe

Spade, spirit level

Rake

Builder's sand, topsoil or pond underlay fabric

Butyl liner

Large stones

Knife

Slates

SEE ALSO

Designing with water
See *Self-contained water feature, pp. 64–65*

Ponds and cascades
See *Styles of water garden, pp. 68–69*

Natural settings
See *Wildlife meadows and ponds, pp. 164–165*

Using a flexible liner to make a garden pond is much more economical than buying a preformed pond shell – and means you can create any size and shape of pond you like. Simple shapes fit into most gardens better than complicated ones, as well as being easier to make. A common mistake is to make a pond too shallow – any pond less than 45 cm (18 in) will be susceptible to changes in temperature, which can stress fish and cause green-water problems.

To make digging out a large pond quicker, it may be worth hiring a mini-digger, either with or without a driver. Check where the machine will enter the garden and what will happen to the spoil – topsoil and any turf removed can be reused but subsoil is best removed from the site. Where a wheelbarrow is to be used to remove spoil, lay down planks to protect beds and lawns.

There are many different materials that can be used for lining ponds, but butyl synthetic rubber is particularly good because it is strong, ages well and can be repaired easily. Although butyl liner is strong, it can be pierced by sharp stones or by the roots of couch grass. Clear the pond site carefully, and if you have couch grass in your garden,

apply a suitable weedkiller, such as one containing glyphosate, before laying down the liner. Butyl liner is easier to lay if it is softened, so unroll it and leave it out in the sun for at least an hour before starting work.

A pond surrounded by leafy greenery makes a tranquil addition to any garden, and this one's curved shape is enhanced by the plants grouped informally around it.

Floating and marginal plants are an attractive way of giving fish shade and a place to hide.

A POND FOR FISH

Any shape of pond is suitable for fish, but the depth and the surface area need to be sufficient to provide fish with a buffer against changing temperatures and to maintain oxygen levels. As a rough guide, part of the pond should be at least 60 cm (24 in) deep and you need an area of 30 x 30 cm (12 x 12 in) for every 3–5-cm (1¼–2-in) length of fish. Check with an aquatic centre: the

type of fish may affect the stocking level, and a filtration system can help to increase it. Oxygenate the water by incorporating oxygenating plants, installing a fountain or adding an air pump, and provide some shade by including marginal plants or an overhang of the pond edging. If there are herons in your area, deter them by building a pond with steep sides, or covering it with netting.

MAKING AN INFORMAL POND

1 Choose the site for the pond, then use a hosepipe to mark out an informal shape. A pond should be sited in full sun and away from overhanging trees.

2 Dig out the pond, incorporating a shelf, 30 cm (12 in) wide and 45 cm (18 in) deep, at one end to make a planting area for marginals. Use a spirit level to check that the bottom of the pond is level, then rake over the soil and remove any sharp objects that come to the surface.

3 To protect the butyl liner, line the hole with a 3-cm (1¼-in) deep layer of damp builder's sand or sieved topsoil, or use pond underlay fabric if the soil is very stony. Drape the butyl liner over the hole, taking care not to overstretch it. Anchor one edge with stones, then get into the pond to fit the liner into the shape – remember to remove your shoes first.

4 Slowly fill the pond with water. As the water pushes down on the liner, pull the liner gently upwards to smooth out any large creases or crevices.

5 Trim off the excess liner, leaving 15 cm (6 in) overhanging the edge. Arrange the slates around the edge of the pond, making sure the excess liner is hidden.

Helpful hints

Most prepacked liners state what pond dimensions they will make. To work out how much you need when you are buying liner from a roll, first decide on the length and width of your pond. Add these measurements together, then add twice the maximum depth and allow an extra 15–30 cm (6–12 in) for the overlap. When you are putting down the protective layer of sand, topsoil or underlay, pay extra attention to where the lowest point of the pond will be. This is where water pressure will be at its greatest, placing most strain on the liner.

STYLES OF WATER GARDEN

PLANTING SUGGESTIONS

Planting in or near your new feature will soften hard edges and enable you to hide pond hardware such as pumps or pipes. To attract wildlife, provide foliage ground cover around the banks of the pond.

Lush planting usually works well on banks and sides of ponds, so think of plants with large foliage first: hostas, rodgersias, and rheum, for example. In an artificial pond, however, the nearby soil may not be moist enough for summer foliage, so be prepared to look for drought-tolerant alternatives, such as ornamental grasses and evergreens.

Where a water feature has no nearby soil, use pots of plants to soften the outlines. Conventional plants, growing in pots, are fine outside the pond, but use aquatic planting baskets for marginal plants that are to be immersed in the water.

A water garden can be, or appear to be, a natural feature like a wildlife pond or an alpine stream. To create a natural style, the setting and the planting need to be considered as carefully as the actual construction. For a feature that makes no attempt to be anything other than a purpose-made construction, however, such as a formal lily pond or a fountain, the materials and style are more likely to reflect the house or other hard landscaping materials already used within the garden. Many different materials are used including glazed ceramics, tiles and sculpture, the style being more in keeping with the house and living space than the garden.

Tiny, discreet pumps are very affordable. This means that the smallest corner, patio, or even balcony can accommodate a water feature. The pump can be temporary, assembled in summer and dismantled in winter.

▶ CASCADES AND WATERFALLS
These water features can be impressive if they are well constructed. In the display shown here, water glides down over the smooth and level lipping stone as a continuous sheet. The lipping stone protrudes from the wall so that water is directed into the reservoir rather than down the wall. Lining under the cobblestones at the bottom collects water, which is then returned into the system.

◀ GURGLE POND
Here a gurgle pond is used to mark the corner of a border. Gurgle ponds are ideal self-contained features for those who want running water without a pond. A reservoir and pump are hidden under the feature (often a millstone or boulder) and an outlet pipe fits into a hole at the top. Water then gurgles up and cascades over cobblestones.

► SCULPTURE
A comical water feature can consist of a sculpture, two wooden barrels, a small pump and a few floating aquatic plants.

◄ METAL SPOUT
In a modern setting, use bold blocks of foliage (here, two ornamental grasses) as a foil for a simple metal spout.

▲ TOWN GARDEN
A formal pond is often much in keeping in a town garden. Here a rectangular pond is framed by paving. A seat faces a fountain. Eye-catching tiles alert people to watch their step. Hostas in pots provide foliage.

► WILDLIFE
A quiet spot with plenty of plant cover will help to create an environment for wildlife. Keep things simple. Here the gravel path and the rough-hewn wooden bridge are perfectly in tune with the planting style.

▲ RAISED POND
If there are problems with the underlying soil, a raised pond can be useful. It is not a quick fix, however. Once filled with water, the liner will slump if it has not been sufficiently supported by sand or topsoil.

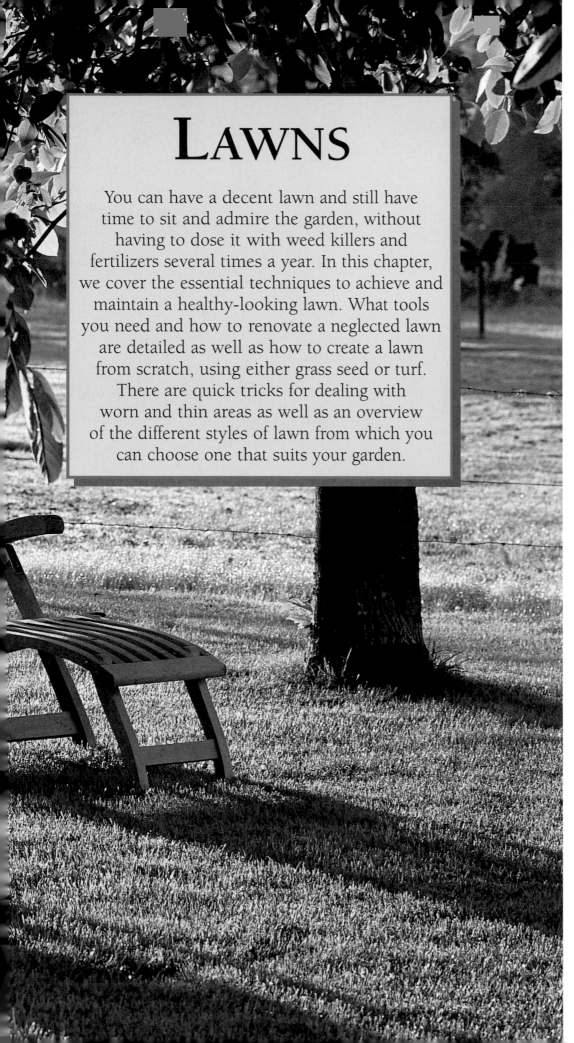

LAWNS

You can have a decent lawn and still have time to sit and admire the garden, without having to dose it with weed killers and fertilizers several times a year. In this chapter, we cover the essential techniques to achieve and maintain a healthy-looking lawn. What tools you need and how to renovate a neglected lawn are detailed as well as how to create a lawn from scratch, using either grass seed or turf. There are quick tricks for dealing with worn and thin areas as well as an overview of the different styles of lawn from which you can choose one that suits your garden.

3

TOOLS FOR LAWN CARE

TRIMMING LONG GRASS

Lightweight (electric) string trimmers have a plastic cutting cord that copes well with long, dry grass and some weeds, although the cord often jams with wet grass or coarse weeds. Heavy-duty trimmers often come with a cutting line plus the option of a metal cutting blade; they can tackle tough weeds such as brambles. Trimmers with metal blades can be potentially dangerous for the untrained user.

Traditional tools such as a scythe or sickle are making a comeback as more people try meadow gardening. These tools offer a way of dealing with long grass and are effective if the blades are kept sharp. To use them correctly and safely, get help from someone experienced. The essential difference is that a scythe has a long handle and is held with two hands, while a sickle has a short handle and is used with one hand.

MOWING

Before you purchase a lawn mower, stop and assess your needs. For a small lawn, a push cylinder mower may be all you require. If the blades are kept sharp, you'll get a clean, even cut with a minimum of work and no engine noise. An electric mower, either battery powered or plug-in, is excellent for a small- to medium-sized lawn. For large spaces, you'll probably want to opt for a petrol-driven machine, either one you walk behind or a ride-on mower.

TRIMMING EDGES

A nylon string strimmer is a quick and easy way to tidy up the edges of your lawn. However, for a really crisp finish, opt for the old-fashioned rotary edger. The multi-toothed cutting blade is fitted to a wheel that rolls along the surface next to the lawn. The blades make a vertical cut that is flush with the sidewalk, driveway, or bed, creating a professional edge. Edge a small lawn by hand with edging shears. A long-handled model exists so you don't have to crawl along the ground.

CUTTING TURF

Lawn turf often needs to be cut, not only when it is being laid but if the shape of the lawn is to be changed or made more distinct. You may also want to cut and peel back turf in order to plant bulbs for naturalizing in grass and to level out any bumps and hollows. An edging iron is a specialist tool for cutting through turf. The blade must be kept sharp and you need a fair amount of force behind it; a sharp spade or an old bread knife is a suitable substitute.

WATERING

In dry climates, where you need to water regularly, the most efficient way to water your lawn is with an in-ground sprinkler system equipped with automatic timers. Other watering options include fixed sprinklers, which are suitable for small areas; oscillating sprinklers, which are adjustable, so you can control how the water is distributed; revolving sprinklers that spin

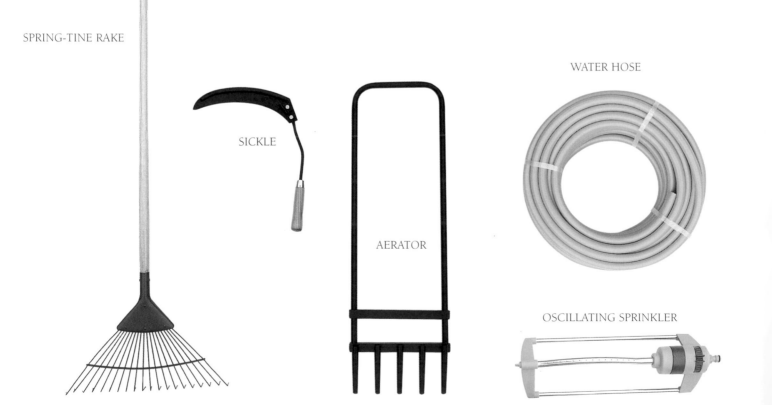

SPRING-TINE RAKE

SICKLE

AERATOR

WATER HOSE

OSCILLATING SPRINKLER

due to water pressure (on better models you can adjust the height and width of the watering pattern); and impulse sprinklers, which break the water spray into small droplets and can be set to vary the watering pattern.

FEEDING

Chemical fertilizers need to be applied to lawns very evenly, otherwise the grass greens up in patches, which can look very strange. For medium or large lawns, it is worth using a fertilizer spreader. These are pushed along the lawn, with a hopper dispensing the correct amount of granules or powder. The machines are set to take certain brands of fertilizer, but it is possible to reset them for other brands if you

calibrate them first. To apply a liquid feed, use a watering can fitted with a rose or a hose with a watering and feeding attachment.

WEEDING

If your lawn has only a few weeds, pull them out by hand; there are various tools, such as fishtail weeders, designed to take out weeds while disturbing the soil as little as possible (see p. 93). There are also spot weeders that will tackle broad-leaved weeds or moss, which will spoil the look of your lawn. Where weeds or moss are widespread, control them by using a combined weed-and-feed, with or without moss killer. These chemicals are applied using a fertilizer spreader.

REMOVING THATCH

Dead grass and dead moss can build up on the soil surface to form a spongy layer called thatch. The thatch can be removed by raking vigorously. Use a spring-tine rake: one with tines that are round in cross-section rather than flat. Where hand raking is too tiring, rent a dethatching machine once every year or two. An alternative is to buy a scarifying attachment, which will fit on to some types of mower.

AERATING

There are various tools that will get more air into a compacted lawn. To spike a small area, a garden fork will suffice, but you

can buy a special hand aerator that will remove cores of earth. This is useful if you want to brush in a soil improver afterwards. For larger lawns, it is quicker to use a petrol-driven machine. As aerating does not need to be done every year, consider renting rather than buying a power aerator.

SWEEPING

A besom broom is useful for sweeping off any morning dew from the lawn before mowing; it can also be used for sweeping up a light dusting of fallen leaves. A spring-tine rake or a leaf rake is more efficient for removing heavy leaf fall in autumn.

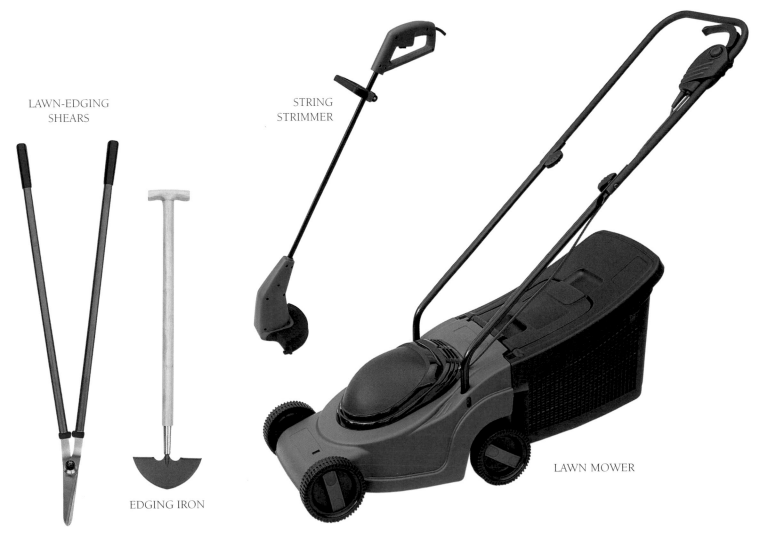

LAWN-EDGING
SHEARS

STRING
STRIMMER

EDGING IRON

LAWN MOWER

TRANSFORMING A POOR LAWN

YOU WILL NEED

Sieved topsoil or soil-based compost

Something to cut the turf, such as a sharp spade, edging iron, old bread knife, or pruning saw

Trowel

Hand fork

Garden rake

Level or straight strip of timber

SEE ALSO

Using lawn tools
See *Tools for lawn care,*
pp. 72–73

Handling turf
See *Laying turf,*
pp. 78–79

Growing a lawn
See *Using grass seed,*
pp. 80–81

Lawn design
See *Shaping your lawn,*
pp. 82–83

Lawn maintenance
See *Caring for your lawn,*
pp. 84–85

A neglected lawn can look awful, yet can soon be restored to health by simple lawn care, such as correct mowing and feeding. Where a lawn was laid without adequate preparation, or has since been mistreated, improvements are still possible but may take a little longer. Grass growing in

waterlogged ground, subject to heavy wear or deep shade, will always struggle even if well tended. In these situations, you need to deal with the cause of the problem or maybe reassess whether a lawn should be there at all. Lawns look their worst during summer droughts and winter floods. In both instances, the best thing you can do is to stay off the lawn and do nothing until autumn or spring; these are the best seasons for tackling lawn improvements.

The first step to reviving a neglected lawn is to cut it back in stages, then assess the grass and the ground. Use a string trimmer, scythe, or sickle to cut down long grass. Let the grass recover and start to regrow, then use a mower on its highest setting.

The results of some lawn improvements, like dealing with bumps and hollows, or repairing edges, are more or less instant; others take more than one growing season to show their effect. If you do not have time to deal with bumps and hollows, use a wheeled rotary mower and temporarily raise the cutting height of the blade to 2.5 cm (1 in).

To distract the eye from a poor or neglected lawn, use strong vertical elements such as obelisks, urns set on pedestals, and colourful containers.

ASSESSING A LAWN

Once the lawn has been cut, you will be able to take a closer look at the sward. How dense is the grass compared to lawn weeds? So long as there is at least 50 per cent cover of grass, a lawn is worth renovating with annual spring lawn care, such as feeding and weeding, plus once-only measures such as oversowing. Where there is less than 50 per cent grass, it is best to start again by

creating a new lawn either with turf or from seed, or perhaps by choosing a completely different surface. Close inspection of the blades of grass can tell you a lot about how the lawn will respond to future treatments. Grasses with thin, fine blades are less tolerant of wear and tear but withstand close mowing well; these are ideal for show lawns. Rye-grass has broad blades and is useful

for family lawns, since it can withstand wear and tear. A lawn that feels spongy underfoot probably contains moss and/or a dead layer of grass and moss on the surface of the soil (thatch). Removing the thatch improves the health of the grass as it allows water and fertilizer to reach the roots. Mowing around a tree can be difficult, so it is best to leave grass unmown around the trunk.

REPAIRING BUMPS AND HOLLOWS

1 Inspect the lawn for bumps and hollows. Grass growing over a bump will be scalped by the mower, while grass in a hollow escapes the blades and is left too long. Cut a cross in the turf right over the bump or hollow, using a sharp spade or edging iron. An easier tool might be an old bread knife or pruning saw.

2 Carefully peel back each of the four corners of the turf, easing the blade underneath it to loosen it from the soil.

3 Use a trowel or hand fork to even out the ground. Any soil causing a bump in the surface must be removed. A hollow needs to be filled in with sieved topsoil or soil based compost; add enough to level the ground. After adjusting the level of the soil, firm the ground to remove any air pockets. Check the result with a level or narrow length of wood if necessary.

4 As soon as the underlying ground has been evened out, replace the four corners of the turf. Use the back of a garden rake to press the turf back in place and to make sure that the grass roots are making firm contact with the soil. Bumps and hollows are best dealt with in spring or autumn since this gives the grass time to recover. Water the area if the weather is dry.

CUTTING BACK

Use either an electric or a petrol-driven string strimmer to clear long grass; a machine that cuts with a plastic cord should be quite adequate. Alternatively, use a hand tool such as a scythe or a sickle. Cut down the grass to a height your mower can manage. Let the grass recover and then use a mower on its highest setting.

Helpful hints

Where you have a large area of long grass that needs cutting, use the mower to cut a wide footpath (or several paths) for access. The grass on the paths can then continue to be cut regularly to a height of 2.5 cm (1 in), while the grass in the other areas can be left to grow (or mown back at another time).

Another approach is to cut grass where the ground is flat, but leave banks and slopes to become meadows. Large areas of grass need not take long to maintain if you choose equipment designed for larger lawns, such as ride-on mowers and dethatching machines.

LEVELLING AND PREPARING THE SITE

YOU WILL NEED

Spade

Sod stripper (optional)

Weed killer (optional)

String and pegs

Length of straight
timber

Garden rake

Spirit level

SEE ALSO

Using lawn tools
See *Tools for lawn care,*
pp. 72–73

Handling turf
See *Laying turf,*
pp. 78–79

Growing a new lawn
See *Using grass seed,*
pp. 80–81

Lawn design
See *Shaping your lawn,*
pp. 82–83

Lawn styles
See *Types of lawn,*
pp. 86–87

The ideal conditions for a lawn are an open, sunny position with a moist but well-drained soil. A lawn will never do well in deep shade, but drainage of waterlogged soils can be improved by installing land drains; consult a drainage specialist if necessary. Flat ground will produce the most uniform sward, so it is well worth taking time to level the ground thoroughly at the

start. Minor undulations in the surface can be easily tackled (see right), but when it comes to moving large quantities of earth (that is, removing all the topsoil), seek advice from a professional landscaper.

The ground for a lawn should be flat but not necessarily level; a slight incline or slope on a lawn is acceptable and often an attractive feature. However, for safety's sake, think twice about having a lawn on a slope of more than 15 degrees. While it is possible to buy commercial mowers with a low centre of gravity which can cope with such slopes, a carpet of ground cover, or a wildflower meadow, might be an easier solution.

The range of grass mixtures available (as both seed and turf) has improved greatly in recent years and suppliers now provide more information on the different varieties, so it should be easier to choose a mixture that is right for your garden. To help you decide whether to use turf or seed, see pages 78–81. Whichever you choose, the initial ground preparation is the same. This work is best tackled either in early autumn or in spring.

While there is no need for a garden roller these days to achieve the perfect, even lawn, thorough ground preparation at the outset will make your lawn easier to maintain.

EDGING

If you are creating a lawn, or altering an existing one, reduce the need to trim lawn edges by installing a mowing edge. This can be very discreet, a single row of bricks, for example, at the edge of the lawn, or it can be a feature such as a path. The secret of successful edging is to install it just below the surface of the lawn so the mower can be pushed over the edge of the lawn, cutting off

all the upright grass. Some grass will grow sideways over the edging but this is not as noticeable and can be trimmed when necessary. To make a brick edge, dig a trench deep enough to hold 2.5 cm (1 in) of mortar, plus 5 cm (2 in) of aggregate, plus the depth of the brick, and still be below the level of the lawn. Assuming a 23-cm (9-in) wide mowing strip, cut a trench 30 cm (12 in) wide.

Compact the trench base with the back of a rake and add rubble to its base. Spread a 2.5-cm (1-in) deep layer of mortar; place the bricks on top. Before the mortar sets, use a spirit level to check the bricks are even. Allow the mortar to dry slightly before adding more mortar to either side of the bricks (sloping it away from the top edges), in order to anchor them in place.

PREPARING AND LEVELLING THE SITE

1 Stake out garden canes around the area of the new lawn, and use a hose or rope to highlight the boundaries. If you are replacing an existing lawn, use a sharp spade to slice through and remove the unwanted turf. For large areas, consider renting a turf stripper. When stripping turf, try to keep as much of the topsoil as possible.

2 Dig over the ground thoroughly, down to one spade's depth. Remove any surface debris and dig out any buried stones. Tree roots can be cut with a pruning saw or severed with a sharp spade. Add soil improvers if necessary (see box below).

3 Clear away old tufts of grass and surface weeds. Deep-rooted perennial weeds will need to be removed by digging them out with a hand fork or by treating with a systemic weed killer. Bear in mind that chemical weed killers take several weeks to work.

4 Rake the soil, breaking up any clods of earth with the back of the rake head. Again, use the back of the rake head to push soil into the hollows and the front of the rake head to pull soil away from bumps.

5 Once the soil is in position and level, tread the whole surface in order to firm it down but without compacting it. Leave the ground until you are ready to turf or seed.

ENRICHING THE SOIL

Grass growing in deep, rich soil will be less vulnerable to pests and diseases. It also should grow vigorously enough to choke out competing weeds. Before amending soil, send samples to a soil laboratory for a full report on the pH and nutrient content. Armed with that information, you will know what you need to add. The best soil enricher is garden compost. It improves the structure of any kind of soil and adds important microorganisms and microbes. Well-rotted manure is another excellent improver.

If topsoil is thin, buy in some good-quality topsoil. Dig it in or rotovate to at least 10–15 cm (4–6 in) deep.

LAYING TURF

Choose a supplier that offers specific types of turf for different uses, such as hard-wearing or ornamental, and which allows you to see samples before ordering. Fresh turf is essential. If recently harvested, the grass will be a fresh green colour; avoid any that smells rotten or is starting to yellow. Well-cut turf has an even thickness of soil. A thin layer of soil may be lighter to move around, but there should be enough soil to hold the turf together when it is handled. Turves will keep rolled up for a day or two after cutting, if the weather is cool and the soil is kept moist. Otherwise, unroll the turves on a patio in a lightly shaded place and keep it watered. When laying a large lawn, it helps to put down planks over the newly laid turf and to work from these. It is easier to lay a square or rectangle of grass, before cutting the lawn into its final shape, such as a circle, at a later date. When laying turves around features such as island beds, always lay the turves flat and cut rather than bend to shape. The best place to start laying turf is against a straight edge at one corner of the lawn. To ensure a straight line, use either a permanent feature, such as a path, or a temporary edge, such as a wooden plank.

Making a lawn from turf gives a mature-looking area of grass quickly. Autumn is the ideal time to lay turf |since grass roots become established quickly in the warm soil, but are not subject to summer drought for many months. However, turf can be laid at any time of the year as long as the ground is not frozen or very dry.

PLANTING BULBS

Many spring-flowering bulbs can be planted under a lawn to flower in the grass. They include: *Anemone blanda, Crocus tommasinianus, C. vernus, Fritillaria meleagris, Galanthus nivalis, Narcissus* spp., *Scilla siberica,* and *Tulipa kaufmanniana.* As long as the grass is not cut until most of the bulbs' foliage has died back (about six weeks after flowering), they will naturalize over the years.

An ideal place for bulbs is an area where cutting can be delayed, such as on a gentle slope or near trees or shrubs. Most bulbs are planted in the autumn. Space small ones 2.5–5 cm (1–2 in) apart and larger ones 15 cm (6 in) apart. Plant at a depth twice the height of the bulb. Bulbs can be planted just before laying new turf or sowing grass seed or in an existing lawn. Use a sharp spade to cut down through the grass to about 2.5–5 cm (1–2 in). Slide the blade underneath so you can peel back the turf. Loosen the ground by pushing in a garden fork to open up the soil. Scatter the bulbs randomly and plant them where they fall. Plant each bulb, growing point upward, with its base in contact with the soil. Replace the soil and grass. Firm down and water thoroughly.

LAYING TURF

1 After levelling and preparing the ground (see pp. 76–77), mark out the area where the turf is going to be laid with pegs and string. Use a builder's square for any right-angled corners. The shapes of any planned island beds or other large features can be marked out as well.

2 Unroll the first strip of turf so that one long side is against a straight edge and press it down firmly with your hands. Kneel on a plank while laying the turf to spread your weight.

3 Position the second roll of turf so that its end is just overlapping the end of the first roll. Always slightly overlap the edges, then press them down hard; this helps to compensate for soil shrinkage later on. Carry on until the first row of turves is complete.

4 For the second and subsequent rows, stagger the joints (as you would with a brick wall) by overlapping at the boundary of the lawn; overlaps can be trimmed off later. When laying turf around obstacles, trim off excess turf where rows meet; use a knife to trim to a slight overlap and firmly press down the edges.

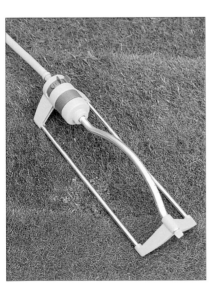

5 Give the lawn a thorough soaking until the soil underneath is wet. The easiest way to do this is to use a lawn sprinkler attached to a hose. Water the grass daily if the weather is dry, paying particular attention to the joints.

6 The overhanging lawn edges can be trimmed using a sharp spade or edging iron. Do this before the first mowing. Mow after two weeks with the mower on its highest setting.

USING GRASS SEED

Using grass seed is an inexpensive and versatile way of renovating an existing lawn as well as starting a lawn from scratch. A sparse sward will benefit from a technique called oversowing, whereas for a few bare patches reseeding is needed. Late August to early September is the best time to sow grass seed; the soil should be warm and starting to become moist, thus enabling the seed to

germinate well. By growing in the autumn the grass can establish itself before the drought and wear and tear of the following year's summer. Grass seed can also be sown in April, but you will probably have to water more often and it will be subject to wear and tear sooner.

Do not be tempted to buy cheap agricultural grass mixtures because they grow too vigorously upward, making a thin sword that needs frequent cutting. Before oversowing or reseeding, get rid of weeds or moss in the lawn; any bare ground that results can then be reseeded. Rake in a general fertilizer to improve the soil if it is low in nutrients.

When oversowing an existing lawn you need, in most instances, to use the same or a very similar seed mix, otherwise your lawn will have patches of grass growing at different rates. When oversowing a fine lawn, use fine grass mixtures to maintain the lawn as an ornamental lawn. However, a lawn containing rye-grass can be oversown with a similar cultivar of rye-grass or a fine-leaved species.

Sowing grass seed will create a fine lawn at just a fraction of the price of lawn turf, but you must protect the newly sown area from heavy wear for three to six months.

Helpful hints

Overseeding is used to thicken up sparse lawns. Use a spring-tine rake (or a powered dethatcher) to pull up any thatch and to straighten flattened grass. Scatter the seed at the recommended rate given in the manufacturer's instructions. The rate for overseeding is generally lower than that for sowing a new lawn, usually 20 g per sq m (¾ oz per sq yd). Often a fertilizer is included in the package as well. Protect the seeded area with plastic mesh. Within a month, the lawn should be thicker as the grass seedlings grow to fill the gaps in the existing lawn. Set the mower blades high while the new grass establishes itself.

RESEEDING

Bare patches in a lawn can be re-seeded. Rake or fork over the ground to make a seedbed; water if the soil is dry. Scatter a general fertilizer – about 28 g per sq m (1 oz per sq yd) – then grass seed at the rate advised on the package. Rake in the seed and use the back of the rake head to firm the surface. Net the patch until germination.

SOWING SEED

1 Lay four 1-m (3-ft) canes on the ground to form a square. Check the recommended application rate because it varies between seed mixtures. If no measure is supplied, make your own by weighing out the amount needed for 1 sq m (1 sq yd) into an empty plastic pot or jar and marking the level.

2 Scatter the correct measure of seed over the square by sowing half the seed in one direction, then the other half at right angles. Pick up three of the canes and make an adjacent square. Carry on sowing seed, 1 sq m (1 sq yd) at a time, until the whole area has been sown.

3 Lightly work the seed into the soil with a garden rake. Firm the ground gently, but firmly with the back of the rake head. This is sufficient to make sure the grass seed is in contact with the soil; there is no need to use a heavy roller.

4 Cover the seeded area with plastic mesh, using large stones or bricks to hold the mesh in place around the edges. Secure the ends over inverted pots on top of garden stakes. Use a sprinkler to moisten the soil in dry spells. Germination should start within two weeks. When the grass is 5 cm (2 in) high, make the first cut, but take off only about 1 cm (½ in).

UNDERSTANDING THE SEED PACKAGE LABEL

A seed package label is full of valuable information. The label should contain the following:

Percentage of pure seed: The label should list each type of grass in the package and the percentage of each. This is based on weight, not number of seeds. Don't settle for less than a total of 80 per cent desirable lawn species. Unless you are overseeding a warm-season lawn for winter, look for less than 3 to 5 per cent of annual grasses. Don't buy if the label states "VNS" – "variety not stated".

Germination: The percentage of live or viable seed; expect a germination rate of at least 85 per cent.

Weed seeds: Accept no more than 0.5 per cent weed seed by weight. Look for the promise "No noxious weeds". Noxious weeds are hard-to-control plants unsuitable in a lawn.

Cultivar names: Many cultivars or trade-named grasses are better than plain species; worth paying more for.

Test date: Don't buy seed that was tested more than nine months to one year before the purchase date.

Inert matter: Percentage by weight of chaff and dirt in the package.

Endophyte-enhanced: Research shows that such grasses are more drought tolerant and pest resistant.

SHAPING YOUR LAWN

YOU WILL NEED

Paving slabs

Sharp spade

Knife or pruning saw

Tape measure

Pegs and string

Sharp sand

Level

Broom

SEE ALSO

Handling sod
See *Laying turf,*
pp. 78–79

Reseeding
See *Using grass seed,*
pp. 80–81

Lawn maintenance
See *Caring for your lawn,*
pp. 84–85

Lawn styles
See *Types of lawn,*
pp. 86–87

A lawn is a very versatile garden feature. If you want to make mowing easier, widen a border, or to change the style of a garden, this can be done easily without any special tools. Simple lawn shapes, such as circles, squares or rectangles, have more visual impact in a small or medium-sized garden than too many fussy edges. Upkeep is also simplified. To maintain the tidy shape of the lawn, you will need to trim the grass around the edges now and again (even though you may have a mowing edge), since it tends to grow sideways and look untidy. If a small section of lawn edge has crumbled away or is damaged, it can be repaired easily, but where a long stretch of edging has crumbled, or has started to merge with a border, it is better to cut the lawn to shape again. Any shaping or repairing is best done in autumn or spring to give the grass time to recover before summer.

Grass paths create a softer look in the garden, compared to paving slabs and cobblestones. Choose a hardwearing variety of seed if your grass is to be used as a walk or play area.

WELL-WORN AREAS

Where parts of the lawn are regularly worn down to compacted earth and no grass, there is little point in reseeding each year, or re-laying fresh turf. The answer is either to use a different surface or to redesign the garden so that those activities responsible for the worn areas are moved somewhere else. Putting in stepping stones along a well-worn route is easier than putting in a proper path. Any type of slab or flat stone will do; it does not have to be square, just big enough to put your foot on. Many interesting patterns can be made by arranging the stepping stones. For example, they can be set on a diagonal, or laid in a grid. Remember to keep the pattern simple, since you will have to trim the grass around them and between them every so often.

Baked earth or sticky mud under children's play equipment can be replaced with a deep layer of bark chips. Make sure you get play-grade material. This costs more but is better quality; it contains chunky pieces of bark, not sharp wood chips. You will need to keep the chips in place and to support the lawn; boards on edge or a roll of edging plastic or metal material are all easy to lay.

CUTTING LAWN TO SHAPE

1 To make a circle, take a length of string slightly longer than the diameter; tie the ends together. Insert a pole into the ground at the centre. Loop the string over the pole, insert a sharp stick (or a container of free-flowing sand) in the other end, and move around the pole, keeping the string taut. Use the stick (or sand) to mark the circle.

2 Using a garden knife or pruning saw, cut along the marked curve. Hold the grass taut, with your free hand, to ensure a clean cut.

LAYING STEPPINGSTONES

1 Position the slabs and try walking over them to ensure they will be comfortably spaced. Cut deep into the turf around each slab; then undercut the turf and lift it out. Remove enough soil to take the depth of the slab and 5 cm (2 in) of sand, plus a bit extra to ensure a correct bedding level.

2 Flatten the bottom of the hole and lay a 5-cm (2-in) deep layer of sharp sand. Place the slab in position. Check that the slab is below the level of the surrounding lawn and make sure it is level. Make any necessary adjustments by adding or removing sand as necessary. Once you are happy with the position, sweep the slab clean with a broom.

REPAIRING LAWN EDGES

1 Use a sharp spade, half-moon cutter or knife and a straight piece of wood to cut out a section of turf enclosing the damaged edge. Undercut the turf so it can be moved.

2 Fill in the resulting hole within the lawn with either sieved topsoil or soil-based compost, firm it so it is level with the ground. The area can now be re-seeded or a new piece of turf can be laid.

CARING FOR YOUR LAWN

YOU WILL NEED

Moss killer

Fertilizer spreader

Spring-tine rake

Lawn mower

SEE ALSO

Lawn repair
See *Shaping your lawn,*
pp. 82–83

Feeding
See *Applying fertilizers,*
pp. 98–99

Weed control
See *Dealing with weeds,*
pp. 102–103

Once you have dealt with any major problems, there are just a few basic techniques needed to keep your lawn in reasonable condition. The lawn will need cutting, but only when it is growing; the number of times you need to mow the lawn depends on the weather in any particular year. If mowing is a chore, see the "Helpful

hints" box opposite. Autumn is the most important time of year to fertilize cool-season grasses. Give a light spring feeding as well if the grass is ailing or your soil is poor. Fertilize warm-season grasses in spring once growth begins and again in August or September. Do not feed warm-season grasses later in autumn. Most weeds can be dealt with by hand-weeding or a spotweeder.

On wet soil or in shaded areas, moss can be a real nuisance; you may have to resign yourself to using a moss killer every year, dealing with soil drainage or eliminating the shade. Some lawns produce a lot of thatch (a spongy layer of dead grass and plant debris on the surface of the soil). Where this is more than 1 cm (½ in) thick, it can be raked out to keep the grass healthy. Any live moss in such areas must first be killed in order to avoid raking it to other areas. Established lawns should not need regular watering in summer; they may turn brown during dry spells but will green up again in the autumn.

With a small amount of attention in spring, followed by a sensible mowing regime that cuts little and often throughout the summer, garden lawns will thrive.

REMOVING MOSS

When moss starts to take over a lawn, it is a sign that conditions are either too wet or too shady for the grass to compete. In the short term, you can kill the moss but it will return unless you improve soil drainage and/or reduce the shade.

Apply moss killer according to the instructions on the package. Small areas can be spotweeded with a hand-held sprayer. For larger areas,

it is worth using a moss killer combined with either a feed or, if necessary, a "weed and feed" product. Most are sold in a granular form and are easy to apply using a fertilizer spreader.

The following week, cut the lawn with the mower blades set on the highest setting. You should see areas where there once was moss and where weeds have started to blacken.

The next week, rake out dead plant debris using a spring-tine rake and then mow as normal. You may now need to reseed bare patches or, if the moss was very widespread, oversow with grass seed to fill in the gaps. Prune any overhanging trees or shrubs that cast shade over the lawn.

Alternatively, try raising the pH level of an acid soil by adding an application of lime.

APPLYING LAWN FEED

Be careful to apply lawn feed evenly, otherwise your lawn will be patchy looking. Powdered or granular feeds can be broadcast by hand or dispensed from a container or wheeled fertilizer spreader. Liquid feeds are diluted according to the instructions and applied using a hose-end sprayer.

HAND-WEEDING LAWNS

Aim to remove the whole weed, both top growth and roots. Weeding tools such as daisy grubbers are designed to ease roots out of the ground without bringing up large amounts of soil. If you do need to remove weeds with a hand fork or trowel, do this when the weeds are young.

REMOVING THATCH

A layer of thatch more than 1 cm (½ in) deep is best removed. Use a spring-tine rake on a small or medium-sized lawn; do this little and often in the growing season (but not in a drought). Rent a powered de-thatching machine (or buy an attachment for your mower) to remove thatch on large lawns.

AERATING A LAWN

For compacted soil, push a garden fork into the ground to a depth of about 10 cm (4 in). Do this all over the lawn. For larger lawns, rent a powered aerator that removes small cores of soil, then spread a thin layer of composted bark or sieved leaf mould over the lawn and brush it into the holes. Aerate in spring or autumn, when the ground is moist.

USING SPOT-WEEDERS

Target problem weeds with a ready-to-use hand-held sprayer. Alternatively, use paint-on lawn weed-killer. Either approach is more sensible than dosing the whole lawn. The treated area can then be protected from children and pets until the chemical is dry.

Helpful hints

There are several ways to make mowing less of a chore. Make sure your mower is the right size; if mowing the lawn is becoming a time-consuming burden, perhaps it is time to get a mower with a wider cutting blade or make your lawn smaller, or simplify its shape. Mowing is quicker and less tiring when you leave the grass collecting box off. The clippings can be left on the lawn as long as they are fine and widely dispersed. They will rot down quickly and feed the grass naturally. Mowing little and often produces the healthiest grass. A minimum cutting height of 2.5 cm (1 in) is adequate for most lawns.

TYPES OF LAWN

PLANTING SUGGESTIONS

Lawns struggle in shade and in dry, sunny sites, but there are other options.

In shade, use low ground-cover plants, preferably ones that are easy to propagate. There are several varieties of bugle (*Ajuga reptans*), a creeping evergreen perennial, in various colours. Ivy is ideal under shady trees if pegged down to stop it from climbing up the trunks. An alternative to ivy, with the benefit of blue flowers, is the lesser periwinkle (*Vinca minor*).

In a warm, dry site, choose a mat-forming herb such as thyme (*Thymus serpyllum*), chamomile (the best for alternative lawns is *Chamaemelum nobile* 'Treneague'), or oregano (*Origanum vulgare*). Most will need trimming; but for drought-tolerance and easy upkeep use lilyturf (*Ophiopogon japonicus*), an evergreen perennial which looks like a dwarf ornamental grass.

Grass is a very versatile surface. You might want your lawn to be neat and crisp, and grown solely for its lush green appearance, or you might prefer a less-than-perfect space which could be suitable for games and pets. The type of lawn you choose will depend upon your lifestyle and the size and layout of your garden. If you are starting with bare ground, you can seed or turf, using a suitable grass species that will cope with, say, close mowing, or wear and tear. Note that some grass species are just not suitable for heavy wear or for growing in shade.

No plant is more resistant to being walked on than grass. But if the growing conditions are not suitable, or if maintenance would be difficult, other plants (such as thyme or chamomile) can provide an alternative.

► DIFFERENT MOWING HEIGHTS The path across the lawn has been mowed short, but the grass between trees has been left long. Naturalized daffodils appear in clumps near the trees; the grass here can be left longer before it is cut.

◄ CLOAK OF GREEN Any low-growing evergreen can be used to create a green carpet. Remember, though, that invasive plants need to be contained by decorative edging, a path or, as shown here, by a stream.

▲ GRASS TILES
This modern approach to planting has created an eye-catching pattern using slabs (which take the wear and tear) interspersed with low-maintenance lilyturf.

▲ SEPARATING PLANTINGS
The broad sweeps of lawn between these island beds are pleasing to the eye and promote a feeling of tranquillity. Grass makes a good surface for paths, provided they are wide enough (in order to avoid excessive wear).

◄ EDGE TO BORDER
Nothing sets off a well-planted border better than a neat lawn. A mowing edge or path between the lawn and the border will prevent plants from spilling on to the lawn and reduce the need for trimming.

SOIL

Before you rush into selecting and buying trees, shrubs and other garden plants, it is important to find out what sort of soil is in your garden and whether it needs improving in any way. Most soils benefit from the addition of well-rotted organic matter, which opens up the soil. Some organic matter can be obtained by collecting and composting grass clippings, prunings, fallen leaves and other plant waste. The tools you need to cultivate the ground for planting are covered in this chapter, which also includes a practical guide to identifying and dealing with garden weeds.

IDENTIFYING YOUR SOIL TYPE

YOU WILL NEED

Spade

Trowel

Waterproof cover

Plant label

4 x 1–2m (3–6-ft) bamboo canes

Saucer

Test kit for pH

Teaspoon

SEE ALSO

Better soil
See *Improving your soil*, pp. 94–95

Feeding
See *Applying fertilizers*, pp. 98–99

Making compost
See *Organic matter from your garden*, pp. 96–97

So you can grow the right plant in the right place, it is worth finding out about your garden soil at an early stage. You can then decide what types of plant will thrive in your garden, and also whether to make any improvements to the soil. To do the basic tests outlined here, you just need common sense and a willingness to get your hands dirty. Most tests can be done at any time of year, except the drainage test, which should be done in late winter or when the water table is at its highest. In a large garden, or where the land has many changes in level, it is worth doing soil tests in several places.

A good place to start is to test the texture: dig down about 10 cm (4 in) and feel a handful of the soil. This will give you an idea whether the soil contains sand, loam, or clay; additionally you might see white or grey lumps of chalk or lots of stones in it. For most gardeners, loam is the ideal soil; this is a mixture of different-sized particles of both sand and clay. Loam can hold moisture in summer but allow water to drain through freely in winter; this means plant roots have access to water for growth without getting waterlogged. Where there is a high proportion of either clay or sand or a lot of

peat, you may need to improve the soil. Fertilizing, liming or adding organic matter to a soil can affect its fertility or moisture-holding ability. To find out more, if for example, you are planning a vegetable or fruit garden, you can send a soil sample to a soil laboratory for a chemical analysis. Take a sample by following step 1 of the acid/alkaline test (you usually need about 500 g [1 lb] of soil, but check with the laboratory). You can buy a simple test kit to see for yourself if the soil is acid, alkaline or neutral. This will tell you enough to decide if you can grow camellias or rhododendrons, but if you want to make an acid soil more alkaline by adding lime, you will need a more precise measure of the soil pH so that you know how much lime to add.

Plants vary greatly in their tolerance to drought and to waterlogged soil. How wet the soil is during winter can also determine how hardy a plant will be in a certain site. Drainage depends not only on the soil type but on the lie of the land and sources of ground water. It is straightforward to find out how well drained your soil is, but improving a waterlogged site can sometimes be difficult, as well as expensive.

TESTING SOIL TEXTURE

1 Squeeze some moist soil in your hand. If it feels spongy, a bit like peat or moss, it has a high organic content, either because it has been cultivated or because it is naturally peaty. Rub some soil between your thumb and fingertips. If it feels gritty that means sand is present. On the other hand, a smooth texture indicates either a loam or clay.

2 Knead the soil and try to work it into a ball. If you succeed, the soil contains some clay particles; if it keeps breaking up, it contains very few clay particles. Roll the ball into a sausage shape, then try to bend it into a circle. A loam soil does not have sufficient clay particles to bind together to form a circle, but a soil heavy with clay does.

DRAINAGE TEST

1 In late winter, dig a hole 45 cm (18 in) across and 45 cm (18 in) deep. If you cannot dig as deep because there is not enough topsoil, just dig as far as you can. Fill the hole halfway up with water, then push a cane into the ground and mark the water level. Put a waterproof cover over the hole.

2 Check the level of water in the hole after an hour and again the next day. If the water has drained away within an hour, it indicates a free-draining soil. Water will drain away overnight on an average or normal soil. If the water is still at its initial level the next day, this indicates heavy clay or waterlogged soil.

TESTING ACIDITY AND ALKALINITY

1 Lay out bamboo canes in a zigzag across the sample area. Using a clean trowel, take some soil at the five points at the end of the canes. Dig down about 10 cm (4 in) so you get to the natural soil rather than mulch or fertilizer. Remove debris such as stones or weeds and crush any lumps of soil. Mix the five samples together in a clean container.

2 To get a rough idea if the soil is acid or alkaline, use a pH kit. Take 2.5 ml (½ tsp) of the soil sample and drop it into the test tube. Add tap water, shake well, and allow to settle. Compare the colour of the liquid with the colour chart supplied with the kit, and read the description.

YOUR SOIL PROFILE

Dig a deep hole in the ground and examine the sides of the hole. You should see layers of different colours and textures of soil. Usually you will see a darker, organic layer of topsoil, then an underlying layer of lighter subsoil. Most plants root in the fertile topsoil, where organic matter, soil creatures like earthworms and microorganisms are found. The underlying subsoil is infertile and should never be mixed with the topsoil or the quality of the latter will be lessened. Checking the soil profile alerts you to future problems.

If a clay soil has been compacted by heavy machinery, a hard layer forms within the topsoil which plant roots cannot penetrate. This hard layer needs to be broken up by systematic digging, otherwise plants will be unable to establish themselves. Sometimes plants cannot thrive because the topsoil has either been destroyed (typically debris or subsoil has been dumped over the topsoil during excavations) or is very shallow (as is the case with many chalky soils). If your garden does not have enough topsoil, it is worth buying some and incorporating good-quality organic matter well in advance of any major planting.

CULTIVATING AND WEEDING

DIGGING

A spade is designed for digging down into the soil; it should never be used to bang in posts or prize up slabs. Digging is strenuous work and hard on the back, so choose a spade with a handle long enough to keep your back straight. Border spades have smaller blades, are less tiring to use and make it easier to work in confined spaces, but take longer to dig over a large plot. Even if you are not planning to do much digging, it is worth buying a spade for planting trees, hedges and shrubs.

FORKING

A garden fork is easier than a spade to push down into stony or compacted ground in order to open it up. A garden fork is also used for lifting out perennials and shrubs from the ground or turning over a compost heap. As with spades, there is a choice of handle length and head size, so it is worth buying one that suits your height and build. Hand forks are much smaller and are used to work the ground between plants or to remove any weeds.

RAKING

After digging or forking, soil is often uneven and full of clods and stones. A garden rake will level out the soil and break it down to create a crumb-like texture ideal for starting off young plants or sowing seeds. As well as raking with the tines facing into the soil, also move earth around by pushing it with the rake held with its tines facing upward. The back of the rake will also break up clods of earth. A rake can also be used to level out

gravel, but it is not suitable for lawns. If you want a variety of rakes, consider buying a multi-change handle that allows various heads to slot in as required.

PLANTING

Bedding plants, small perennials, and young vegetable plants are planted by making holes in the ground using a trowel. It gets a lot of use so buy a good-quality trowel that feels comfortable in your hand. Narrow-width trowels with a more pointed blade are also available; these are useful

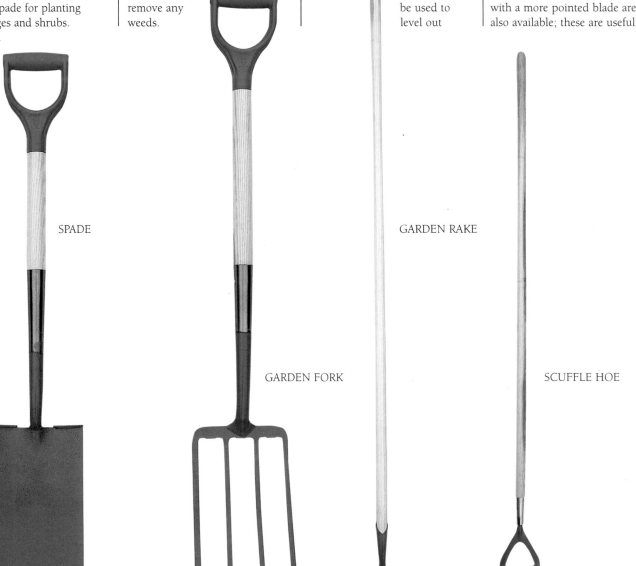

SPADE

GARDEN FORK

GARDEN RAKE

SCUFFLE HOE

for weeding in confined spaces and for planting bulbs. When planting larger perennials, shrubs, climbers and trees, use a spade rather than a trowel. A quick way to plant seedlings, transplants or small bulbs is to make a hole in the soil with a dibber. Bulb planters take out a core of soil at a known depth and then release it over the planted bulbs. They can be quicker than using a trowel or dibber if the soil is workable.

HOEING

Hoeing is the act of cultivating the surface of the soil to get rid of weeds and to break up the surface or to prepare a seedbed. To slice through annual seedlings use a scuffle hoe; the sharp blade is pushed and pulled just below the surface of the soil. It is worth using a scuffle hoe between rows of seedlings on vegetable plots and where outdoor sowings need to be kept free of weeds. A draw hoe is used with a chopping action to get rid of larger weeds, but it can also be used to carve out rows for seeds or troughs in prepared seedbeds.

HAND WEEDERS

There are numerous weeding tools with both short and long handles used to cultivate or weed around established plants. If you have a site that is tricky to weed, it is worth looking for a specialist tool. To cut out weeds growing between cracks in paving, use a paving weeder; the one shown below has a cutting edge and a hook to pull out the weeds. For removing weeds growing in rock crevices, use a fishtail weeder. To extract the roots of perennial weeds in lawns without having to disturb lots of soil, use a daisy grubber or taproot weeder.

MULTICHANGE HEADS

A multichange tool system allows you to have a range of different tool heads without having to buy a handle each time. You can buy a single handle, adjustable in length in order to suit your height; thereafter, just buy specific tool heads as required. There is usually a wide choice of heads, including various rakes, cultivators and hoes. Such systems can work out cheaper and make tools easier to store and transport. The drawbacks are that you are limited to one company's products and only one tool can be used at any one time.

APPLYING WEED KILLERS

Most spot-weeders come ready to use, so for a small area, no special tools are needed. To tackle a large overgrown area it will be more economical to buy a concentrated weed killer and dilute it in either a watering can or a sprayer, which must be reserved for that purpose only. When buying a watering can (or sprayer) to apply chemicals, choose one in a different colour from those used for watering plants, and fit it with a dribble-bar to apply the product evenly over lawns or paths. Compression sprayers come in various sizes. To use them, you pump up the reservoir containing the diluted weed killer to increase the pressure, then squeeze the trigger to control and direct the spray.

HARVESTING

Bare hands remain the best tools for harvesting garden produce, but an extendable fruit harvester is extremely useful for reaching tree fruits. It is fitted with a soft cloth bag to ensure that the fruits are not bruised when they are being picked.

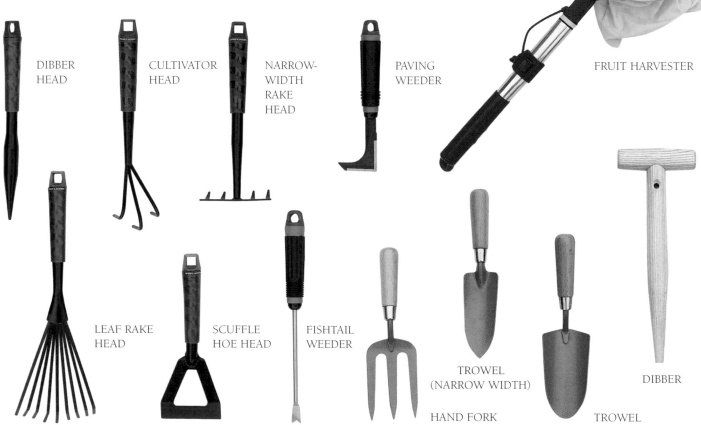

DIBBER HEAD

CULTIVATOR HEAD

NARROW-WIDTH RAKE HEAD

PAVING WEEDER

FRUIT HARVESTER

LEAF RAKE HEAD

SCUFFLE HOE HEAD

FISHTAIL WEEDER

HAND FORK

TROWEL (NARROW WIDTH)

TROWEL

DIBBER

IMPROVING YOUR SOIL

YOU WILL NEED

Spade

Pegs

String

Well-rotted organic
matter

Wheelbarrow

SEE ALSO

Soil type
See *Identifying your soil
type, pp. 90–91*

Making compost
See *Organic matter from
your garden, pp. 96–97*

Feeding
See *Applying fertilizers,
pp. 98–99*

*Once a garden bed is
crammed with plants, full-
scale soil improvement is
difficult to carry out,
so aim to do as much as
you can before or just
after planting.*

Nearly all soils (apart from peaty soils) are improved by adding organic matter, such as garden compost, grass clippings or a green manure. It improves the moisture-holding abilities of free-draining soils such as chalky, stony and sandy soils, and opens up heavy clay soils, improving structure and allowing water to drain away.

Organic matter can either be dug in or mulched, that is, laid on the surface of the soil and left for earthworms to complete the task. Mulching is less strenuous than digging, but cannot tackle underlying problems such as soil compaction. Digging opens up compacted soil, aerates it and improves drainage. At the same time as boosting your soil, you can remove perennial weed roots and incorporate bulky organic matter. For most soils, single digging (see box opposite) will suffice as a once-only treatment, followed by mulching each year thereafter.

If you have hardpan (compacted earth) deep in the soil, you may need to double-dig to break it up. This involves digging over and removing the topsoil, prior to digging down another spade's depth, breaking up the

Helpful hints

If your garden contains rubble or subsoil, the problem must be tackled at the outset. A professional landscape contractor can clear away or level subsoil and then lay the required topsoil. The latter must be of good quality, with a soil structure that holds moisture without waterlogging, and with an acceptable pH. The nutrient content of topsoil is less critical because it can be adjusted at a later date by using fertilizers. After the soil has been allowed to settle, you can start planting. Topsoil that is on the shallow side can be made deeper by adding organic matter each year.

hardpan, and adding organic matter. Double-digging is time-consuming and hard work, but you should need to do it only once.

The best time to dig is in late autumn or as the soil is drying out in spring. In autumn, you can leave large clods of earth on the soil surface for the frost, snow and rain to break down. By spring, the clods will form a layer of crumbly soil. On light sandy soils, wait until spring before digging, since a hard crust forms on the surface over winter.

ACID AND ALKALINE SOILS

Most garden soils are between pH 5.5 and pH 7.5 (acid to alkaline, pH 7 being neutral). Most plants prefer a slightly acid soil (pH 6 to pH 6.5). A very acidic soil (pH 5.0) is suitable for such species as rhododendrons, although adding lime will enable a greater range of plants to be grown. Add lime to the soil in the autumn and wait until spring before applying manure or fertilizer; nitrogen can be lost if both are applied at the same time. It is not easy to make an alkaline soil more acid, but there are many lime-tolerant plants and any acid-lovers can always be grown in pots of peat-based soil mix.

WORKING ON WET SOILS

1 Digging helps to open up compacted clay soil, but if it is a very wet site you will need to carry out the digging either when the soil is dry in the autumn or is drying out in the spring. Avoid walking over or compacting wet clay soils. Put down planks to spread your weight, or put in proper paths with raised beds.

2 Adding organic matter can help to improve the drainage of a wet, clay soil. Grit makes an immediate improvement in wet peat and clay soils. Digging it in can be hard work and expensive. Use 3mm (⅛ in) grit. A wheelbarrowfull will cover 2–3 sq m (20–30 sq ft) of soil.

MULCHING

1 Spread organic matter on the surface of the soil in a deep layer, at least 5 cm (2 in) thick. Avoid covering the stems or crowns of plants. The best time to apply a mulch is in mid-spring. A thick mulch prevents weed seeds from germinating and keeps soil moist. Water cocoa husks after laying so that they bind together and do not blow away.

2 Keep dogs away from cocoa husks and deter cats from mulches by moistening the surface or putting in some sharp sticks. In time, earthworms will drag the mulch into the soil where it will rot down. Reapply or add more mulch every spring. Raise the height of the beds by using a brick or wooden edging in order to help retain the mulch in position.

SINGLE DIGGING

When faced with heavily compacted soil or a new plot that has never been cultivated, single digging of the soil is needed to provide the best possible start for your plants. Although it may seem a daunting task, console yourself with the fact that it rarely needs to be carried out more than once on a bed.

First, mark out the area to be dug into a square or rectangle.

Spread an even layer of organic matter over the soil surface so that it will be mixed into the topsoil as you dig. Excavate a trench about 30 cm (12 in) wide to the depth of the spade. Moving only the topsoil, not the underlying subsoil, transfer it to a wheelbarrow or place it to one side on a plastic sheet. Remove any weeds, roots, stones or other debris in the bed as you come across them.

The soil from this first trench will be used in the last trench. Dig out a second trench alongside the first, and move its topsoil to fill the first trench. Then, dig out a third trench, and move its topsoil to fill the second trench. Repeat this procedure until you are left with the final trench. To fill this trench, use the soil that was set aside from the first trench.

ORGANIC MATTER FROM YOUR GARDEN

YOU WILL NEED

Compost bin kit

Garden fork

Composting material

Old carpet or sacking

Waterproof compost bin cover

Watering can

Four 1-m (3-ft) canes

Plastic or wire mesh

SEE ALSO

Better soil
See *Improving your soil*,
pp. 94–95

Feeding
See *Applying fertilizers*,
pp. 98–99

Well-rotted organic matter is any material of plant or animal origin that has been composted down for use as a soil improver. Recycle as much as you can from your own garden and kitchen in order to make garden compost and leaf mould. The most efficient way to get started is to collect all the material together in a bin and provide the right conditions for it to rot down quickly. The ideal size and shape for a workable compost bin is 1 m (1 yd) for each dimension (that is, width, depth and height). Any smaller and it is hard to keep the material warm enough to ensure composting. The bin should be placed in a shaded area, away from the kitchen and seating areas, but with good access so it can be filled regularly. Leaf mould can be stored in a container of any size in any suitable out-of-the-way place.

There are numerous types of compost bin available. Most are not particularly attractive, so consider screening them from view, either by building an enclosure made from fence panels or trellis or by using evergreen shrubs or hedging plants. Allow space around the bin for a wheelbarrow for times when the bin is to be filled up or emptied. A traditional compost bin is made from wood. You can either make one yourself using fence posts and rough-sawn timber or you can buy one in kit form. Plastic bins are also available, some of which are closed systems that keep out vermin. Rather than being filled little and often, plastic bins are filled up once and then left. Leaf mould enclosures are simpler structures than compost bins and can be rigged up using whatever materials you have on hand.

You may need to supplement your home-made organic matter with horse manure. Spent mushroom compost (manure, peat and lime) is another alternative, but it is very alkaline: it is good for the vegetable plot, but not for acid-loving plants. Some processed bagged soil improvers are also alkaline, so check the packaging for details. Animal manure from local sources may cost next to nothing, but it is usually fresh and needs to be composted before use. Stack it in a site where any liquid will not run into nearby ponds or streams. Water the material if it is dry, then cover it with a waterproof sheet secured at the edges. The manure should be ready to use in a couple of months.

Helpful hints

Turn the contents of the compost bin once every six weeks. Fork out the contents either on to the ground, and then back in again, or into a vacant adjacent bin. Within a year you will have a dark, crumbly garden compost. The following materials can be composted: fruit and vegetable waste, shredded newspaper (in moderation), grass cuttings, green prunings, remains of bedding plants, top growth from perennials, used potting soil from containers, and woody prunings if shredded. Do not add eggshells, meat products, weeds, or diseased or pest-ridden plants.

SHREDDED MATERIAL

The quickest way to make compost is to shred woody prunings into small pieces before adding them to the heap. Use an electric or petrol-driven shredder to make light work of piles of prunings. For your own protection, wear safety gear, such as goggles, earplugs and heavy-duty gloves.

MAKING YOUR OWN GARDEN COMPOST

1 Assemble the compost bin according to the instructions; here the sides are made of removable slats that make the bin easy to fill and empty. The bin needs to be strong and of good quality because when it is full, its contents exert quite a force on the wood.

2 The bin should be on free-draining soil (not on concrete or paving), so that worms and insects can migrate into it and help aerate the compost. If the soil is wet, put a layer of twigs under the bin.

3 Fill the bin with alternating 15-cm (6-in) deep layers of green waste and woody material. The more you chop up the waste, the sooner the compost will form. You can add a handful of nitrogen fertilizer or a shovelful of garden soil to get the process going.

4 Cover the top layer with a square of old carpet or sacking to keep the contents moist and warm. The contents may need watering in dry spells. Shredded newspaper, in particular, will rot down more quickly if watered. In spells of heavy rain, place a waterproof cover over the bin to prevent its contents from becoming slimy.

MAKING LEAF MOULD

1 Gather up autumn leaves by using a hinged leaf rake, a spring-tine rake or a leaf collector. To speed up the breakdown of the leaves, run a mower over them to cut them up prior to storage. Leaves are broken down by fungi (unlike compost, which relies on bacteria), so there is no need for any warmth to aid the process.

2 Make a simple enclosure to hold the leaves. Use plastic or wire mesh wrapped around four tall stakes. There is no need to cover the leaves; just wet them if they are dry. Leaf mould takes from six months to two years to form, depending upon the types of leaf.

APPLYING FERTILIZERS

YOU WILL NEED

Liquid feed

Watering can

Bamboo cane

Hand held sprayer

SEE ALSO

Soil types
See *Identifying your soil type, pp. 90–91*

Better soil
See *Improving your soil, pp. 94–95*

Making compost
See *Organic matter from your garden, pp. 96–97*

Garden soils already contain some nutrients, and any organic matter added to improve the structure of the soil will also contribute to soil fertility. Animal manures, especially poultry manure, are rich in nutrients. Cocoa husks and garden compost also have useful amounts, but leaf mould and chipped bark contribute very little in the way of nutrients. The organic approach to gardening is to feed the soil with natural and composted (that is, organic) matter, rather than rely on fertilizers. If your soil is low in nutrients and you cannot add sufficient organic matter, fertilizers offer a quick and easy way of supplying your plants' needs. Fertilizers can be formulated to release nutrients slowly (pellets, sticks or plugs) or quickly (liquids, fine powders or granules).

Slow- or controlled-release fertilizers are usually applied annually, at the start of the growing season. Fast-acting fertilizers should be used only when plants are actively growing. Nitrogen, phosphorus and potassium are the three major nutrients that may need to be added to soil. Soluble nitrogen (nitrates or ammonium salts) are easily washed out of soils during heavy rain. Free-draining soils, such as sandy or chalky soils or potting composts, are most likely to leave plants short of nitrogen. Both phosphorus and potassium are usually present in sufficient quantities in garden soils, but if in doubt get your soil analysed. Extra potash, such as a tomato feed or rose fertilizer, will boost fruiting and flowering plants.

Although you can grow many types of plant without adding fertilizers, those that are harvested or cut back regularly will need feeding.

ORGANIC FEEDS

You may find organic feeds are useful if you are waiting for soil fertility to build up, if growing a greedy crop or if a plant is showing signs of nutrient deficiency. Organic fertilizers include blood, fish and bone meal, green sand and pelleted manure (a form which is relatively odour free).

Organic liquid feeds such as those based on seaweed extract are useful for counteracting trace-element deficiencies.

Some gardeners also make homemade feeds, often referred to as "tea", using compost or manure soaked in water. Other possible ingredients include stinging nettles, which produce a feed that is strong in iron, magnesium and sulphur, and comfrey, which provides a high-potatassium liquid feed.

MAKING UP LIQUID FEED

1 Measure out the concentrated liquid into a watering can using the cap or other measure provided. Fill with the appropriate amount of water. A typical watering can holds 7.5 litres (2 gallons). Stir with a bamboo cane to mix thoroughly. You can make up and then store liquid feeds..

2 To deliver feed directly to the roots of a particular plant, insert an empty plastic pot, with drainage holes, into the soil near the plant when planting up. Filling this up will direct the feed to the plant's roots via the holes in the pot.

TOP DRESSING

Wearing gloves, take a handful of powder or granules and scatter it over the soil or mulch, following the application rate given on the package. Apply it on a windless day and avoid spilling any on plant foliage. Rain will wash the fertilizer down into the soil.

USING FEEDSTICKS OR PLUGS

Insert feedsticks or plugs of fertilizer into pots of compost at the start of the growing season (spring). The fertilizer is formulated to release its nutrients into the compost as the temperature rises. You may need to supplement with liquid feed as the growing season progresses.

TYPES OF FERTILIZER

Balanced or general fertilizers, such as blood, fish, and bone meal, contain more or less equal amounts of nitrogen, phosphate, and potash. To find out if a fertilizer is balanced and what percentage of nitrogen it contains, look on the package for the nutrient ratio expressed as N:P.O:K. For example, a balanced or general fertilizer has a ratio of 7:7:7, making it ideal for soils lacking the three major nutrients. Straight fertilizers add just one nutrient, so a soil with plenty of phosphorus and potash can be topped up with nitrogen, by applying sulphate of ammonia or nitrochalk.

Helpful hints

As a quick emergency measure to rescue a starving plant, spray a foliar feed on plant foliage. Foliar feeding is not a routine technique, but may be used to save a favourite plant that is suffering from a lack of nutrients. Use foliar feeds only on a dull day, since strong sunlight may cause the feed to burn the plant. Damage to the roots is usually the cause of the problem and will need to be addressed before the next growing season. Perhaps the plant needs to be moved to more suitable soil during the dormant season or, if grown in a container, it may need to be transplanted to a larger pot.

TYPES OF WEED

The same plant can be a weed to one person and a wildflower or butterfly plant to someone else. A lot depends on your style of gardening and whether the native plants are contributing to your garden or simply getting in the way and competing with the plants you have chosen to grow. Often it is not so much the weed itself, but where it is growing, that is the problem. For example, ivy might be welcome to colonize an old tree stump or wall but not to smother a young, recently planted hedge. Similarly, weeds in dense shade where few other plants thrive may be best left where they are.

Knowing how a weed spreads gives you a better chance of controlling it. If you can identify the weed and know its Latin name, you can find out more about its method of reproduction from a reference book. Often the same species has many different common names, and weeds vary from place to place. It is therefore important to obtain a book that is relevant to your situation. An alternative is to observe the life cycle of the weeds in your garden – the first step in tackling any weed is to decide if it is an annual or a perennial plant. If it is a perennial, you will also need to know what sort of root system it has.

ANNUAL WEEDS

Annual weeds grow, set seed and die all in the same year. The principal problem with annuals is that they set a large quantity of seeds. These can then lie dormant in the soil for many years. Once you start cultivating the soil you will find that you get flushes of seedlings erupting as they are brought to the surface by digging, forking and planting.

The best way to control annual weeds is to prevent light from reaching the soil through mulching or planting ground cover, and to remove any weeds that appear before they flower. Some weeds are actually biennials and so spend their first year overwintering as a rosette of leaves. These weeds are controlled in the same way as annuals.

(Left to right) Annuals such as hairy bittercress produce masses of seeds. Different perennial roots: lesser celandine (bulbil root); dandelion (tap root); couch grass (runner/rhizome root); horsetail (deep root).

HAIRY BITTERCRESS
Cardamine hirsuta

LESSER CELANDINE
Ranunculus ficaria

DANDELION
Taraxacum officinale

PERENNIAL WEEDS

The weeds you really need to watch out for are the perennials, which come up year after year and are difficult to remove. If you cut a weed down or pull it out and it grows again in the same spot, it is probably a perennial. Although many weeds flower and set seed, it is their roots that help them spread unseen. Perennial weeds may have runners, rhizomes, bulbils, tap roots or deep roots. As well as the top growth, the roots need to be tackled, by digging them up and destroying them, applying systemic weed-killer or by smothering with heavy carpets or plastic matting. Perennials need persistent control measures, often over several years, before the roots are sufficiently weakened or eradicated.

In the right place, many weeds can be an asset. A wildflower border at the bottom of a garden not only looks pretty but provides valuable food and shelter for wildlife.

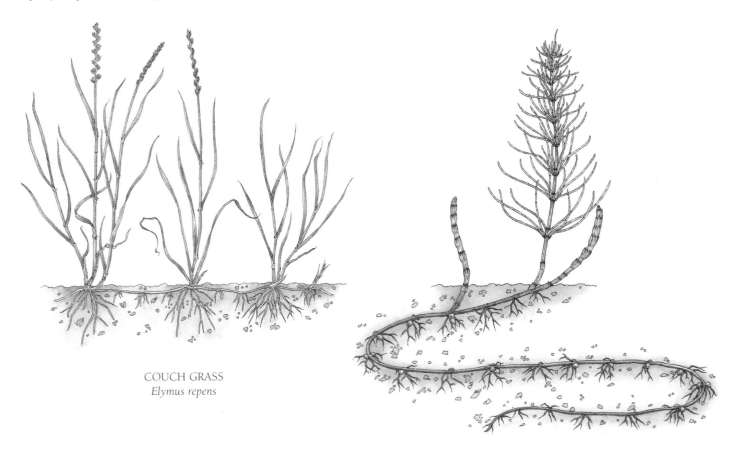

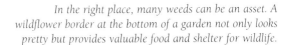

COUCH GRASS
Elymus repens

HORSETAIL
Equisetum spp.

DEALING WITH WEEDS

YOU WILL NEED

Scuffle hoe

Hand fork

Other hand weeders, such as fishtail weeder

Spot weeder

Compression sprayer

Weed killer

Sheet mulch

Loose mulch

SEE ALSO

Garden tools
See *Cultivating and weeding, pp. 92–93*

Identifying weeds
See *Types of weed, pp. 100–101*

Annual weeds are best dealt with by not allowing their seeds to germinate. Cover bare soil in spring with ground-cover plants or a mulch. Annual weed seeds germinate readily if the soil has been disturbed by digging or planting. However, covering newly dug soil is not practical where you are planting out or are sowing seed. In that situation you are better off hoeing to sever the weed seedlings. Annual weeds set prolific numbers of seed each year; aim to deal with them early in the year before they flower.

Perennial weeds flower and set seed but also spread via their root systems, so you need to tackle the roots as well as the topgrowth. Digging up the entire plants will help, but some are very deep-rooting so you might want to use a systemic weed killer. These take longer to work than contact weed killers, but they do kill off the whole plant including the roots. Perennial weeds can grow very large, and their woody stems and waxy foliage can resist the penetration of weed killers. A useful technique is to cut back the topgrowth, with a string strimmer, brush cutter or pruning shears, and wait for new growth to appear and then spray that. If you do not want to use chemicals, cut the weeds back and cover them with a sheet mulch secured to the ground with large stones; it may then take a year for the weed roots to die.

It is always easier to clear weeds from a bed before planting or sowing, rather than having to remove weeds growing in among garden plants. Aim to start with weed-free ground; then either sow plant seed in rows and hoe between the rows, or lay down a sheet mulch with planting holes. Established borders of shrubs and perennials can be kept weed free by mulching each spring with a 5-cm (2-in) deep layer of loose mulch. Smothering weeds with old carpet or sheet mulch will eventually kill them, but you may have to leave it down for a year to make sure the roots are dead.

To reclaim an overgrown or neglected garden, it is worth considering using a weed killer to help rid it of deep-rooted perennial weeds. For a large area, the most economical method is to buy concentrated systemic weed killer containing glyphosate and dilute it in a compression sprayer reserved for the purpose. Spray weeds when they are actively growing in late spring to ensure the weed killer is taken down into the roots.

WEEDS IN HARD SURFACES

Weeds that come up between cracks in paving can be cut out with a special weeding knife or old bread knife. Try to remove as much root as possible or the weeds will simply regrow. Where the whole surface contains weeds, you will have to resort to a path weed killer. These often incorporate a weed inhibitor, so you should need to treat it only once a year. To avoid having to use path weed killers, lay down woven polypropylene under new hard landscaping; this prevents weeds from emerging. Weed seedlings often establish in gravel, but they can easily be pulled out by hand. Where large areas need to be treated, save money by purchasing concentrated path weed killer and dilute it. Apply with a watering can or sprayer reserved for the purpose.

SUPPRESSING WEEDS

1 Sheet mulch, such as woven polypropylene, can be pegged down permanently over the soil to block out weeds. Cut crosses in the sheet where you want to plant.

2 After planting, cover the sheet with a thin layer of chipped or shredded bark or gravel, to improve the appearance of the bed

DIGGING OUT ROOTS

Where a few perennial weeds are growing in among garden plants, it is often easiest to dig them out by hand rather than attempt to use weed killers. When the soil is moist, insert a hand fork or other weeding tool into the ground and ease out the whole plant, root and all. Burn it, or put it in the rubbish bin. Do not use it for garden compost.

HOEING

Use a scuffle hoe with a sharp blade to sever weed seedlings while they are young. Push and pull the hoe just below the surface of the soil, taking care not to damage any adjacent garden plants. If you hoe on a warm and windy day, the seedlings can be left on the ground to shrivel and die.

SPOTWEEDING

You can target problem weeds that grow among plants, or in paving, by painting, spraying or smearing weed killer on their leaves. Ready-to-use sprayers save you having to handle concentrated weed-killer; wear waterproof gloves as a precaution against getting poison on your hands. Lawn spotweeders are also available.

Helpful hints

If roots of perennial weeds are creeping under your neighbour's fence and invading the back of your border, dig a trench about 15 cm (6 in) deep and line it with heavy-duty plastic, or slabs, and then fill it in with soil. The weed roots will find it impossible to penetrate through the plastic or slabs. When buying plants in pots, in addition to removing weeds from the surface, remove the top 1 cm (½ in) or so of compost; it could contain weed seeds. Cover stacked soil improvers and mulches to prevent weeds from seeding in them and finding their way into your borders.

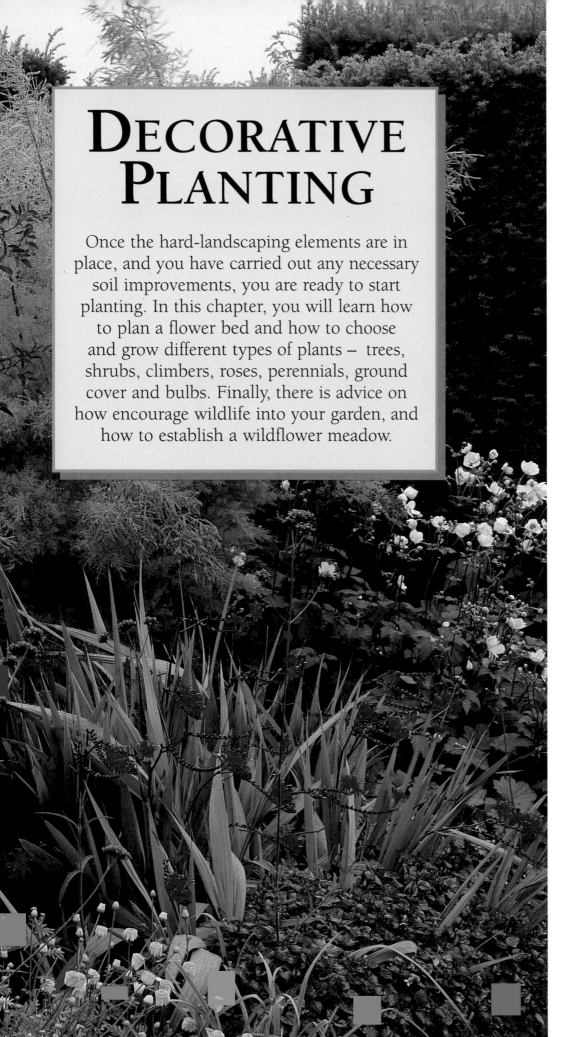

DECORATIVE PLANTING

Once the hard-landscaping elements are in place, and you have carried out any necessary soil improvements, you are ready to start planting. In this chapter, you will learn how to plan a flower bed and how to choose and grow different types of plants – trees, shrubs, climbers, roses, perennials, ground cover and bulbs. Finally, there is advice on how encourage wildlife into your garden, and how to establish a wildflower meadow.

5

PLANNING A FLOWER BED

When you have a flower bed to plan, the first things to consider are its function, and its position in relation to the rest of the garden. Is it an important dividing bed, screening and separating one area from another? In this case, you will need some large shrubs, including some evergreens for year-round coverage. Does it lightly enclose a seating area? Here, scented flowers or foliage might be placed to great effect. Can it be seen from the house? If so, you may want to incorporate plants that will provide an attractive view in every season.

STYLE OF PLANTING

Once you're clear about the function, think about the style of planting you want. If you have decided on the style of the garden, you can follow on from this with planting styles that fit well with the general look. You can also have different styles in different parts of the garden. Keep it simple and make sure there are clear divisions between each area. Use the checklist opposite to help you with the planting look. Otherwise, create your own categories, particularly if you are keen on plants that thrive in a particular habitat or have a certain type of foliage – woodland plants, for example, or grey-leaved plants that add up to a Mediterranean look.

COLOUR

When planning a flower bed, colour is of paramount importance. The foliage will be what you see for most of the year, so always bear leaf colour in mind at the start. A deep red and pink scheme may include a large proportion of red-leaved plants, such as *Cotinus coggygria* 'Royal Purple', intertwined with pink climbing roses, such as the attractive 'Pink Perpétué', to give a vibrant effect. Alternatively, a background of plain

It might look random and natural, but this garden has been carefully planned, balancing yellows, whites, blues, purples, and foliage.

green or some green and white variegation – *Weigela florida* 'Variegata' has pretty leaves as well as pale pink flowers – will be softer.

One of the strongest year-round colour schemes is based around plants with bright or yellow-green foliage, like *Paeonia lutea* 'Ludlowii' and lady's mantle (*Alchemilla mollis*), enhanced with yellow flowers in season, from early daffodils through to potentillas and on to *Hypericum* 'Hidcote' in late summer. You can use different colour schemes in different areas, but the eye will "read" colours from the whole view – so an overall balance needs to be achieved.

Roses lend a dreamy air to this wall and archway. Colours have been splashed around in a refreshing way.

CHOOSING A PLANTING STYLE

Remember to look first at the function of the bed or border and plan your planting to suit it. Then either concentrate on the style of the planting you wish to achieve or work from the colour scheme. When working on a colour scheme, start off with the foliage colour and plan for year-round effect. It is often better to keep to one colour scheme throughout the year in case plants flower early. Remember that colour schemes that clash may spoil the overall effect – so don't forget to include a division between beds.

PLANTING STYLE	GARDEN STYLE	FOLIAGE AND FLOWERS	EXAMPLES
Meditative	• Modern architectural, cottage, Japanese formal	• Green, green and white, or grey foliage. Pale flowers, with one or two deep red.	• *Aconitum* 'Ivorine', *Adiantum venustu*, *Corylopsis pauciflora*, *Dicentra eximea* 'Pearl Drops', *Ruta graveolens*
Romantic	• Cottage, English country	• Green, grey and red foliage, with red, pink, purple or white flowers.	• Cabbage roses, camellias, peonies, tulips, scented plants
Grand	• Formal townhouse	• Mainly green foliage. Any flower colours, but not too many different ones.	• Camellias, galtonias, lilies, magnolias, pieris, rhododendrons
Bright	• Cottage, English country, modern architectural	• Green, green and yellow foliage; yellow, orange, red, blue and white flowers.	• Forsythia, *Ilex* 'Golden King', *Kerria japonica*, *Rosa* 'Golden Showers', rudbeckias, *Spiraea* 'Goldflame', sunflowers
Modern sculptural	• Modern architectural, formal townhouse	• Any well-shaped foliage, and bold combinations of colours for the flowers.	• Aristolochia, arundinaria, *Fatsia japonica*, hostas, *Rhus typhina*, *Viburnum rhytidophyllum*
Mysterious	• Architectural, English country	• Green foliage, any colour for the flowers.	• Helleborus, *Euphorbia* spp., Mahonias, *Garrya elliptica*, *Rheum palmatum*
Fairy tale	• Cottage, English country	• Green, green and white, and grey foliage; and flowers with soft colours.	• Delphiniums, lavender, phlox, *Rosa* 'Ballerina', *Weigela florida variegata*, wisteria

CHOOSING PLANTS FOR A FLOWER BED

SHAPELY SHRUBS

Buddleja alternifolia

Hebe (*Hebe rakaiensis*)

St John's wort
(*Hypericum* 'Hidcote')

Viburnum davidii

Weigela 'Bristol Ruby'

STRIKING STEMS

Arundinaria murielae

Dogwood (*Cornus alba*
'Elegantissima')

Kerria japonica

SEE ALSO

Choosing a style
See *Planning a flower bed*,
pp. 106–107

What to buy?
See *Buying plants*
pp. 110–111

Designing with plants
See *Styles of planting*,
pp. 112–113

Once you have decided on the general style of your flower bed, noted the function it fulfils in relation to the rest of the garden, and chosen the colour scheme that will blend with the overall effect, you need to take account of each bed's microclimate. Consider whether the bed is in full sun all day, or if it is at the base of a sunless wall. Or is it something in between – perhaps dappled shade, or in the sun for part of the day? You will know the general soil condition of your garden by now, but look closely at this bed – is it damper or dryer than the rest? Perhaps the soil is thinner here for some reason, or years of leaf fall from the neighbour's tree have created a good dark topsoil from old leaf mould. It is essential to take these factors into consideration when choosing plants.

Before buying new plants, check whether there are any established ones in the bed that you can keep. It takes time for plants to reach a good size, and if you can incorporate

This thrilling yellow to red-purple spectrum shows how carefully positioned flowers can yield spectacular effects, especially when they are planted in groups.

an existing plant you will give the bed a more established appearance right from the start. You can reshape an overgrown bush to improve its appearance, but do not expect to reduce its size. If a plant is too large and you cannot design the bed around it, then you will have to remove it.

The next step is to choose large structural plants, which will probably help to fulfil any practical function of the bed. If you want to incorporate screening, consider whether you need evergreens for thick cover or whether two or three large deciduous shrubs, which create a lighter effect, will be sufficient.

The foliage colour of these plants will form the base note of the bed. It is best to avoid too many extremes, such as several different shades of red, or various yellow variegated bushes dotted around. The aim should be to blend the tones, using a soft neutral like a green or grey, enhanced with one or two

Blue-green foliage and white and yellow flowers form the base colours of this attractive bed. Note how the different leaf shapes lend the bed a varied and interesting texture.

Pinks, reds, purples and blues form the sultry backdrop for highlights of paler colours. Groups of colours add intensity and increase the visual impact.

deeper tones or contrasts. Think of the plants' shapes, and again blend these carefully. An arching shrub with lower rounded bushes below, for example, or a series of upright stems, such as bamboo, together with a flat bed of wispy grasses are careful combinations that will look far more effective than a mixed jumble of shapes.

CONTRAST AND UNDERPLANTING

Once you have the general grouping of the structural plants, you can add contrast in colour or leaf shape – a pale, furry grey such as *Senecio* 'Sunshine' against the glossiness of *Choisya ternata*, or the dark spikiness of *Mahonia* combined with the bright green, rounded leaves of *Rosa rugosa*, for example. The same principles of blending the tones or choosing contrasts apply to flower colour, and you also need to take the flowering season into account.

When you have chosen the tall plants for a bed, consider the lower shrubs, keeping in mind the same principles. You may choose to concentrate on perennials rather than adding

more shrubs – these will often have a longer flowering time, but some are less effective in winter. Again, place the larger, striking plants first, either singly or in small groups, and then surround them with lower plants. For ground cover, the best effect is generally achieved when you plant large numbers of one or two plants. Choose plants that grow well here – there is no point in having a bed filled with hostas if you are plagued with slugs, for instance, because the elegant foliage will quickly become riddled with holes.

PLANNING TIPS

When choosing structural trees and shrubs, remember to leave enough room for their ultimate height and spread. While they are growing, you can fill the gaps temporarily with tall perennials that can be uprooted later. Make sure you have enough early-spring and late-autumn plants in the bed because these tend to be sparser than late-spring and summer-flowering plants. If you are in doubt about which ground cover to choose, try a few different plants. Mulch heavily between the plants to suppress weeds, until you know which plants you want to use. Ground-cover plants are often good weed suppressors.

BUYING PLANTS

YOU WILL NEED

List of plants or plant attributes

Spade

Catalogue (optional)

SEE ALSO

Which tree?
See *Buying and planting trees, pp. 118–119*

Hedging plants
See *Choosing a hedge, pp. 120–121*

All kinds of climbing plants
See *Choosing climbers and wall shrubs, pp. 126–127*

All kinds of roses
See *Choosing roses, pp. 130–131*

Which shrub?
See *Buying and planting shrubs, pp. 138–139*

The simplest way to buy plants is to go to a garden centre where you can see what you are buying. The danger is impulse buying, and this is where your planning will come in useful. Many plants that fail to thrive are impulse buys! You should have a clear idea of the colours, sizes and attributes of the plants you want, even if you haven't decided exactly which plant. A list that says something like: "shrub, 1.8 m (6 ft) high, deciduous, arching shape, white flowers, tolerates some shade" will be a great help. You can also order from nurseries, many of which will have a different range of plants, specializing in clematis or roses, for example. Ask for advice if you are not sure – most places will have at least one very knowledgeable person on the staff.

Most plants are sold in containers, which is the most expensive way to buy them but also the easiest. With a container plant, the most important thing is to make sure that the roots are not potbound. With your hand around the plant and over the top of the pot, tip the pot upside down. If you can see roots trying to force their way out of the hole at the bottom, the plant is potbound. The roots will be coiled tightly around the inside of the pot, and will never grow out into the surrounding soil. It is not worth buying a shrub or tree in this condition. However, many herbaceous plants can be more easily divided and will happily grow, so you will get two or three plants for the price of one – this is good value. On the other hand, it is not worth buying a plant that has just been potted on; you will pay extra for the larger size, and all you'll get is more earth, since the roots won't have had time to grow into the pot.

Bare-rooted plants are a less expensive way to buy roses, shrubs, hedging plants and trees; garden centres also sell a few of these, particularly of fruit trees and roses, or they can be ordered from nurseries and will be delivered after lifting in autumn, until early spring. They should be planted in mild, damp weather if possible, and must be heeled in (see opposite) if you do not plant immediately. Water heeled-in plants regularly in dry weather, but do not leave them too long before planting because they will start to grow and their roots will become entangled so that you damage them again when you plant them in their final position.

EXAMPLE OF GOOD PLANT

This plant has lots of strong, healthy stems growing from the base. Each stem has healthy, glossy foliage, and new shoots can be seen developing. The growth is evenly spaced around the stem so that the whole plant has a balanced shape.

EXAMPLE OF BAD PLANT

This plant has only one strong shoot, which is bare at the base but has sprouted leaves at the top. The other shoots are spindly and weak, although they have produced a few flowers which give a more appealing effect. Some of the leaves are browning and there are suspicious patches and spots on them.

CONTAINER-GROWN PLANTS

Most plants are grown in containers, where their roots grow and develop in the shape of the container, so that when you lift the plant out of the container, the roots remain covered in soil, and are not disturbed. This means that they can be planted at any time of year, although in dry weather they will need regular watering.

PLUG PLANTS

Plugs are tiny seedlings, often of expensive bedding plants, sold before they are potted on. Because you are buying them at an early stage of development, they are less expensive, but you will have to pot them on yourself, and for tender plants you will need a warm, bright place to keep them until the weather has warmed up.

SEEDS

Seeds are sold for all vegetables, annual flowers and some herbs and perennials. It is possible to buy pelleted seeds for easier germination of more difficult plants. Seeds lose their viability over time so that fewer seeds will germinate if they are old. Don't buy packets that aren't dated for the current year. Even in a sale, old seed may not be a bargain.

BEDDING OUT

Many of the cheaper bedding plants and some perennials are sold in trays with strips of tiny plastic planting cells. You can either buy the entire tray – usually of four strips – or break off as many strips as you want. Again, this is an inexpensive way to buy bedding plants. Plant them out as soon as possible into their final positions, carefully separating their roots.

HEELING IN

If bare-rooted plants cannot be planted immediately on delivery, they must be heeled in. Prepare a site in a sheltered position, and dig a hole, or a trench if you have several plants. Unwrap the plants from their packing and lay them in the trench. Trees should be laid at an angle so that they are not blown over. Cover the roots with soil and firm down.

Helpful hints

You can plant a container plant at any time of year, since the damage to roots is minimal. If you can, though, plant at the traditional times – for all except frost-tender plants (which should be planted in spring) this is early autumn, once the heat of the sun lessens and the soil is damp. At this time there is warmth in the soil, which allows for good root establishment before winter. Mulch around the base of the plant to keep the roots warm as the weather cools, to maintain moisture and to minimize weeds.

STYLES OF PLANTING

PLANTING SUGGESTIONS

Plants have their own individual character, which is built up from a combination of their colour, shape and foliage effect, and their scent, as well as the associations in the mind of the beholder. You may find the flowering cherry a glorious sight in spring, ideal for your country garden; others merely think of the messy blossoms and prefer a formal line of tulips. Generally, roses are seen as romantic, especially the old varieties with evocative French names such as 'Honorine de Brabant' and 'Baron Girod de l'Ain'. Camellias, with their beautiful glossy leaves, can be formal or romantic, depending on how and where they are planted, while a tall and angular *Mahonia*, spiky *Helleborus foetidus*, and the snakily marbled *Arum italicum* 'Pictum' are sinister, slightly wicked-looking plants.

There are infinite ways and styles of planting. You can draw up a style checklist to help decide on your garden's overall look, or make up your own categories from your favourites: shrubs or trees, perennials, biennials or annuals, as well as herbs. You may also incorporate fencing or walls and lawn or paving into the scheme. Some of the gardens shown here stick closely to a colour theme, while others concentrate on form and foliage texture and shape. If you opt for a glorious mixture of plants, you may risk an indeterminate mess or you may strike it lucky and achieve a unique effect. It is always fun to experiment, especially with perennial plantings, which are quick to establish.

▶ POPPY MEADOW
This stunning meadow of California poppies (*Eschscholzia*), dotted through with a few cornflowers, and misty blue mountains rising in the distance, is like an Impressionist painting. Such a dramatic effect requires space – and the courage to keep it simple.

◀ FIRE AND FLAMES
Plants of different shapes and warm-toned colours fill this garden bed, reflecting the warm, sunny climate in which it is located.

▶ A COUNTRY COTTAGE GARDEN
Charmingly planted with flowers in mainly white and bright gold tones, this cottage style is set off by the old wall with its coping of traditional tiles.

▲ SOFT HUES
In this English
country garden, the
perennial *Clematis*
is set amid such
annuals as zinnia
and petunia.

▶ WATER'S EDGE
A meditative, even
mysterious planting
has the accent on
sculptural foliage in
various greens.

◀ LEMON-LIME
Yellow flowers and
warm green foliage
make an attractive
colour scheme.

CHOOSING TREES

GOOD TREES

Birch (*Betula jacquemontii*)

Crab apple (*Malus* 'John Downie')

Ornamental pear (*Pyrus nivalis*)

Prunus 'Shirotae'

Snowy mespilus (*Amelanchier laevis*)

Sorbus 'Joseph Rock'

SEE ALSO

All kinds of trees
See *Styles of tree planting, pp. 116–117*

Which tree?
See *Buying and planting trees, pp. 118–119*

Trees are structural plants and, together with hard landscape features such as fences and pergolas, form the bones of the garden. They will be the ancestors in your garden, standing as a blessing or a curse on those who come after you, depending on how well you choose what to plant. So think carefully – trees are not impulse buys.

FUNCTIONS

Decide what you want from your tree before you start to choose one. If it is to be a focal point, consider the shape you want and the requirements of the site. For a key point in a shrub bed, you will need a fairly small tree that casts light shade. A flowering cherry, such as the pale pink *Prunus* x *yedoensis*, and the Judas tree (*Cercis siliquastrum*), whose flowers appear before the leaves in spring, are good choices. For a tall, dark spire to catch

Foliage and shape are the key points in this easy-to-care-for shrub border, and a few tall, slim trees, such as these dark green conifers, bring contrast and vertical highlights.

the eye and provide a counterbalance to a building, the Italian cypress (*Cupressus sempervirens*) is the classic choice. You could also try *Chamaecyparis lawsonia* 'Columnaris', a blue-grey column, especially if you have a smaller garden. For a lawn, the silver birch (*Betula pendula*) is effective underplanted with bulbs in spring. It casts very little shade, but can grow to 21 m (70 ft), so needs space. A smaller option is Mount Etna broom (*Genista aetnensis*), which produces its yellow flowers in summer.

Screening is one of the most common reasons for choosing a tree. It is also the most problematic, since the tendency may be to go for something fast-growing. To hide a view, it is better to build a screen and plant a suitable tree to fill the same function in a few years' time. If wind screening is needed, shrubs or

Trees with attractive bark make excellent sculptural features. Here, the trees have been spaced to create a stark contrast to the profusion of flowers below.

hedging plants may be better than trees, because they have leaves at ground level. Trees for shade are unrivalled for their cool, refreshing effect on hot days. A spreading shape is needed – a sweet chestnut (*Castanea sativa*) is excellent if you have the space, or you can choose one of the smaller oaks, such as *Quercus rubra*. A magnificent evergreen shade tree for milder climates is the Pohutakawa (*Metrosideros excelsus*), which produces brilliant red flowers in summer.

For seasonal interest, both spring and autumn colour are important, and some trees offer both. The Amur maple (*Acer ginnala*) has clusters of white flowers in spring and bright red autumn leaves. Crab apples give blossom and fruit – in the case of *Malus* 'Golden Hornet', attractive golden yellow clusters. If wildlife is your interest, choose a native tree, which will support a whole world of its own, from mosses and lichens to beetles and birds. (See also pp. 162–165.)

Autumn is the time when many trees come into their own, giving impressive displays of vivid reds, oranges and yellows.

A trees makes a good focal point in a lawn, but make sure it has enough room to spread.

POINTS TO CONSIDER

When choosing a tree, consider carefully its size compared to that of your garden – forest trees are beautiful but are out of place in a small plot. Find out how large your chosen tree will be when it reaches its full height and spread, and allow for this when planting – you may want to use other plants to fill the gaps temporarily. The size that the tree reaches and the speed of its growth will be affected by the soil type and aspect – make sure that the tree's preferences will be met by the planting site. Questing tree roots can cause problems, damaging the foundations of a nearby building, especially if the tree is planted in a clay soil. Willows and poplars are notorious for their vigorous root systems, but it is best not to plant any large tree close to your house.

STYLES OF TREE PLANTING

PLANTING SUGGESTIONS

For autumn colour, maples (*Acer*) are renowned, yet other species such as snowy mespilus (*Amelanchier lamarckii*) and American mountain ash (*Sorbus americana*) also produce brilliant colours, and have the added attraction of berries for the birds.

Conifers form the bulk of evergreens, but other options include *Eucalyptus*, with its steel-blue disc-shaped leaves. The holm oak (*Quercus ilex*) is imposing but grows slowly.

Silver birch (*Betula*) has beautiful silver bark; that of *B. papyrifera* is a dazzling white and peels off in layers. The dark brown stems of the paperbark maple (*Acer griseum*) also peel as they age. Shoots of the poplar (*Populus*) and willow (*Salix*) are brightly coloured in spring, as are many dogwoods (*Cornus*).

Many people avoid planting trees in their gardens because they fear the problems of size and shade, yet there are many smaller trees that will add an essential quality to any planting scheme. If you have space for only one tree, try to choose a variety that will give interest in more than one season, such as flowers and fruit or leaves that change colour before they fall. Or try a species that will provide a major focal point for your entire garden.

Using a variety of shapes – spreading, pyramidal, conical, weeping, round-headed, arching and columnar – will add interest, as will special features, such as leaf shape, size or colour, and trees with berries or attractive bark.

The planting of a woodland or a group of larger trees, however, if carefully chosen and placed, is a generous act, which will be appreciated by your descendants, or those who follow on the land after you.

▲ CONIFERS
Tall conifer spires contrast strikingly with smaller rounded bushes and soft foliage in this woodland garden.

► FOCAL POINT
Clipped pointed bushes and a well-manicured lawn are a perfect foil for the horizontal tiers of the trees.

▲ SMALL TREE
The Judas tree (*Cercis siliquastrum*) bears its bluish pink flowers on bare branches in late spring before the leaves unfold. The tree forms a rounded shape, is slow growing, and can also be grown as a shrub.

▲ OLD CHARM
The beauty of ancient trees adds irreplaceable character to a garden, lending an air of calm and maturity. In Japan, old trees are treasured and carefully preserved, often propped up with wooden posts.

► JAPANESE CHERRY
A stunning sight in spring, the Japanese cherry is covered with pale flowers. Its value also lies in the spreading habit, which will remain gracefully elegant all year round.

BUYING AND PLANTING TREES

When buying a long-lived plant such as a tree, it is important to use a reputable nursery or garden centre where you can ask advice from an expert who will know your locality and can help you choose the best specimen. Many reputable outlets will offer a replacement if a tree dies within one to two years of planting. Look for a well-balanced branch system and a good, fibrous root system.

You may not be able to plant the tree straightaway. Pot-grown trees can be kept in their pots and watered but you must heel in bare-rooted plants (see p. 111). It is worth planting at the right time and in the right weather – clay soil, for instance, should not be worked in wet weather. While you are waiting, you can clear away any encroaching shrubs, to allow in plenty of light and air for the tree.

It pays to prepare the soil very thoroughly – the more care and attention you give now, the better the plant will grow. The hole must be at least twice the size of the rootball, more in poor soil. When digging a hole in a lawn, remove the turf and stack it to one side first; keep the topsoil on one side and dispose of the subsoil elsewhere. Loosen the soil at the bottom of the hole and put in the saved turf, grass-side down. Backfill the hole, using organic matter and, if the soil is poor, a slow-release fertilizer. Then you are ready to drive in the stake and plant (see opposite).

The gnarled, twisted trunk of a weeping maple (Acer spp.) contrasts with its feathery canopy of leaves. The finely shaped, colourful foliage looks particularly beautiful when the sun shines through it.

PLANTING A TREE IN A CONTAINER

1 Put stones or bits of broken terracotta in the container to ensure good drainage. Put in some soil-based compost with added organic matter. Position the tree and add the rest of the soil. Firm around the rootball. The soil should be 2.5 cm (1 in) below the rim of the pot. Water in well. If watering washes the soil down around the roots, add more soil.

2 To make the best impact in a small space, plant a dwarf conifer in a container. The visual interaction of pot and plant is important, so test your conifer in various containers to see which looks best. Make sure you choose a slow-growing tree, and be prepared to repot it in a few years before the rootball gets too big to remove it from the pot.

PLANTING A TREE

1 Hammer the stake into the hole at a position near the centre but on the windward side, and to a depth of about one-third of its length. The height of the stake above the ground should be a third of the height of the tree or less – this will allow the tree to move and so strengthen the trunk as it grows.

2 Place the tree in the hole to check the depth of its roots – it must be planted so that the soil surface is the same as it was in the container or the ground. Put the tree to one side, cover the roots with sacking to keep the sun off, and backfill with improved soil to the correct level for the plant's rootball.

3 Place the tree in the hole again, and tie it loosely to the stake to keep it steady while you work. Spread out its roots carefully and start to backfill over them; rock the tree gently every now and again to shake soil down among the roots. Keep filling until the soil reaches ground level.

4 Press gently around the tree with your foot to firm the soil around the roots. Water in thoroughly with a hose, and if the soil sinks a little, add more soil to the original height. Retie the trunk with an adjustable tree tie. Nail the tie to the stake before fitting it around the tree trunk.

CHOOSING SITES

Before planting a tree, check the chosen site. Consider how much shade the tree will cast when mature, and whether it will shade out any favourite sun-loving plants. If it is too near a pond, leaves can be a nuisance in the autumn. If you are planting a specimen in a lawn, you will have to mow around it. Make sure you have allowed enough space for the roots to grow without damaging paving or building foundations. Bumps and unevenness can occur where the tree grows and, in its search for water, invasive roots can heave and crack patios and walls, and even damage your house foundations.

Helpful hints

Use a plastic tree guard to protect the tree's stem from rabbits and deer, if these are a known problem in your area. Trees less than 1.2 m (4 ft) in height when planted do not need staking; otherwise use a hardwood or treated wooden stake for extra stability.

Loosen tree ties regularly, or the trunk will grow over the tie, girdling or choking the tree, which will result in poor growth. Remove all ties and stakes after a few years. Keep grass away from under the tree until it is well established so that the grass does not compete with the tree for water or nutrients.

CHOOSING A HEDGE

GOOD VARIETIES

Escallonia
'Donard Radiance'

Firethorn (*Pyracantha* 'Orange Glow')

Holly (*Ilex aquifolium* 'J C Van Tol')

Cotton lavender (*Santolina chamaecyparissus*)

Rugosa rose (*Rosa rugosa* 'Typica')

SEE ALSO

Hedge design
See *Styles of hedge, pp. 122–123*

Laying hedges
See *Planting a hedge, pp. 124–125*

Protecting your garden
See *Weather protection, pp. 174–175*

Hedge maintenance
See *Caring for hedges, pp. 186–187*

Before you choose the plants for your hedge, it is important to establish its function. Do you need a boundary that gives privacy from the neighbours? In this case, you probably need a tall, substantial hedge. This may also be suitable for enclosing a separate garden area – some of the classical rose gardens have beautiful dark yew hedges, to set off the brilliant colours of the roses. For your front garden, you may want a lower hedge that defines the boundary area but allows passers-by to see your flowers – or privacy may still be an issue and a higher hedge more appropriate.

In a coastal area, you may need a windbreak grown from salt-tolerant plants such as *Escallonia*, *Pyracantha* or *Elaeagnus ebbingei*. Then there are hedges that are more decorative in intent, ranging from a simple path edging of lavender or a sharply clipped box hedge restraining an exuberant mixed cottage border, to the elaborate clipped designs of a knot garden, outlined in cotton lavender (*Santolina chamaecyparissus*).

Low hedges are an excellent way of framing separate areas of the garden, or softening the edges of a pathway.

FORMAL HEDGES

You also need to decide whether you want a hedge that can be closely clipped to give a formal appearance, or a more sprawling informal hedge. For tall formal hedges, yew (*Taxus baccata*) gives a sharp outline and has the added advantage of growing well in shade. Leylandii (*Cupressocyparis leylandii*), *Chamaecyparis lawsonia* and other conifers can give a similar effect. Because they are fast-growing, they are useful for quick screens but need to be clipped twice a year once they reach the desired height.

Holly (*Ilex aquifolium*) gives a softer outline, but its prickly leaves can make it unpleasant to maintain. Privet (*Ligustrum ovalifolium*) is semi-evergreen, and a popular choice. *L. o.* 'Aureum' is golden-tinged for a brighter

A neatly clipped hedge brings a formal air to the garden and can be used to create an architectural effect. Here, it leads the eye towards a statue as a focal point.

effect, while beech (*Fagus sylvatica*) keeps its russet leaves all winter. Low formal hedges are traditionally made with box, such as *Buxus sempervirens* 'Suffruticosa', lavender, or cotton lavender, all of which will respond to close clipping. *Lonicera nitida* (Chinese honeysuckle) is often used instead of box, which it resembles – it is cheaper and grows faster. It can become straggly, but you can cut it right back to the base to sprout again.

INFORMAL HEDGES

Many shrubs can be used for informal hedges. These need more space than formal hedges, and should be gently pruned into shape when necessary, rather than sheared into strictly kept lines. They give a more rounded, bushy effect than formal hedges. Plants that are most suitable for informal hedges are multi-stemmed and bushy, and take frequent clipping.

Plants that make excellent informal hedges include the species roses, such as *Rosa rugosa*, and evergreens such as *Cotoneaster lacteus* or *C. simonsii*, *Griselinia littoralis*, *Escallonia macrantha* or *Viburnum tinus*. *Berberis* and firethorn (*Pyracantha*) both make prickly evergreen hedges that may deter intruders – although the thorns make them difficult to maintain. For lower informal hedges, *Berberis thunbergii* 'Atropurpurea Nana' or *Potentilla fruticosa* both work well.

The traditional English country hedges were often grown from hawthorn (*Crataegus monogyna*). This plant was also known as quickthorn and was valued for its speed of growth. Other common local trees or shrub plants used included blackthorn (*Prunus spinosa*), field maple (*Acer campestre*) and wild privet (*Ligustrum vulgare*). If you are lucky enough to have inherited one of these hedges, preserve it, and maintain it by relaying (see pp. 186–187).

Here, an informal hedge creates a natural backdrop to throw the bright colours of a country flower border into emphasis, as well as providing an effective screen and garden boundary.

If space is very tight, you can use a climber, such as clematis, to create the effect of a hedge.

PLANNING TIPS

You can brighten up a dull hedge by planting flowers in the border in front of it to provide contrast and colour. For a dark green hedge, such as yew or box, think of using pale colours – white foxgloves or yellow roses work well, for example. A hedge variegated with yellow will lend itself to a warm colour scheme of oranges and reds, with a touch more of yellow or red foliage – but will quickly look too busy if you add too much colour detail. Alternatively, a brightly coloured, non-vigorous climber, such as *Tropaeolum speciosum* looks good grown through an evergreeen hedge. An informal flowering hedge can form a major attraction and focus for colour by itself – firethorn, which produces clusters of colourful berries in autumn, gives excellent value.

STYLES OF HEDGE

PLANTING SUGGESTIONS

In front of a formal dark hedge, plant pale or brightly coloured specimens. A deep red-leaved bush such as *Cotinus coggygria* will form a dull picture against a yew hedge. Paler foliage, or grey leaves such as those of *Senecio* 'Sunshine', will be enhanced by the contrast. Alternatively, silhouetted plants, such as the tall-spired *Verbascum* or the ethereal white *Crambe cordifolia*, will show up well against such a background.

However, with a variegated hedge such as *Ilex* 'Golden Queen', avoid other variegated plants in front. Choose plain green plants, perhaps with yellow flowers, such as a *Hypericum* or *Kerria*. If you are really confident, continue the warm tones into orange-coloured plants, such as *Spiraea* 'Goldflame' and *Euphorbia griffithii* 'Fireglow'. Include a large proportion of green, to avoid a hectic, feverish effect.

Hedges are often associated with formal garden styles, where their crisp lines help to delineate the shape of the garden, often marking paths lined by pyramidal shapes or possibly ornate entrances enhanced by topiary work (see p. 158). Use a low hedge of boxwood, santolina or lavender to outline a flower bed or an herb garden, or to form a boundary between patio and lawn, for example. For these uses, the plants must be kept neatly clipped and in good condition.

However, an informal hedge can be useful either as a soft edge to a bed, or as a boundary, where its appearance will blend in with other shrubs in front of it. Its flowering habits and the time it takes to mature should be taken into account. Such hedges can form windbreaks, noise barriers and shelters, and provide privacy. They will also attract wildlife, such as nesting birds.

▲ CLASSICAL STYLE
In a formal layout, box and lavender edging and a shaped conifer, clipped into a high arch to form a window, elegantly frame the bust and statuary beyond.

▲ PAVED WALK
Red brick steps and clipped hedging, leading to a paved walk, contrast with sloping flower beds and informal shapes of climbing roses and foliage plants.

◄ GREEN GLOBES
The soft green contours of these shaped hedges contrast well with the towering flowering spikes.

◄ BOLD COLOUR
In a generously sized flower bed, an informal flowering hedge, which does not require clipping, contrasts with the formal clipped topiary shapes. Make sure you choose species and varieties that will not grow too large for the size of your garden, unless you are willing to prune more often to keep the hedge to size.

◄ STRUCTURED HEDGING
Tiers of hedging interspersed with other plants and topped with a loose citrus hedge, give varied tones. The brick paving emphasizes the formal lines.

▲ STRONG CONTRAST
Neat box edging is a perfect foil for billowing roses. The contrast in shape and texture makes for a satisfying combination. A clipped hedge is essential for this effect.

PLANTING A HEDGE

YOU WILL NEED

Shovel or spade

Stakes

Rubber mallet or hammer

String or twine

Measuring tape

Soil enrichers

Mulch

Water

SEE ALSO

Basic blueprint
See *Designing your garden, pp. 20–21*

Hedging plants
See *Choosing a hedge, pp. 120–121*

Hedge design
See *Styles of hedge, pp. 122–123*

Heeling in
See *Buying plants, pp. 110–111*

A hedge, particularly a long one, is a big investment in plants. Spend some time before you purchase the plants to decide which type will serve you best. Fast-growing shrubs tend to be shorter lived (20 years or so) than slow-growing ones. If you want a hedge quickly and choose a plant that will grow feet instead of inches a year, be aware that it will need pruning more often in order to keep it tidy. Remember also that it will grow old and decline much sooner than traditional hedging materials such as box or yew, some of which can live for hundreds of years.

Once you have decided on the type of plant (or mixture of plants) you want for your hedge, you need to work out how many plants you will need. First measure the length of the proposed hedge, and then find out the expected mature width of the trees or shrubs you will be using. Since you cannot count on a plant growing to its optimal mature size (soil, light, moisture, and other factors all influence the final size of any plant) and you want the plants to merge into each other to make an uninterrupted line, reduce the expected width of each plant by one-third. Then divide the width into the length of your hedge. For example, *Buxus microphylla* (small-leafed box) grows to about 1.5 m (5 ft) wide at maturity. Reduce that to 1 m (3 ft) to ensure a gap-free hedge, and divide that number into the length of the hedge. If your hedge is 10 m (30 ft) long, you will need about nine plants. If you want the new hedge to fill in more quickly, add another plant or two and space them all closer together. For a denser and wider hedge, plant a double staggered row (see opposite).

The staggered, stair-stepped hedges along the perimeter and the hedge-framed beds in the centre create a formal, tailored garden rich with pattern and texture.

WILLOW WEAVING

Willow stakes can be made into a woven fence; the uprights will quickly root in the ground so that it becomes a living wall. Use varieties such as the common osier (*Salix viminalis*) and the white willow (*S. alba*); because willow prefers damp soil, you can try dogwood (*Cornus sanguinea*) if your site is on the dry side. You will need some stout stakes made from two- year-old stems to form the uprights. Drive these into the soil along the line you have chosen and trim them off roughly to an even height. Take lengths of flexible one-year-old stems and weave them in and out of the stakes, pushing them down tightly for a dense screen, or make a less dense, "see-through" fence. There are one-day courses where you can learn this technique.

PLANTING A HEDGE IN A STAGGERED ROW

1 Keep the shrubs well watered until you are ready to plant them. Soak the roots of bare-rooted plants in water overnight before planting. If you cannot plant bare-rooted shrubs immediately, heel in the plants in a sheltered position. Trim away damaged roots.

2 Stretch a string between stakes along the hedge line. Measure off where the plants should be placed on either side of the centre line. They should be equidistant from each other and staggered so that no two plants are directly opposite each other. Allow growing space at each end, and mark each plant's position with a trowel.

3 Dig a hole for each plant twice the width of the container (or root spread) and several centimetres deeper. Fill the hole with water and allow it to drain. Backfill the hole with a small quantity of enriched soil and put the plant in the hole with the top of the rootball just above ground level. Backfill with the rest of the improved soil, pressing down firmly.

4 Water the plant slowly so that the roots are thoroughly moistened. Mulch around the plant and along the length of the hedge to reduce weeds and water evaporation. If the topgrowth is heavy compared to the spread of the roots, prune back a little so that the roots can concentrate on growing rather than on having to support lots of excess foliage.

RENOVATING AN OVERGROWN HEDGE

Many shrubs can take severe pruning. In warm climates, you can cut shrubs such as rhododendrons, azaleas and mountain laurels right back to the ground. To increase the chances of plants surviving, prepare them ahead of time. Starting about a year before you cut them back, give them a heavy feed of organic fertilizer such as fish, blood and bonemeal or well-rotted manure. This feeding will give

the plants extra vigour. The safest time to cut back these shrubs is in late winter or early spring when the plant is sending out new shoots. If you are feeling bold, cut it right back to the ground. If you are feeling more timid – and have several years to get the shrub back into shape – cut back severely, but leave some growth. Repeat the process every spring to get the perfect shape.

CHOOSING CLIMBERS AND WALL SHRUBS

Climbers are among the most useful and versatile plants in the garden. In a small space, where there is no room for large shrubs or trees, they add the essential ingredient of height to the garden picture. In a larger garden they can be used to cover a trellis or fencing, again adding height.

Among true climbers, there are some that climb by means of suckers – self-clinging climbers such as climbing hydrangea (*Hydrangea petiolaris*) or Virginia creeper (*Parthenocissus quinquefolia*) – and others that twine around any available support, such as honeysuckle (*Lonicera* spp.). Annual climbers such as the cup and saucer plant (*Cobaea scandens*), and the beautiful blue morning glory (*Ipomaea*) give a quick effect. Scarlet runner beans such as 'Painted Lady' were originally grown for their bright red flowers. Try some up a trellis, to gain the benefit of both the flowers and the beans.

If you are after evergreen cover, ivy is the best-known and one of the best all-round climbers. It is self-clinging, can take dry shade but is happy in sun, and its foliage range is enormous – from the deep green crinkles of *Hedera helix* 'Ivalace' to the icy grey-tinged leaves of *H. h.* 'Glacier' or the almost completely yellow *H. h.* 'Buttercup'. However, ivy can be damaging to walls in poor repair, since its aerial roots work into mortar and loosen it further.

Honeysuckle is one of the most common scented climbers, and there are evergreen varieties, such as *Lonicera japonica* 'Halliana', and deciduous, such as woodbine (*Lonicera periclymenum*) or the Early Dutch honeysuckle (*L. p.* 'Belgica'). Grown near a window, their scent can be delightful on a summer evening. Common jasmine (*Jasminum officinale*) and many climbing roses also have wonderful perfumes.

A tumbling mass of climbers effectively disguises a garden fence. It also creates the perfect frame for the ebullient growth in the flowerbed, and provides a delightful scent for the seating area.

It is important to look up the habit of growth of climbers, and their eventual size. Honeysuckle, jasmine and *Clematis montana* are better scrambling over large structures in a wild part of the garden, since they tend to get bare and woody at the base They are not really suitable for a porch or house wall. Some climbing roses such as the glorious *Rosa* 'Kiftsgate', with its bunches of white flowers, can climb up to 10 m (30 ft). A large tree can support them, but not a small shrub.

Once they are established, climbers are usually quite hardy plants. But they will benefit from routine care. Feed them once a year with a good compost, and keep the soil at the base moist. Prolonged flowering can be achieved by deadheading.

WALL SHRUBS

There are many shrubs that can be grown as climbers – the most obvious is the rose, but other shrubs such as the Japanese quince (*Chaenomeles*) and firethorn (*Pyracantha*) can be used either as freestanding specimens or wall plants. In a small garden, wall shrubs add an extra dimension and, where there is not enough room for many shrubs, it is worth experimenting with different species such as *Hydrangea*, *Syringa* or *Spiraea* against walls or up trellises where they would not normally be seen. Myrtle, *Ceanothus dentata*, *Magnolia grandiflora* and *Piptanthus*

laburnifolius are other evergreens with the advantage of flowers in season – they are all shrubs that do well as espaliers. They benefit from a warm, sunny position, which makes them good subjects for a house wall (a large wall in the case of the magnolia).

In general, shrubs are easier to control than true climbers, but any plant that is too big for its planting position will be a nuisance and cause unnecessary work.

This riotous display uses a climber to connect the separate window boxes, and makes for a more flowing effect. The rich green foliage of the climber also provides a fine base colour for the brightly coloured flowers.

Climbers provide wonderful texture and are a much kinder backdrop than bricks and mortar.

PLANNING TIPS

House walls are an ideal situation for climbers or wall shrubs, and the relative shelter they provide can allow you to grow some of the more tender plants, especially on a sunny or sheltered wall. Grown over an old tree or mature shrub, climbers can extend the season of interest – many shrubs such as lilac and forsythia are very dull out of season, and a clematis can be most effective

scrambling through the branches. It is best in this situation to use a late-flowering clematis that can be hard pruned each year and will not throttle its support plant. Some climbers can also be left without a support so that they spread out horizontally – creating effective ground cover. Be sure to select a less vigorous variety to avoid an invasion into beds and borders.

PLANTING AND TRAINING CLIMBERS

Different types of wall plant need different training and care. If you have a true climber, check whether it is self-clinging or not. People frequently put up expensive latticework on a house wall, and then plant ivy or Virginia creeper, which ignores the trellis and grows up the wall behind it. Self-clinging climbers need just a little help in the first year – a couple of bamboo canes will suffice to train the plant back to the wall or fence.

If your climber grows fine tendrils, it will want something to cling to – a framework of wires, attached to the wall with vine eyes, or stiff plastic mesh is the best option. Be careful to attach the netting firmly at regular intervals to a wooden framework or it will pull away under the weight of the plant. Plastic mesh can also be used for growing climbers up trees, as well.

Trellis is the best support for wall shrubs and climbing roses. The squared trellis is the strongest. Extending diamond trellis is made of quite flimsy wood and needs to be strengthened with a capping beam. Shrubs should be trained flat against the framework, and their main stems spread out in any number of espalier patterns (see pp. 224–225) or fan fashion. Climbing roses will produce strong new stems each season; these can be tied to bamboo canes, making it easier to prune the old stems. Bend the stems horizontally to encourage flowering shoots.

A wall-trained climber, Stephanotis floribunda, *creates a dramatic effect with its dark green arch above the statue. Green tendrils reaching for the statue add a romantic touch.*

PLANTING A CLIMBER

1 Generally, the soil at the base of walls is very dry, so it pays to prepare it thoroughly. Dig a hole 50 cm (20 in) wide and the same depth. Loosen the soil at the bottom of the hole and remove any rubble, old bricks or stones.

2 Place the climber at least 30 cm (1 ft) away from the wall, where rainwater will fall on it. Then position the cane so that the plant can lean back towards the wall for support. Backfill with soil that has been heavily enriched with moisture-retaining matter such as leaf mould. Firm in gently with your foot and water thoroughly.

TRAINING CLIMBERS

1 Hammer the wire-supporting nails into the mortar between the bricks, starting at about 45 cm (18 in) above the ground. Space the nails about 45 cm (18 in) apart over the area you wish to cover. If you take the framework higher than 1.8 m (6 ft), you will need a ladder for subsequent pruning and care.

2 Thread the wire through the holes and make a wire framework, first across the base and then up to the next layer. Include some diagonal lines, as well as vertical and horizontal ones. Cut the wire and twist it around, to fasten it about halfway up. This ensures that the whole framework will not come loose if one nail pulls out.

3 Carefully disentangle the shoots of the climber and spread them out on the ground. Remove any shoots that are damaged or weak and prune the others back to a healthy shoot.

4 Using the bamboo canes, prop the plant against the wall. Tie the shoots loosely on to the framework with twine, using a loose loop and knot so that there is plenty of space for the shoot to expand.

CLEMATIS CARE AND PRUNING

Contrary to popular opinion, clematis do not need any addition of lime or rubble to the soil. They do, however, like a good rich soil with well-rotted manure added. As they are voracious feeders, clematis should not be planted near the roots of trees or shrubs. If you wish to grow a clematis up a tree, plant it at least 1.8 m (6 ft) away and train it towards the tree. Always plant a clematis 5 cm (2 in) below the surface of the soil so that if it is struck by clematis wilt, it can make new shoots from below. Clematis like shade at the roots; you can provide this with low ground-cover plants or by covering the soil around the roots with stones or tiles.

Depending on the variety, there are three different pruning methods for clematis. Keep the label so that you know which variety you have. Those that flower on the new growth, such as the 'Jackmanii' and *Clematis viticella* groups, can be hard pruned in early spring to 1 m (3 ft) above ground level. Prune *C. florida* and *C. patens* groups and *Chanuginosa* Candida after flowering. Many of the species clematis, such as *C. montana*, *C. macropetala* and *C. alpina*, do not need pruning.

CHOOSING ROSES

RELIABLE ROSES

'Ballerina'

'Cornelia'

'Frühlingsgold'

'Golden Showers'

'Nevada'

Rosa glauca

Rosa rugosa 'Roseraie de l'Hay'

SEE ALSO

Rose growing
See *Planting roses, pp. 132–133*

Say it with roses
See *Styles of rose garden, pp. 134–135*

Shrub maintenance
See *Caring for shrubs, pp. 170–171*

Pruning techniques
See *Pruning shrubs, pp. 182–183*

For many people, a garden is not complete without a rose. Fortunately, they come in so many shapes and sizes that there is a variety to suit everyone's taste. Here, we have divided them into three groups for ease of reference. In the first group are what are now known as bush or large-flowered roses (formerly hybrid tea) and cluster-flowered roses (formerly floribunda). These give a long-lasting display of flowers, but apart from the flowers, the plants are not attractive, tending to look stiff and bare, especially after pruning. They can be used to best effect in a mixed border, where their flowering adds to the general effect and other plants serve to hide their bare legs. Good cultivars in this category include the popular white-bloomed 'Iceberg', and the pinky red 'Fragrant Cloud'. Standard and weeping standard roses also fit into this group – they can be used to bring useful height to a formal layout, but tend to sucker determinedly from the stem.

Standard roses often have a formal, stiff appearance. Here though, they have been grown to show off an abundance of 'Pink Bells' and make a lush centrepiece to a rose garden.

SHRUB ROSES

These roses are more densely stemmed with fewer flowers to leaves than the bush roses. They also remain attractive throughout the year because they are not pruned as harshly.

Lavender is a classic plant to use as the edging to a rose border – as well as bringing its traditional charm and sweet scent to the garden, it screens the plants' stems from view.

Helpful hints

A rose is a long-lived plant so it is worth spending some time checking out which varieties you like best before choosing one to plant. The best time to see a rose is in summer after a wet spell – this is when the colour is at its best and the smell at its strongest, and you can also see how the plant stands up to rain. Check that the foliage looks healthy too, then note the variety's name. Order bare-rooted plants for planting in autumn.

In this group are the species roses, which are the healthiest of all and have lovely foliage, such as the ferny leaves of the Scotch rose (*Rosa pimpinellifolia*) and dark glossy foliage of *R. rugosa*. The pure species bear red rosehips in autumn, while the cultivars have larger flowers, such as *R. rugosa* 'Roseraie de l'Hay', with red blooms, and *R. pimpinellifolia* 'Stanwell Perpetual', with blush-pink flowers.

Recently "old-fashioned" roses have become popular, and these can also be classed with shrub roses. Some are ancient, such as the *Rosa mundi* (12th century), which is splashed white and crimson, and 'York and Lancaster' (pre 1551). Many date from the 19th century, and originate from France, such as 'Souvenir de la Malmaison'. Their flowers tend to be double or many-petalled cabbage types, often heavily scented. Newer roses have now been developed that are similar in style to the old roses, but are often lower growing and with greater disease resistance.

Another newer development by the rose breeders are the ground-cover roses, which are easy-to-grow, healthy plants with spreading habits. 'Nozomi', with pearl-pink blooms, is an older variety of this type, while 'Red Bells' and the double, white 'Avon' are among the newer ones.

CLIMBERS AND RAMBLERS

Climbing and rambling roses are probably the showiest of the flowering climbers – and many varieties have longer flowering periods than clematis. They also tend to be less prone to disease, although some such as 'Iceberg' are more prone to mildew and greenfly attack than others like the scented, white-flowered 'Mme Alfred Carrière', which can also take some shade. It can often be difficult to distinguish ramblers from climbers, but most climbers, such as the shiny-leaved, shell-pink 'New Dawn', will be repeat flowering, while ramblers, such as the warm salmon-pink 'Albertine', generally produce only one flush of blooms. Ramblers tend to be more vigorous than the climbing roses, making them more suitable for large structures and wild areas of the garden.

Gloriously red 'Trumpeter' and 'Colour Break' burst into bloom as the summer highlight of this border.

PLANTING ROSES

Roses can be used in many parts of the garden, both formally and informally, wherever a long, brilliant floral display is needed. There is a rose for every planting style. A romantic effect is made with a trellised rose arbour covered in deep red roses – this can be lightened with pale and pretty pink and white, tiny China roses, such as *Rosa* 'Cécile Brünner'. A front garden can be blazoned in red or yellow and orange with bush roses, or shrubs such as the soft apricot *R.* 'Buff Beauty'. A grand rose avenue might be made with the crimson, classically shaped rose *R.* 'Royal William' underplanted with box; or an English cottage-garden effect could be created with roses around the door. The white *R. rugosa* 'Blanche double de Coubert' could scent a meditative retreat, while the shocking *R.* 'Pink Perpétué' makes for a dramatic colour combination growing through *Cotinus coggygria* 'Royal Purple'; steel-blue purple-leaved *R. glauca* combines with pink panicles and huge leaves of *Rheum palmatum* 'Atrosanguineum' to make a mysterious corner.

Roses will grow in a range of conditions, although they prefer a clay to a chalk soil, and respond best in fertile ground. Generally, roses like an open position and do not like to be overhung by trees, although the bright shade of a north wall is suitable for some climbing varieties such as the sunny yellow *R.* 'Golden Showers'. Many roses are prone to disease, particularly mildew, rust and black spot. To avoid the need to spray repeatedly, look for a rose that is listed as being disease resistant and plant it among other shrubs or perennials. Do not plant a new rose where a diseased one grew previously unless you are prepared to remove and replace the topsoil.

A preformed metal archway makes a strong support for a vigorous climbing rose. Make sure the arch is sufficiently high and wide, so you don't need to duck to avoid thorns.

RENOVATING A ROSE BORDER

If you have inherited a neglected rose border or garden, you will need to examine all the bushes to decide whether they are healthy enough to keep. In cold climates, this is a job best done in late winter or early spring, which is the best time for pruning roses. It is likely that some will be overgrown by suckers; in extreme cases you may have only a briar rose left – the wild rose that the variety was grafted on. Dig these out first, and remove suckers on any other plants by severing them at the point where they grow from the rootstock. Look at the other roses and see if they have strong healthy shoots growing from above the graft. (A graft looks like a lump in the stem, at or close to ground level, see box opposite.) Remove any roses that have no new growth, that have been planted too high, or are unsteady. By now you will probably have half the number of roses that you started with. Prune the rest, removing any spindly or diseased stems and shortening strong shoots to an outward-pointing bud. Keep the centre of the rose plant open so that air can circulate. After pruning, add a thick mulch of manure or compost to the bed.

PLANTING A POT-GROWN ROSE

1 Dig a small hole where you want the rose to go, and position the plant, still in its pot, to make sure you like the placement. If you are happy with the look, enlarge the hole to at least 40 cm (15 in) deep; keep the topsoil separate from the subsoil, and backfill to the level of the base of the pot with soil-based compost with organic matter added.

2 The rose should have been soaked for at least one hour beforehand. Slide it out of the container and loosen any tightly bound roots. Set it in position and backfill with enriched soil mix so that the finished level is the same as in the container. Firm it in with your foot; then water well. Repeat the watering often when weather is dry.

PLANTING A BARE-ROOTED ROSE

1 Before planting, soak the roots in water for a few hours, but no more than 24. Trim away any broken roots. Inspect the graft (the bumpy joint between the green stem growth and roots) and make sure there are no suckers shooting directly from the roots below. Remove any old leaves and twiggy side shoots at the same time.

2 Dig a hole deep and wide enough for the roots when they are spread out, without having to twist them around. Build up a mound in the center of the hole to support the roots. Spread the roots evenly over the mound.

3 Backfill with the topsoil mixed with compost or manure, and shake the plant gently so that the soil settles between the roots. When it is about half-full, firm the soil gently with your heel. Complete backfilling until the hole is full; firm it down again and check the level. Water thoroughly.

Helpful hints

The recommended depth for planting a rose varies across the country according to the average winter temperature. Where winter temperatures drop below -23°C (-10°F), the bud union, or point of grafting, should be 5 cm (2 in) below soil level so that it has some degree of protection from freezing conditions. In areas where winter temperatures range between -23°C and -12°C (-10°F and 10°F), the bud union should come just above soil level. In temperate climates, where winters are warmer than -12°C (10°F), the bud union should be 5 cm (2 in) above the ground.

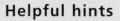

STYLES OF ROSE GARDEN

PLANTING SUGGESTIONS

There are so many colours and styles of roses that it is better to keep your rose garden simple, yet elegant. It is probably not a good idea to have a bed dedicated solely to roses, because in winter there will be no foliage and no colour. Think carefully about where you will position your roses and how to combine them with other plants in order to give the best overall effect throughout the year. Scented roses should be planted near paths or at the edges of lawns so you can appreciate the aromatic flowers in their full glory.

▶ FORMAL DESIGN
In this classical formal garden with rose arches, clipped box and statuary, use is made of all the rose colours – from yellows through to bright reds. This would give too fussy an impression were it not softened by the deep green hedging.

The rose is the universal symbol of romance. Luckily for us, it is also one of the most reliable flowering plants we have. There is little in the garden to rival the rose, for its range of colours, scent and length of flowering time. In contrast, winter is a sad time for roses, when they show only their bare stems, so a good solution is to plant them within hedges of box or lavender.

Roses' colour range is wide, containing all except purples and true blue. However, it is often more effective to choose one or two colour from the palette, to provide more subtle effects. The classic colour romantic rose, is deep red which, combined with pink, makes a sumptuous picture, especially if the roses chosen are double or old-fashioned "cabbage roses" and heavily scented. In contrast, yellow and orange roses give a much brighter, warmer effect, while white roses give an impression of purity in a meditative garden.

▲ ROSE LOLLIPOP
To add height in this garden, the standard rose 'Pink Bells' emerges from a low hedge of lavender, giving a varied colour scheme.

► SOFT HUES
Too many roses can
be overpowering. It
is a good idea,
therefore, to plant
them with other
flowers, such as the
white iris shown in
this garden. The
colour of the iris
echoes the tones of
the climber above.

▼ STRIKING
DISPLAY
Sometimes a
rose display is so
stunning that it
needs only one
sharp contrast to
set it off. In this
instance, the
white seat is all
that is needed to
complete this
dramatically simple
composition.

▲ FLOWERING POT
Roses can also be grown in terracotta pots,
to give a bright, colourful, eye-catching
display. In this example, the rose is being
trained into a conical shape, to make a
dramatic and prominent feature.

CHOOSING SHRUBS

EASY-GROW SHRUBS

Eunoymus japonicus

Firethorn (*Pyracantha*)

**Flowering quince
(*Chaenomeles*)**

Forsythia

**Oregon grape
(*Mahonia japonica*)**

**Mock orange
(*Philadelphus*)**

Viburnum

SEE ALSO

Which shrub?
See *Buying and planting
shrubs, pp. 138–139*

Shrub maintenance
See *Caring for shrubs,
pp. 170–171*

Pruning techniques
See *Pruning shrubs,
pp. 182–183*

Shrubs, together with trees, form the backbone of every garden. They are more rapidly effective and less longlived than trees, but still require careful thought and planning. Check on their hardiness and requirements for sun or shade, dry or moist conditions, and acid or limy soil. Make sure that you allow enough room for them to grow to their full size or you will forever be snipping at them – pruning is often unnecessary if you have chosen well.

There is a huge variety of shrubs to choose from, and they vary in size from the low, evergreen mounds of plants such as *Cotoneaster dammeri*, to bushes that grow and look like small trees, such as lilac. First of all, you need to decide whether you want an evergreen or deciduous shrub. Evergreens usually give a more solid effect. They give essential weight to a border, but may need lightening with deciduous species.

Shapes of shrubs can be roughly divided into four categories: rounded, arching, flat or tiered and upright. Many evergreens are rounded or domeshaped, from large ones such as *Elaeagnus* x *ebbingei* and *Ceanothus* to lower bushes such as lavender and hebe. Deciduous rounded bushes include *Viburnum carlesii* and *Potentilla*.

Arching or weeping shrubs are mainly deciduous, from *Spiraea arguta* to the many fuchsias. The classic tiered shrub is *Viburnum tomentosum*, which looks like a wedding cake when covered in white flowers in early summer; Japanese maple (*Acer palmatum*) is another, with the added attraction of lacy leaves and, in some varieties, red foliage.

Forsythia is a typical example of a deciduous shrub that is upright to pointed, and *Mahonia* and pittosporum are both evergreen types. Some upright shrubs will become more arching with age.

Exuberant azaleas and rhododendrons make a strong impact behind a large pond. They need acid soil and lots of space.

Foliage is often crucial to the effect a shrub gives. A shrub may be rounded with glossy evergreen leaves, like *Choisya ternata*, or soft green circles, like *Cotinus coggygria* – the effect is quite different. There are rough, leathery textured leaves such as those of *Viburnum rhytidophyllum*, and elegant ribbed leaves like those of *Viburnum davidii*. Some foliage is shiny and light-reflecting, such as that of the camellias, and some is almost dusty such as *Senecio* 'Dunedin Sunshine'. There are lacy leaves like *Rhus glabra* 'Laciniata' and deeply incised leaves like those of *Paeonia lutea* 'Ludlowii'.

Leaf colour is more permanent than flower colour, and there are a few guidelines to follow; the most important of these is restraint. Coloured foliage is attractive but can give a restless effect and should be used with care. Plain green can be enlivened with variegation, from the white of *Cornus alba* 'Elegantissima' to the bright yellow of *Elaeagnus pungens* 'Maculata' – white gives a calmer impression than yellow. The orange-tinged *Spiraea* 'Goldflame' gives a glowing look to a border.

Grey-leaved plants group together well. Many of these, such as *Cistus*, *Halimium*, and cotton lavender (*Santolina chamaecyparissus*), are sun-lovers that originate from the Mediterranean – they are often highly aromatic. Reds, such as the deep red of

Cotinus coggygria 'Royal Purple', look good with sunlight behind them, but over-used can be dreary and darken a border.

When considering flower colour, think of the overall impression. Some flowers are dainty, like yellow, white and orange potentillas, while others, notably the rhododendron varieties, have an almost overpowering impact. White can be used in large quantities, where red and orange may need more prudence. True blues are hard to find – *Ceanothus* is the best-known clear blue – but there are many purples.

A shrub border is a must for the easy-maintenance garden. Once the plants are established, it requires the minimum of attention.

Grow scented shrubs over an arch and enjoy the fragrance whenever you walk through it.

PLANNING TIP

The scent of shrubs is most noticeable in an enclosed area – a sunny corner, around a seat or just beneath a window are the ideal places to grow aromatic shrubs. Aromatic plants grown over an archway or in a raised bed also work well. The perfume is emitted by the flowers or the leaves, and in some cases, such as the spring-flowering *Choisya ternata*, both. For good flower scent, think of the deciduous *Azalea mollis* varieties, and the orange-blossom perfume of mock orange or honeysuckle. For plants with aromatic foliage, herbs are a good choice, particularly rosemary, thyme and sage. However, perhaps one of the most powerfully scented plants is *Cistus purpureus*. It needs planting with care, since it can be difficult to establish.

BUYING AND PLANTING SHRUBS

YOU WILL NEED

Spade

Wheelbarrow

Stake, rubber mallet

Tree ties

Secateurs

Compost

Bark chips

Plastic or wool
mulch mat

SEE ALSO

All kinds of shrubs
See *Choosing shrubs,*
pp. 136–137

Plant design
See *Creating shapes with*
plants, pp. 158–159

Caring for your plants
See *Looking after your*
plants, pp. 168–169

Shrub maintenance
See *Caring for shrubs,*
pp. 170–171

More pruning
techniques
See *Pruning shrubs,*
pp. 182–183

Once you have a short list of shrubs, make sure they will be happy in your garden. This means that you must be aware of the microclimate of the site (see p. 16). With each shrub, check its requirements for sun or shade, as well as protection from winds or frost. With a planting using several large shrubs, you will in effect be creating a new microclimate – once these shrubs grow and spread to their full size, they will create partial shade themselves, and if you are planting lower shrubs to combine with them, the larger shrubs will need to tolerate this.

Remembering your soil type (see p. 90), make sure that your plant is suitable – first, does it like acid or alkaline soil? It is important to keep calcifuge (acid-loving) plants separate from others, and if you really want to grow rhododendrons and azaleas in a chalky soil, you will have to plant them in a separate container, preferably in dappled shade, which they love. Does the plant need rich soil or will it grow better in dry, poor conditions? Some Mediterranean plants, for example, grow very fast in rich moist soil, but over time they will become soft and sappy, and they are less likely to resist harsh winter conditions.

Most plants are relatively fragile until they have established themselves, so it pays to protect newly planted specimens from harsh sun and wind for a few months, and to ensure that they do not dry out. A plastic or wool mulch mat around the base of the plant will protect the roots both from weeds and from encroaching perennials, and will also help to conserve moisture.

How large and wide will your shrub grow, and how long will it take to reach maturity? This will vary, but some shrubs, such as rhododendron and *Pieris*, are naturally slow-growing, which is why large specimens cost so much in your garden centre. However, many grey-leaved plants such as lavender are quick growers, so it is not worth buying a large one to start with. It is very important to allow enough room for your shrub to grow to its full size or you will be constantly snipping at it – pruning of some species is unnecessary if you have positioned them well. With slower-growing specimens, you can fill in the gaps with perennials while it is growing to full size. These must be removed in time to allow the shrub to fill out. Remember, it was the slower-growing plant you chose for that position in the first place.

TRANSPLANTING A SHRUB

1 Transplant only in cool, damp weather, during the dormant season. Cut down around the roots with a sharp spade, taking care to dig underneath the shrub as well, to sever its lower roots. (This process can be done in two halves for more mature plants, cutting around half the roots one year and half the next.) Water well.

2 Dig and prepare the new site. Carefully lift the shrub out of its old position, place it in a wheelbarrow and move it to the new site. Trim any damaged roots. Lift it into its new position and backfill. Drive a stake into both sides of the new hole, and tie the plant from each side. Prune one-third of the topgrowth of the shrub.

BALLED-AND-BURLAPPED SHRUBS

1 Bare-rooted plants are dug from the growing field with the soil around their roots, and then wrapped in hessian (or a similar synthetic material) to keep the soil in place. You can leave natural hessian on the rootball since it will decompose, although you should cut the string holding it in place. Synthetic wrapping will not break down, so remove it.

2 Dig a hole twice as big and 15 cm (6 in) deeper than the rootball. Backfill the hole with 15 cm (6 in) of soil with compost added. Fill the hole with water and let it drain. Water the rootball thoroughly. Place the plant in the hole and backfill with soil, tamping down with your foot to remove air pockets. Water again

PLANTING SHRUBS IN GROUPS OF THREE

1 Cluster shrubs in groups of three to anchor a corner in the garden or to add mass to a design where there is too much open space. To work out the planting distances, find out the expected mature spread of each shrub, then subtract a few centimetres to ensure that the shrubs overlap slightly when mature.

2 Choose the location for the first shrub and mark that spot on the ground. Measure out at an angle from that mark to find the position for the second shrub. The third shrub should be equidistant from the first two to create the final point on the triangle. Notch a stick at the distance you want to separate the shrubs, to use for easy measuring.

3 Dig planting holes slightly larger than the rootball for each shrub. Backfill the hole with soil with compost added. Fill the hole with water and let it drain away. Water the shrubs thoroughly, remove them from their pots and plant them, making sure they are at the same soil level they were in their pots, or 2.5–5 cm (1–2 in) higher in clay soil. Water well and mulch.

Helpful hints

Plant pot-grown specimens at any time of year, since damage to the roots of these plants is minimal. The traditional planting time for all other types of plant is early autumn, when the weather is less hot, but the soil is slightly damp. Plant frost-tender species in spring, when the soil is warming up, to allow roots several months to establish before they have to withstand winter temperatures. Mild, damp weather is always best for planting. A plastic or wool mulch mat around the base of the plant will protect roots from weeds and encroaching perennials and help conserve moisture.

CHOOSING PERENNIALS

TOUGH PERENNIALS

Euphorbia

Iceplant
(*Sedum* 'Autumn Joy')

Lady's mantle
(*Alchemilla mollis*)

Lamb's ears
(*Stachys byzantina*)

Michaelmas daisy
(*Aster* 'Lady in Blue')

SEE ALSO

Dividing perennials
See *Lifting and splitting
plants, pp. 200–201*

Which perennials?
See *Planting perennials,
pp. 142–143*

Everlasting flowers
See *Styles of perennial,
pp. 144–145*

Caring for perennials
See *Looking after
perennials, pp. 168–169*

erbaceous perennials are plants that
have no woody stems. Generally they
die down in winter, either disappearing
completely until the spring, like peonies, or
maintaining just a flat rosette of evergreen
leaves, like the peach-leaved bellflower
(*Campanula persicifolia*). Some, such as the
stinking hellebore (*Helleborus foetidus*) and
Bergenia cordifolia, remain all year, and their
evergreen leaves are useful ground cover in
winter. Many perennials have been usefully
improved by plant breeders, who have
introduced new colours, disease resistance,
and other properties valued by gardeners.
Unfortunately some of the character of the
species is often lost in the process. For
example, the introduction of extra-large
flowers (in chrysanthemums, for instance)
tends to overbalance the plant, and shorter
flower stems (in delphiniums, in particular)
may be useful for a small garden but are not
usually as graceful as the originals.

*It's hard to beat bright salvias for late colour, but dahlias
offer an outstanding range. Both combine with pelargoniums
here for an eye-catching display of pink, white and purple.*

VERSATILE PLANTING

Perennials have many attributes to please the
gardener. They can provide a mass of colour,
and be used to correct a seasonal imbalance
in the larger shrubs – to fill the gap after the
roses have finished their first flush of flowers,
for instance. Most are fastgrowing, so they are
useful in the early years of a garden. Because
of this, they can be divided quite soon. If a
plant is really expensive, you can buy only
one and propagate it yourself – although
you'll have to wait a little longer for the
effect. Look at foliage as well as the flower
when you buy, and for a labour-saving
garden, avoid plants that need special
treatment, such as staking or protecting or
spraying. When visiting other gardens, it is

*A deep border gives plenty of room to plant in large groups
and build up layers of textures and masses of colour. This
one highlights reds and yellows in a burst of warmth.*

worth taking note of the name of any plants that particularly strike you, and noting how they are combined with other plants.

You may be choosing perennials because you have a whole new garden to fill, and you have already chosen the shrubs (see pp. 136–137), or perhaps one border is looking boring or empty, or you have a difficult area to fill. Frequently, once shrubs mature and spread, the perennials beneath them die away for lack of light. At this point, you need to choose perennials that are happy under other plants, enjoying woodland edge conditions. Foxgloves (*Digitalis*) or columbines (*Aquilegia*) are excellent choices here. Some parts of the garden are difficult to plant, but you can generally find a few tolerant perennials which will grow almost anywhere. The base of a wall, for example, makes an ideal spot for a few drought-tolerant plants, such as sun-loving artemisia or the shade-tolerant acanthus.

Perennials are excellent for addressing garden problems that are evident when you step back and look at the whole grouping of plants. Are there repeating shapes and colours, or does it need pulling together with one or two unifying ground-cover plants? Perhaps there is a dull space halfway along the border, needing something to draw the eye after the spring bulbs have died down. One of the showy plants like colewort

(*Crambe cordifolia*), with its huge cloud of white flowers, or a mass of crimson phlox would help here. As usual, if you decide what you want the perennials to do, you are more likely to achieve the desired effect.

The green foliage and flowers of Helleborus foetidus *blend with* Rubus cockburnianus *for subtle texture in a shady site.*

PLANT HABITATS

A dark woodland edge is a perfect home for some perennials, such as Bergenia cordifolia.

Perennials are often the plants that fill all the most awkward spots in a garden, but you need to bear in mind your microclimate and harmonize your planting with it. Some perennials, such as blanket flower (*Gaillardia*) and coneflower (*Echinacea* spp.), are open-ground plants, which can take harsh, dry conditions with no problem. Woodland and woodland-edge perennials like shady areas and can often tolerate a dry soil. Rock plants do well in stony places, generally enjoying hot sun and a cool root-run – they are ideal for filling gaps in paving and gravel. It is often the case that plants suited to a particular habitat, such as woodland or damp meadows, grow well with each other, creating an attractive effect, so it is worth combining a few species.

PLANTING PERENNIALS

As a rule, perennials look best planted in clumps of three or five of one plant type. Arrange the plants in drifts that weave into each other for a natural, appealing flow. Start with small plants (to save on cost) and space them to allow for their mature size. There are one or two exceptions, of course. Some large perennials, such as goatsbeard (*Aruncus dioicus*), look more effective standing alone; and those that are short lived but seed easily, such as clary sage (*Salvia*

sclarea), will show you the best position by seeding themselves in some unexpected but beautiful places!

Many early perennials, such as bleeding heart (*Dicentra spectabilis*), are unsightly after flowering, when their leaves die down completely. Others, such as Oriental poppy (*Papaver orientale*) for example, tend to flop around as the flowers fade. Plant these toward the middle or back of a border, so that their old foliage is not so noticeable.

Plants that have been highly bred generally like an open soil – and a richer soil than their wilder relatives – and should be planted on their own. Those from woodland habitats, in particular, can grow together gradually, mixing and spreading at random, forming long-lived groups that require little maintenance and prefer not to be disturbed. However, all perennials will need regular weeding and watering in their first season. If you plant in early spring or autumn, watering will be less of a problem and plants should establish themselves more quickly.

This planting combines many different colours successfully because it uses a large base of green foliage. Spire shapes of tall perennials, such as delphinium, contrast with the flat plates of Achillea *and soft, rounded, lilac-coloured phlox.*

PLANTING OUT

When planting new perennials, check the label to make sure that you know the correct conditions for your plants and that you have the perfect location. Prepare the planting site with extra manure for any greedy feeders, and make sure that there is good drainage for any dry-soil lovers. It is a good idea not to combine plants that have very different requirements; for example, acid lovers and plants from chalky areas do not live happily together. Because most perennials grow fast, it is really not worth paying extra for large plants. Save money by buying the smallest size possible. If you have no choice, buy a large plant that is well established (sometimes last year's stock is on sale at reduced prices in garden centres). If it has several growing crowns, you can divide the large specimen into several pieces before planting out.

PLANTING A NATURAL-LOOKING PERENNIAL BED

1 Prepare the whole bed by loosening the soil with a fork and removing weeds. Spread a layer of rich organic matter on top and incorporate it into the earth as you plant. Position your key plant (singly for a large plant or a small bed, or else in threes); survey it in relation to neighbouring shrubs and trees. If you are happy with the site, plant it.

2 Now position the groups of plants that are less dominant, keeping the spring-flowerers away from the very front of the border, where their leaves tend to flop untidily after flowering. This space is best kept for later-flowering plants, whose leaves are attractive for the months before they flower. Again, stand back and survey the balance before planting.

3 Fill in the spaces with ground-cover plants, using only one or two varieties kept in separate swathes and divided by the taller perennials. Make sure that there is enough room for continuous sweeps of carpeting. At least one-third of all the plants should be ground-cover specimens.

4 When all the specimens are planted, carefully mulch between them with bark chips. In the first two seasons after planting, make sure that the area around each plant is kept weed free.

PLANTING IN TRIANGLES

Use odd numbers, a minimum of three, unless it's a feature plant. Five or seven plants will quickly join together to look established. Group them together in a rough triangle, according to the planting distances. Dig a hole large enough for each plant, adding a handful of compost. Position the plant, loosening any tangled roots, fill with soil, firm in, and water well.

Helpful hints

If a newly planted perennial has made a great deal of top growth, pinch each shoot back to about one-third of its height before planting. This means it has less leaf area from which to lose water while it is developing its root system; this is especially helpful in hot weather and for bare-rooted plants. Pinching out the tips of the shoots at least a month before flowering is also useful for established plants such as Michaelmas daisy (*Aster novi-belgii*) and phlox, which can become too tall and leggy. They will respond by branching out from below the cut and will become bushier. Flowering may be a little later but more profuse. Use this technique to prolong the season by applying it only to certain plants.

TYPES OF PERENNIAL

PLANTING SUGGESTIONS

Many gardens rely heavily on shrubs, and while these are attractive and practical, they lack the gaiety and variety of perennial plants. It is advisable, therefore, to include a good range of perennials when you design your plant schemes.

Most perennials give a far quicker flower effect than shrubs, so they are a godsend for that period when you are impatiently waiting for your shrub garden to mature.

When combining perennials with shrubs, look for form and shape of the foliage, as well as the flowers. Use these characteristics to balance the framework of the shrubs. The shrubs will give a permanent structure and extend the season of interest.

The true old-fashioned English herbaceous border consisted almost entirely of perennials – hence its usual American name, "perennial border" – ranging from enormous plants at the back of the border down to smaller, lower plants at the front. In Gertrude Jekyll's designs, any gap would be filled by sinking in a large pot of lilies or a well-developed annual plant, both of which would be grown specially for this purpose. These borders were often designed to have their greatest effect in certain seasons only, with high summer to early autumn being the best period of show.

A new fashion is for "near-natural planting", where borders are composed mainly of perennials, although they are often planted around one or two shrubs or trees. The planting is based on species plants, which do not need extra care such as staking, rather than the highly bred hybrids. Because they are chosen extremely carefully in order to match both their natural habitats and habits of growth, the plants need less intensive cultivation than those in the classic herbaceous border. To provide interest over as long a period as possible, use some evergreen perennials and choose subjects with sculptural dried flower stems and grasses with tawny leaves, for example.

▲ PRETTY SIMPLICITY
These *Allium nigrum* and *Gladiolus byzantinus* silhouetted in the sun's rays are a simple yet stunning contrast of plant form and colour.

► ENCHANTING AND WHIMSICAL
Eryngium 'Miss Willmott's Ghost' self-seeds and its ghostly, spiky skeleton flowers appear in unexpected places.

◀ COLOUR AND HEIGHT
Tall *Verbascum* give a strong columnar effect to any planting scheme. The eye is drawn to their bright colours and height.

▶ SCULPTURAL FOLIAGE
Using such plants as *Gunnera manicata* and *Hosta sieboldii* adds a sculptural look to a bed. Dainty white irises stand out against the dusky blue grey of the hosta.

▶ WARM AND BRIGHT
An effective autumn border at Great Dixter in Sussex; the style is English country garden. The plants are bright and friendly, the warm yellows and oranges of dahlias and *Gaillardia* being well backed by the cooler tones of the *Cornus alba* behind.

CHOOSING GROUND COVER

SEE ALSO

Best use of space
See *Design solutions, pp. 28–29*

All kinds of shrubs
See *Choosing shrubs, pp. 136–137*

Planting in crevices
See *Planting in rocks and gravel, pp. 148–149*

Easy care
See *Low-maintenance gardening, pp. 190–191*

The bare soil beloved of tidy gardeners is never found in nature, and will rapidly fill with weeds unless you plant to cover it. Ground-cover plants grow to form a carpet of leaves that makes an effective weed suppressor once established. They can be used in combination with more dominant, feature plants (see p. 142) or thickly planted on their own to form an underplanting for shrubs or trees.

Ground-cover plants grow and increase in various different ways. Some have stems that fall over and create new root systems as they grow, others grow as clumps or hummocks, slowly increasing in size, and some increase by means of underground suckers. These last can be over-vigorous and cause a problem in small garden plots.

Before choosing a ground-cover plant, consider the site, and the height that it will ultimately reach. Flat, mat-like plants form a low layer of ground cover that makes an attractive, as well as useful, addition to the flower border. They range from tiny plants such as *Veronica prostrata*, which has evergreen leaves and bright blue flowers, and the creeping thyme (*Thymus serpyllum*) to *Persicaria affinis*, with its small pinkish flower spikes, and furry, grey-leaved lamb's ears (*Stachys byzantina* 'Silver Carpet').

LARGE AND SHADY SITES

Carpeting spreaders that send out sprawling shoots can be a nuisance in smaller beds. It is worth checking carefully which one you are choosing; for instance, *Lamium maculatum* gives good cover in shade and has pretty variegated leaves, while its larger relative *L. galeobdolon* is a rampaging spreader only suitable for woodland settings. Similarly, the small periwinkle (*Vinca minor*) reeps along neatly and is a better choice than the related

A close planting of catmint creates a haze of blue to edge informal flower beds.

Vinca major, which is invasive. Ivy (*Hedera helix*) makes an excellent evergreen carpet, but again should be used only in large areas. Many of the most useful ground-cover plants for large areas are hummock plants, although they can be slow growing, such as the epimediums, whose delicate flowers appear in spring. Deciduous cranesbills (*Geranium* spp.), with flowers of white, blue or pink, *Tellima grandiflora*, which is evergreen with greenish cream flower bells, and lungwort (*Pulmonaria*) are all good choices.

Most of these are happy in shade, as is the indispensable lady's mantle (*Alchemilla mollis*), with its pretty pleated leaves and yellow-green flowers. Hostas are a sculpturally attractive ground cover for a shady site. However, use them only in areas where slugs are not a problem since they are a favourite food of these pests. Comfrey (*Symphytum*) is another clump-forming ground-cover plant for shady sites and an excellent weed suppressor, but it can be invasive.

USING SHRUBS

Many low-growing shrubs can be used with herbaceous plants for ground-cover purposes. For dry sunny areas, the grey cushiony *Hebe pinguifolia* 'Pagei' is ideal, and rock roses (*Helianthemum*) give good evergreen cover and brilliantly coloured flowers. Heathers (*Erica* and *Calluna* spp.) are tough plants that form a natural ground cover in the Scottish highlands, but most will grow only in acid soil. For shady sites, *Euonymus radicans*, Rose of Sharon (*Hypericum calycinum*) and *Cotoneaster dammeri* are useful evergreen carpeters – although the last two are best used only in larger areas.

Sweet-smelling lavender forms neat clumps and is a popular choice for ground cover in beds and borders.

An underplanting in a woodland area mimics the layer of plants that covers the forest floor.

PLANNING TIPS

Plant the ground cover after the trees, shrubs and key herbaceous plants are in place. Before choosing the plants, check on your soil conditions, aspect (shade or sun), and the size of the area you wish to fill. Prepare the ground well, clearing it of perennial weeds, to give the plants the best possible chance of establishing quickly. You can combine various types of ground cover for a textured display but it can be more effective to plant many small plants of the same variety. They will knit together and form a thick layer in between one and three years, depending on how closely spaced the planting and what species is used. Once they are established, most ground-cover plants need little aftercare and will suppress any annual weed growth.

PLANTING IN ROCKS AND GRAVEL

YOU WILL NEED

Gravel

Rocks

Driftwood (optional)

Sheet mulch such as
woven polypropylene

Ground staples
(U-shaped metal staples)

Plants

Scissors

Garden rake

Spade

Trowel

Watering can or hose

SEE ALSO

Low-growing plants
See *Choosing ground
cover, pp. 146–147*

Plant design
See *Creating shapes with
plants, pp. 158–159*

Easy care
See *Low-maintenance
gardening, pp. 190–191*

A drought-tolerant gravel garden is an attractive alternative to a lawn. You can use rocks and gravel to create a special feature reminiscent of a mountain scree, rocky outcrop or dry riverbed. Whatever your choice, make a feature that is part of the overall design of the garden and not merely a hasty afterthought. Most plants associated with rocks and gravel are alpines or other drought-tolerant plants. For a wide choice of

plants, provide them with a sunny, open position and a well-drained soil. South- or west-facing slopes are ideal, since rocks look most at home on a hillside. If you have a flat, slightly shaded site, your best option is probably a simple gravel surface, or a site resembling a dry riverbed, sparsely planted.

When working on a level surface, such as a path through a gravel garden, lay down sheet mulch between the earth and the gravel. The best sheet mulch is woven polypropylene; this is more expensive than black plastic, but well worth it. This is because it is easier to lay and also because water drains through it, rather than forming puddles on the surface. Plant large specimen plants first and then fit the sheet mulch around them. However, most of the plants will be small fillers and holes can be cut in the sheet mulch to take these. Start with a site that has been cleared of weeds, particularly when building a rock garden where it is not practical to put down sheet mulch. Perennial weeds, such as grasses, are difficult to get rid of once the feature is built.

Combine large boulders, rocks, driftwood and decorative gravel with bold foliage and architectural plants to create an eye-catching low-maintenance garden area.

CHOOSING STONES

Where possible, aim to buy rocks locally. The stones will fit in better with their surroundings. In addition, you will be able to see examples of how they age, and save on the cost of transport. Visit a quarry or a stone dealer yourself so you can pick out specimen rocks of the right size. If you are concerned about the environmental damage caused by extracting certain materials (such

as water-worn limestone) look for alternatives such as secondhand or reclaimed materials. Good-quality synthetic stones can look realistic and are light to move, but they do not keep the roots of rock-garden plants as cool. Moving large rocks is difficult and dangerous, but smaller ones can be arranged to give the appearance of larger rocks. Gravel varies a great deal in size and

colour, so look around several outlets to see what is available. It is less expensive to buy gravel loose from a builders' yard than in bags from a garden centre. Small gravel, with a diameter of about 1 cm (½ in), looks good, but a larger size (2.5 cm/ 1 in) stays put more easily and will not be used as cat litter. To re-create a dry riverbed, use smooth or rounded boulders and pebbles.

MAKING A GRAVEL GARDEN

1 Plants with large rootballs should be planted in their final positions and watered in well. For safety's sake, any large, heavy rocks should also be put in position at this stage. One-third of the rock should be embedded below ground level. Firm the soil down, and make it even, with the back of a rake.

2 Lay down the sheet mulch. To secure its edges, make a 10-cm (4-in) deep V-shaped trench and push the edges down into the trench with a spade. To join two sheets, you need a 2.5-cm (1-in) overlap before securing the sheets in place with ground staples every 1 m (3 ft). Cut the sheet to fit around large plants.

3 To plant small filler plants (those you would normally plant with a trowel), cut a cross in the sheet mulch. Peel back the corners and dig a hole. Take the plant out of its pot and insert it in the hole, making sure the roots have full contact with the soil. Replace the peeled-back sheet. Carefully place gravel around the plant.

4 Cover the space between plants with gravel 2.5–5 cm (1–2 in) deep. Use a garden rake to level it out. Position any finishing touches, such as larger rocks or driftwood. Finally, water the gravel to rinse off any dust.

PLANTING BETWEEN ROCKS

1 To give the impression of larger rocks, select small rocks with similar markings and place them so the markings are running the same way. Tilt the rocks slightly so that they lean back into the rock garden; this will direct any water back into the soil. Fill in the gaps with soil-based compost combined with grit and leaf mould.

2 Water the plant and allow it to drain. Meantime, pack some soil into the crevice. Take the plant out of its pot and squeeze the rootball gently to make it less than the width of the crevice. Insert it between the rocks, making sure its roots are in contact with the soil. Water it again and replace any soil that washes away.

CHOOSING BULBS, CORMS AND TUBERS

Among the first flowers of the season are bulbs – snowdrops (*Galanthus nivalis*), crocuses and winter aconites (*Eranthis hyemalis*). These plants thrive in woodland edge conditions, such as the areas under trees and shrubs where the lawn grows thinly. They naturalize well and are shown to their best advantage when planted in generous sweeps rather than in small pockets.

The early daffodils, such as *Narcissus* 'February Gold', herald the real start of spring. Daffodils come in many sizes and types, from the large single trumpet daffodils, to tiny species such as *Narcissus triandrus* 'Thalia'. Colours range from white through cream and yellow to pale salmon-pink and the two-toned white and orange of scented *Narcissus poeticus*. All these bulbs can be naturalized and planted in large groups, but the best types for this are the smaller varieties that do not blow over in windy conditions. Double varieties and those that have more artificially coloured flowers are not suitable for wild areas because they look unnatural.

Close plantings of dark purple irises and scarlet rock roses stand out at the back of a summer border.

PLANNING TIP

Always plant bulbs after you have finished all the other planting – otherwise you may slice through a stray bulb. After flowering, do not cut down the leaves of bulbs until they have died down or gone yellow – the dying foliage will feed the bulb for next year. For this reason, it is best to place taller bulbs at the middle or back of a planting, where their dying foliage will not show.

Great sweeps of bluebells (*Hyacinthoides non-scripta*) make an unforgettable sight in their native beech woods. However, they can be a nuisance since they spread rapidly and are persistent, so should be planted only in wild areas of a large garden. The dainty *Cyclamen coum* and *C. neapolitanum* make good carpeting plants, and can take extremely dry conditions. They bloom from winter to early spring, as does the small blue-flowered *Iris unguicularis*.

SUMMER AND AUTUMN COLOUR

Apart from the species, tulips are the best bulbs for formal plantings. The range of colours is enormous, and many have subtle or dramatic colour effects in the petals, such as the green streaks of *Tulipa* 'Viridiflora' and the rose-and-white splashes of *T.* 'Sorbet'. As well as the species tulips, which have small, single, early flowers, there are tall Darwin hybrids, the elegant lily-flowering types, the fluffy doubles such as 'Angélique', and the later parrot-flowered varieties with their attractively fringed petals.

Lilies produce the most glamorous bulb flowers for the summer garden, but they can be difficult to cultivate. They like moisture as well as good drainage, and are subject to various problems – they are vulnerable to drying out, and to viruses, diseases and pests.

Most lilies prefer semi-shade and slightly acid conditions, although the white Madonna lily likes full sun and limy soil. Being tall plants, they generally need staking. Varieties range from the speckled orange tiger lily (*Lilium tigrinum*) and hotly coloured Bellingham hybrids to the distinctive Turk's cap or Martagon lily, with its recurving petals. The bedding hyacinth comes in white, pink, red and yellow. The scent is exquisite, but the stiff blooms make them difficult to place, and they may be best planted in pots.

Bearded irises grow from rhizomes, where the bulb is effectively above the ground rather than below it. The common flag iris is purple, but these plants have a large and subtle colour range. They grow best in dry, sunny conditions. Alliums are easy subjects, and range from chives (*Allium schoenoprasum*) with their small round heads to *Allium albopilosum*, which has huge spheres. The flowers are usually purple, although some varieties have pink, white or yellow flowers.

For summer and autumn, gladiolus hybrids and dahlias are extremely popular, and provide long-lasting colour for the formal garden. They are generally lifted after flowering and stored in frost-free conditions over winter. Gladiolus hybrids are stiff plants that need careful placing, but the species, such as *Gladiolus byzantinus*, are dainty and fine and do not need lifting. All prefer sunny positions. Autumn-flowering crocuses make good carpets in beds or under trees.

The distinctive round heads of ornamental alliums make an unusual addition to the flower border. Alliums are easy to grow but need a well-drained soil and plenty of sunshine.

Daffodils are traditional harbingers of spring, and look particularly good when grouped naturally in the lawn or under trees. Larger varieties make a strong impact but smaller species stand up better to wind.

PLANTING BULBS, CORMS AND TUBERS

Bulbs, corms and tubers all store food in the swollen base of the plant. After flowering, leaves die back, returning nutrients to storage for the following year. Many bulbs have evolved to deal with long periods of drought, either hot, dry summers or the dry shade of woodland after the trees unfurl their leaves. Most bulbs are very tough: one or two old crocuses or tulips will survive to flower year after year.

Bulbs appreciate feeding and will benefit from a good soil-based compost, especially one rich in potash. They must have adequate drainage or the bulbs will rot. Plant them deeply – at least twice their height. They will tend to go deeper year by year, by pulling themselves down by their roots.

You can plant bulbs in bedding displays, in pots or among perennials in a mixed border. Naturalistic planting is becoming popular, but certain bulbs, such as tulips, hyacinths and many lilies, do not suit this type of planting since they look too stiff and formal. It is better to plant them in dramatic ways, such as straight lines of white tulips against a dark hedge. Bulbs can be used in a more formal manner: daffodils in regular clumps down a drive, or crocuses forming pools of bright colour among shrubs. The more highly bred or unusually coloured varieties are suitable for a bold display – Madonna and regal lilies both look marvellous in big pots on either side of a front door.

In a woodland setting, clumps of white-flowered bulbs, such as this arum lily, can create a dramatic effect with the delicate white blooms contrasting with the green trees.

NATURALISTIC PLANTING

For naturalistic planting, you need to know the natural habitat of your bulbs. Do they prefer shade, damp or dry conditions in which to grow?

Many bulbs originate in woodland areas and will be happy in the dry shade found under deciduous trees and shrubs. Snowdrops, daffodils, winter aconite and bluebells come into this category. Some lilies, such as the common turk's-cap (*Lilium martagon*), will grow in semi-shade.

Snake's head fritillaries (*Fritillaria meleagris*) grow naturally in damp meadows, so a dampish shady lawn will suit them; but remember to leave the lawn unmown until the foliage dies back.

The little magenta *Gladiolus communis* subsp. *byzantinus* likes dry grassland; it originates in the southern Mediterranean, where it grows in wasteland.

Rock and gravel gardens provide good naturalistic conditions for bulbs such as alliums and autumn crocuses (*Colchicum*). Other lovers of these same hot, dry temperatures are various tiny irises: the dwarf bearded *Iris pumila*, from Eastern Europe to the Urals, and *I. unguicularis*, from Algeria, Tunisia, Turkey and Greece.

FORCING BULBS

1 Put potting compost in the bottom of the pot and position the bulbs on top, so the tips of small bulbs are 2.5 cm (1 in) below the rim; large bulbs can have their tops showing above the rim. Add compost to just below the rim, then water and allow to drain. If using a pot with no drainage holes, take care not to overwater the compost – it should be moist but not sodden.

2 Wrap the pot in newspaper and put it in a cool, frost-free shed or indoors in a dark, cool cupboard. Leave for two to three months until shoots show; then bring into a light but cool place. Water the soil, if necessary, and leave for a week until the shoots turn green. Move bulbs into a warm room, keeping the soil moist. Tall varieties may need staking with split canes.

PLANTING IN DRIFTS

1 Work out roughly where you want the plants to go and clear the ground of weeds, loosening the soil well and adding compost on top. Kneel down so that you are near the soil's surface. Take a handful of bulbs and, with a gentle sweeping motion, strew them over the soil.

2 Survey how the bulbs have naturally fallen, and separate any that are on top of each other. Take a trowel or bulb planter and plant each individual bulb in position. Roughly outline the position of the bulbs with sticks and repeat the process in the ground next to them until you have run out of bulbs or filled the spot.

LAYERS IN CONTAINERS

Place 2.5 cm (1 in) grit in the bottom of the pot for drainage; add 2.5 cm (1 in) of compost. Stand the first layer of bulbs, roots down, shoots upward, with a gap between. Settle them firmly into the compost, then sprinkle more soil around the first layer until only the tips are showing. Firm the soil; then continue with a second layer.

Helpful hints

Tulips and bedding hyacinths are traditionally lifted every year once the leaves have turned yellow. Sort the bulbs; clean off dead leaves and roots and discard small and damaged ones. Store in a well-ventilated room or tool shed. These bulbs may well survive, even without lifting, but they will tend to produce smaller blooms. However, this is suitable for a more natural look.

Snowdrops should be brought inside if at all possible; this means moving them while they are growing and their leaves are green, rather than waiting until they are dormant. Many other bulbs, such as lilies, benefit from being treated in this way, and some special bulb nurseries can supply them in this form.

CHOOSING CONTAINERS

BEST MATERIALS

Terracotta

Wood

Plastic

Stone

Concrete

Aluminium

Fibreglass

SEE ALSO

How to plant a pot
See *Planting a container,
pp. 156–157*

Plant design
See *Creating shapes with
plants, pp. 158–159*

*Most garden centres offer
an array of containers. As
well as terracotta, wood
and plastic, common
materials include cement,
stoneware, earthenware,
reconstituted stone, and
stone-concrete mixes. You
can also buy "feet" to keep
containers off the ground,
and prevent waterlogging.*

Growing plants in containers of compost rather than planting them into the ground is a popular way of creating decorative plantings. It lends itself particularly well to smaller spaces or where there is little or no suitable garden soil. The most visually effective container plantings are those where the container reflects the style or type of garden and is a suitable size and shape for the plant it holds.

The size of a container will have a direct bearing on how well the plant will grow. Roots in a small pot will be subject to more extremes from the environment than roots with more soil around them, and this will mean more caretaking duties for you. In general, the larger a container the better and easier things are – but move small plants up gradually into large pots as they grow. From a practical point of view, avoid putting long-term plants like shrubs and trees into pots that are narrower around the rim than they are at the base since you will have to break the pot when it comes to repotting them.

There is a wide choice of materials to use for containers, and you can recycle many old items, such as watering cans or half-barrels, for use as planters. Stone or concrete containers age well, but are heavy to move

The portability of containers makes them uniquely flexible. This garden at the Chelsea Flower Show in London combines planted and potted plants to pleasing effect.

around. Metal is enjoying a revival, but modern taste is for aluminium rather than lead containers. A good modern material is fibreglass, which is light but durable. However, the most popular materials for containers are wood, terracotta and plastic. Each has its advantages, and may be more suitable for some plants rather than others.

WOOD

Wood is a versatile material, and there are styles and finishes to fit in with any garden. Half-barrels are good value for money and offer rustic charm suitable for climbing roses or to house a leafy gunnera. Versailles tubs offer a more formal look, which is ideal for standard roses or clipped bay. Wood is one of the best materials for window boxes since it can be painted to match the colour of the building. It is also frost resistant and protects plant roots from temperature extremes. It is hard to clean out wooden containers and they can rot, so they are best lined with polythene before planting. You will also need to paint or stain them.

PLASTIC

Plastic is inexpensive compared to other materials, and this is particularly noticeable when you are buying large containers. It is lightweight, which makes it ideal for roof gardens and balconies, but a liability for top-heavy plants such as standards. Less watering may be required for plants in plastic pots, since moisture is not lost through the container's walls. Some types also contain self-watering reservoirs.

Plastic is easy to clean, although less expensive pots may become brittle, discolored, or misshapen. The main disadvantage with plastic is that the plant's roots can overheat during hot spells in summer and the potting soil can become waterlogged in winter. Plastic pots are particularly suitable for vegetable growing.

TERRACOTTA

Many gardeners would not consider any other material. Terracotta manages to look the part in both natural and styled gardens. It also ages well and so matures and blends into a garden. Terracotta is porous (unless glazed), so compost is less likely to become waterlogged than that in plastic pots, and roots are kept cooler in summer. Small pots are reasonably priced, but those over 30 cm (12 in) in diameter are expensive. Although long-lasting, terracotta pots are heavy and easily broken if mishandled. The porous walls are prone to drying out in hot summers – but this suits drought-tolerant plants like pelargoniums and Mediterranean herbs.

The top three: terracotta, plastic, and wood (left to right). The green plastic window box has two built-in water reservoirs, making it handy for someone who has little time for watering.

You can be as adventurous as you like in your choice of container. Here an old rowing boat makes a riverside idyll of a bed.

PLANTING A CONTAINER

YOU WILL NEED

Hanging basket

Liner

Lightweight hanging-basket compost

Small piece of plastic

Small trailing plants for sides

Feature plant for the top

Small upright plants for the top

SEE ALSO

Trees in pots
See *Buying and planting trees, pp. 118–119*

Bulbs in pots
See *Planting bulbs, corms and tubers, pp. 152–153*

Pots and more pots
See *Choosing containers, pp. 154–155*

Plant design
See *Creating shapes with plants, pp. 158–159*

Easy care
See *Low-maintenance gardening. pp. 190–191*

Container plants can be enjoyed on hard-surfaced patios, in ornamental urns and troughs, or in tiered planters; in particular, hanging baskets and window boxes are very useful to would-be gardeners who have little or no growing space. Tender plants provide temporary summer displays and allow you to replant the container each year with a new planting scheme. Try growing two different displays a year in one hanging basket by

replacing spent summer-flowering plants in the autumn with hardy bedding that will flower the following spring.

Long-term plants, such as small trees, shrubs and perennials, can be grown in containers for many years if care is taken to protect the plants and their pots from winter weather. Remember, too, that you need to allow enough room in the container for the plant to grow. Plants can be moved on to larger pots every other spring, or the roots trimmed (or perennials divided) and returned to their pot along with some fresh compost.

The essential point when planting up a container is to make sure water can drain through the compost; if it becomes sodden for long periods, the plant roots will die. A good-quality compost of sufficient depth will make watering easier because it will retain moisture for long periods yet not be prone to waterlogging. For hanging baskets, use a lightweight compost, such as one based on peat, coir or bark rather than soil. For top-heavy trees and shrubs, a soil-based compost provides more stability for the plant.

The shape of this urn makes repotting difficult without breaking it. The best solution is to insert a lining pot into the urn and plant it in that.

PLANTING A FREESTANDING CONTAINER

1 Put the tub in its final position before filling, resting it on small clay "feet" to improve drainage. Cover the drainage holes by placing pieces of broken pots (crocks) concave side down or use large flat stones. Add a 2–4 cm (1–1½ in) layer of gravel or polystyrene chips, then add the compost, breaking up any lumps with your fingers.

2 Tip the main, feature plant out of its pot. Position the plant in the centre of the container and cover the rootball with compost. Firm it down with your fingertips. The surface of the compost should be at least 2–4 cm (1–1½ in) below the rim of the pot, to allow for easier watering. Water the container after planting.

PLANTING UP A TRADITIONAL HANGING BASKET

1 To hold the basket in place, rest it on the rim of a bucket. Insert a moulded liner or place moss on the bottom and halfway up the basket. Half-fill the basket with compost, breaking up any lumps with your fingers.

2 Plant the sides of the basket first, using small plants with a trailing habit. Hold the plant with one hand outside the basket and gently poke or squeeze the roots with the other hand, or hold the plant inside the basket and poke or pull the topgrowth through. Cover the roots with compost, and firm it gently into place.

3 Cover the rootballs of the side plants with compost, and then add a large upright plant in the centre. Plant smaller plants, either upright or trailing, to fill in around it. Top off with the compost and firm down, leaving a 1-cm (½-in) gap between the surface of the soil and the top of the basket.

4 Remove any damaged foliage or flowers, water the basket, and leave it to drain. Keep baskets of tender plants somewhere light and frost free, so that they gradually acclimatise to being outside. Baskets have chains that hook on to brackets attached to the wall. Make sure the brackets are strong enough for the basket and are well secured.

BASKET AND LINERS

If you want to use a loose material for lining your wire-mesh basket, you need not restrict yourself to moss. Consider alternative materials such as coir, wool or even conifer clippings. Rigid, premoulded liners made from biodegradable materials and sheet ones made from plastic, foam or coir matting are other options, but to plant up the sides you need to cut holes in the liner. For quick-and-easy displays, opt for the plastic hanging baskets with solid sides so that you can dispense with liners altogether and plant vigorous trailing plants like 'Surfinia' petunias or a trailing fuchsia in the centre.

Helpful hints

Keep the compost moist by watering it when required. About four weeks after planting up, start regular liquid feeding unless you used a slow-release feed at the start of the growing season. Remove faded flowers promptly to encourage more flowers. Before you go on holiday, protect your plants against drought and heat stress, by grouping containers together and placing them in a slightly shaded area. Put small pots inside larger empty ones to insulate the rootball. If you will be away for a few days, put a sprinkler in the centre of the cluster of pots and connect it to a timer so that pots are watered daily.

CREATING SHAPES WITH PLANTS

YOU WILL NEED

Rooted cuttings

Pots of increasing sizes

Compost

Stakes/canes for support

Ties

Wire-mesh basket and
staples (for weeping
varieties)

Heated greenhouse

SEE ALSO

Designing with plants
See *Styles of planting,*
pp. 112–113

Hedge design
See *Styles of hedge,*
pp. 122–123

Flower shape
See *Types of perennial,*
pp. 144–145

It is very satisfying to create your own shapes starting with young plants, but you can buy mature specimens already trained. Plants with a long clear stem with the leaves and flowers at the top are often called "standards" or "half-standards". Depending

on the variety chosen, the top growth can be bushy and upright like a lollipop or lax and weeping. A young fuchsia plant is easy to train, but choose a variety sold as being suitable for standard work. The principle is similar for many other plants, although a few, such as roses, obtain their shape by grafting one variety on to a long stem of another.

Clipping evergreens, such as box, is another approach to shaping plants. The simplest shapes are domes, spheres and cones. These are cut with the tips of one-handed shears or pruning shears and can be done by eye or, in the case of a cone, with a simple guide. It will take several years for the shapes to form if you use box, but for a quicker effect you can twist stems of ivy around frames to create a "false topiary". Once the initial training has been done, the plants need a bit of routine clipping or pinching back to maintain their shape. This pruning is usually done at intervals throughout the growing season. Topiary grown in containers needs watering and feeding just like any other container plant.

Container-grown box plants lend themselves to training and shaping. Here, a grouping of spirals and small lollipop-shaped plants makes an attractive feature.

STANDARD ROSES

Standard roses are created in nurseries by grafting one variety with desirable flowers on to a tall clear stem of another (usually *Rosa rugosa*). To maintain their shape, you need to stake standard roses along the length of their stems.

Because roses are hardy, the standards can be planted in the ground to become a long-term feature in the garden. Alternatively, they can be kept in a container or tub and moved on to the patio when they are in flower.

Annual pruning will be needed to keep the head of the plant compact and to prevent any lopsided growth. Prune the head as you would a bush rose of that variety; that is to say, assume the graft union of the two species to be equivalent to ground level. To keep a clear stem, it is important to pinch out any suckers between finger and thumb as soon as you notice them. Not only will suckers spoil the clean line of the stem but they will sap the plant of energy.

CLIPPING TO SHAPE

For a young plant, use a permanent frame fitted over the pot, or put on a template when clipping. To make a cone template, use a wigwam of three bamboo canes tied at the top and held in place with three or four circular wires. Start clipping at the top of the plant and work down, stepping back periodically to check the overall effect.

TWISTING AROUND A FRAME

Place the young plant at the centre of a pot. Insert the frame over the plant and push the feet securely into the soil. Gently tease out the stems and spread them over the outside of the frame. Then take each long stem and twist the stems around the wires of the frame, aiming for an even coverage. Use the shorter stems to fill in any gaps.

TRAINING A STANDARD FUCHSIA

1 You can either take cuttings in the summer and grow them over the winter to form flowering specimens the following summer, or purchase young plants early in the year. Select several rooted cuttings and plant each one in a small pot with a split cane for support.

2 As the cuttings grow, tie the stem loosely to a more substantial cane at regular intervals to keep the stem straight. Remove any side shoots that form, but keep any leaves on the main stem intact. After a few weeks, select the strongest growing plants for further training.

3 When the stem has reached the desired height, pinch out or cut off the growing tip and keep the side shoots from the top four sets of leaves. Shape the head as you would a fuchsia bush, pinching out the growing tips of the side shoots when they have four pairs of leaves. Pick the leaves off the main stem.

Helpful hints

Standard sweet bay trees with the added attraction of plaited stems are stylish. It is possible, but rather tricky, to make your own. The secret is to start with young stems and work them when they are pliable. You need a plant with three young stems (single-stemmed plants can be cut back to a 8-cm (3-in) stump in winter, and several stems will then appear the following growing season). Keep the young plant under glass so it will grow fast. Maintaining a high humidity by misting will help to make the stems easier to plait. Support the stem with a stake until it fuses together and stiffens.

WILDFLOWER AND WOODLAND GARDENS

PLANTING SUGGESTIONS

You don't have to have acres of land to encourage wildlife into your garden. Grow plants that produce berries or have edible seeds or scented flowers. Wildflowers will bring birds, bees and butterflies, and a small pond will attract all sorts of creatures.

In a larger garden, you might create a small woodland coppice by grouping a few trees and shrubs, with a path winding through. If you have plenty of lawn area, you could set aside a space for sitting and playing ball games, while allowing other parts to grow longer so that flowers bloom in the grass; you can even plant wildflowers to form a meadow (see p. 164).

In addition to being environmentally friendly, wildlife gardens can be beautiful in their own right. They tend to be calm, peaceful places, without the brilliant, almost hectic colouring given by hybridized plants. It is just as important, however, to design the layout carefully. Many people think that "wild" means simply letting it all go, and it is possible to do just that. But a more enjoyable effect is achieved by careful planning of paths, seating and shelter, as with a conventional garden.

▲ ATTRACTING BIRDS
In the first year, the biennial teasel (*Dipsacus fullonum*) grows only a rosette of leaves, but by the second year 1.8-m (6-ft) tall flower stems with distinctive seed heads appear.

► A WALK IN THE WOODS
A simple but charming woodland walk, surfaced with bark-chip mulch, leads through a grove of white-stemmed silver birch. White and yellow flowers, including the Welsh poppy (*Meconopsis cambrica*) grow at their base.

► MEADOW PATH
This mown grass path leads through a lovely meadow garden where herbaceous perennials grow in a near-natural manner.

▲ BUTTERFLY TRAP
Stone crop (*Sedum spectabile*) attracts butterflies in late summer, is easy to grow, tolerates shade and needs little water.

▼ WATER'S EDGE
This lakeside garden and the woodland behind are so beautiful that they need only the simplest of planting, such as water lilies and rushes, to complete the effect.

WILDLIFE GARDENING

PLANTS FOR BIRDS

Cotoneaster frigidus 'Cornubia'

Elder (*Sambucus nigra*)

Sea buckthorn (*Hippophae rhamnoides*)

Spindle tree (*Euonymus europaeus*)

Symphoricarpos

Viburnum lantana

Whitebeam (*Sorbus aria* 'Lutescens')

SEE ALSO

In the wild
See *Wildflower and woodland gardens*, pp. 160–161

Natural settings
See *Wildlife meadows and ponds*, pp. 164–165

If you have the space for it, plant a native woodland to provide a haven for wildlife for generations to come.

As its name suggests, a wildlife garden is a garden designed to attract as much wildlife as possible. You may wish to concentrate on particular types of wildlife, such as birds or butterflies. However, since natural ecological systems are interconnected, your best bet is to provide a habitat with a wide range of food, shelter and, if possible, a source of water. This will attract many different types of wildlife – and one will, in any case, often bring the other.

Many gardeners prefer to use native plants, particularly trees, when planning a wildlife garden. Although it is perfectly possible to create a welcoming environment without them, native trees may attract a wider variety of insects. Whether you opt for a native garden, or a mixture of indigenous and imported plants, choose those that will thrive in your site while at the same time providing food and/or shelter for the animals and insects you want to attract.

There are many different sorts of wildlife garden, ranging from desert and dry grassland to woodland or wetland and

Use a nesting box to encourage birds into your garden. Place it in a sheltered spot by the middle of winter to give birds a chance to investigate it fully before nesting time.

swamp. Your choice will be limited by your local climate and fauna. Some climates allow for an interesting combination of two or more habitats, thus attracting a much wider range of creatures to your garden.

WOODLAND

Before starting to create a woodland area, take some time to survey your site and see what plants are already in place. The ideal is a balance of mature tall trees, young, lower-growing trees, and a range of shrubs and wildflowers at the lower levels. You may need

Helpful hints

To attract wildlife to an existing garden, use plenty of plants that bear fruits, berries and seeds. Do not be too tidy, but leave fallen logs in piles to rot down and allow leaf litter to collect in corners and underneath shrubs. Let the grass grow a little longer and leave some unweeded, neglected patches.

to clear away overgrown undergrowth, especially if it consists of alien species. If you have a combination of native trees and exotic species, it might be worth removing the exotics to clear the space for the addition of some indigenous species such as ash (*Fraxinus excelsior*), hornbeam (*Carpinus betulus*) and wild cherry (*Prunus avium*).

Work out where you want your paths to go, and surface them with crushed stone, obtained from a local supplier, bark chippings or other suitable rustic material. This will prevent the paths from becoming slippery when the leaves fall in autumn. After this, add the under layer of smaller woodland trees and shrubs, with plants such as rowan (*Sorbus acuparia*), spurge laurel (*Daphne laureola*), woodbine (*Lonicera periclymenum*), guelder rose (*Viburnum opulus*) and tutsan (*Hypericum androsaemum*).

Once the structure of your woodland is established, plant the field (ground) layer of wild flowers in drifts and clumps. For spring there are the attractive woodruff (*Galium odoratum*), Solomon's seal (*Polygonatum multiflorum*) and wood anemone (*Anemone nemorosa*), and later come others, such as yellow archangel (*Lamium galeobdolon*) and ground ivy (*Glechoma hederacea*). Make sure these plants have adequate water during the first season and maintain a leaf mulch to keep in moisture.

Whatever plants you choose, you can follow the basic steps of clearing, laying paths, planting trees, then shrubs and finally the field layer, but check that plants will be happy growing in your area. Your local wildlife organization will be best placed to advise you about plants and conditions; they will also tell you where you can obtain plants of local provenance.

HEDGEROWS

If you don't have room for a woodland garden, you could replace a fence with a wildlife hedgerow, or alter an existing hedge. Traditional hedgerow species are hawthorn

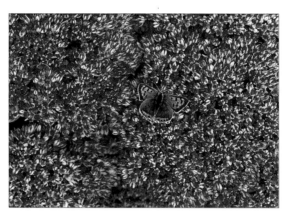

Fill borders with plants that attract wildlife. Thistles make a striking visual impact, and are a major food source for birds.

Include plenty of nectar-giving flowers to entice butterflies into the garden.

(*Crataegus monogyna*), blackthorn (*Prunus spinosa*), dog rose (*Rosa canina*), hazel (*Corylus avellana*), holly (*Ilex aquifolium*) and dogwood (*Cornus sanguinea*), but every area differs a little, and it is worth finding out what plants grow well in your area.

Plant according to the hedgerow instructions detailed on pp. 124–125, then after two or three years, when the shrubs have become established, introduce plantings for a herbaceous layer. Suitable plants here could include foxglove (*Digitalis purpurea*), campion (*Silene dioica*), primrose (*Primula vulgaris*), violet (*Viola riviniana*), bluebell (*Hyacinthoides non-scripta*) and cuckoo pint (*Arum maculatum*).

WILDLIFE MEADOWS AND PONDS

A wild grassland or meadow needs a reasonable amount of space, but can attract numerous insects and, therefore, their predators to the garden, as well as providing a place for growing wildflowers. Generally speaking, the poorer the soil, the wider the range of wildflowers that will grow. This is because in a rich soil the coarse grasses and weeds will tend to smother the finer ones. Stripping off a layer of topsoil will ensure a better result. Before beginning to choose plants, test your soil to find out whether it is alkaline or acid. Select your plants from a list of local grassland species. For a country-style meadow, decide whether you want an early- or late-flowering show. Choose all the plants accordingly, since the effect is maintained by mowing. An early-flowering meadow, with a mass of ox-eye daisies (*Leucanthemum vulgare*), cowslip (*Primula veris*) and birdsfoot trefoil (*Lotus corniculatus*), is mowed in the summer, after the flowers have set seed.

Colourful poppies and other summer-flowering plants recreate the charm of a countryside meadow.

Make a pond frog-friendly by giving it shallow sides and creating a wetland area at the edge.

PLANNING TIPS

Although a wildlife garden consists of various different areas with specific purposes, the areas that are most prolific in wildlife are those that provide an interface between two habitats. A woodland edge that connects with a field habitat is an ideal combination. Make the interface as long as possible by curving the edge of a hedge, and opening up glades in your woodland. Another excellent site for wildlife is the water margin that blends water and land. A wetland provides an excellent site for many water-loving plants, as well as providing shelter for insects and frogs and other amphibians. It is easily made by extending the flexible liner when making the pond – keep a wide curve at the edge of the pond to make this a larger area.

A late-summer meadow that is filled with yarrow (*Achillea millefolium*), field scabious (*Knautia arvensis*) and greater knapweed (*Centaurea scabiosa*) is cut in the autumn and again in spring to hold back the growth of any vigorous grasses.

It is worth establishing flowering species first and allowing grasses to colonize later, since they tend to be more vigorous. If your lawn is growing on poor soil, a quicker way to establish wildflowers is to cut out patches and plant into these, taking care to protect the plants from the surrounding grasses until they are established. You can obtain seeds for many wildflowers, but they can be tricky to germinate. Plants are easier to establish, but make sure that you obtain them from a reputable supplier – occasionally plants are taken from their native habitat by unscrupulous dealers.

PONDS

Water is essential for wildlife, even if it is as small as a bubble fountain or a tiny pond in an old bathtub or half-barrel (see p. 65). If you are making a pond, make it as large as

you possibly can, and make sure that it is at least 60 cm (24 in) deep in some parts. The edges should be shallow, so that wildlife can climb in and out easily – these will double up as a wetland habitat.

For any pond, you need a combination of plants, including oxygenating plants, which grow and spread beneath the water and also give food and shelter. Floating plants, such as water lilies, root in the bottom of the pond while their leaves float and provide shade for the water, reducing algal growth and giving platforms for water insects. Emergents grow at the shallow edges and marginals grow in the damp soil at the edge of the pond.

Combining all these plants will encourage wildlife to visit. Be sure to use only native plants; water is such a fertile growing medium that exotics can easily invade and swamp the natives. Take advice on this, and if you get your plants from an existing pond, find out if the owners have problems with invasive plants. If you wish to encourage dragonflies and other water insects, and your pond is not very large, don't have fish because they will eat the larvae.

A profusion of bluebells, left, makes a shimmering sweep across a woodland area. These plants are too invasive for small plots but make a beautiful addition to a large wildlife garden.

Water-living species will come to make their home in a garden pond, right, and many birds and insects may also come to drink or bathe.

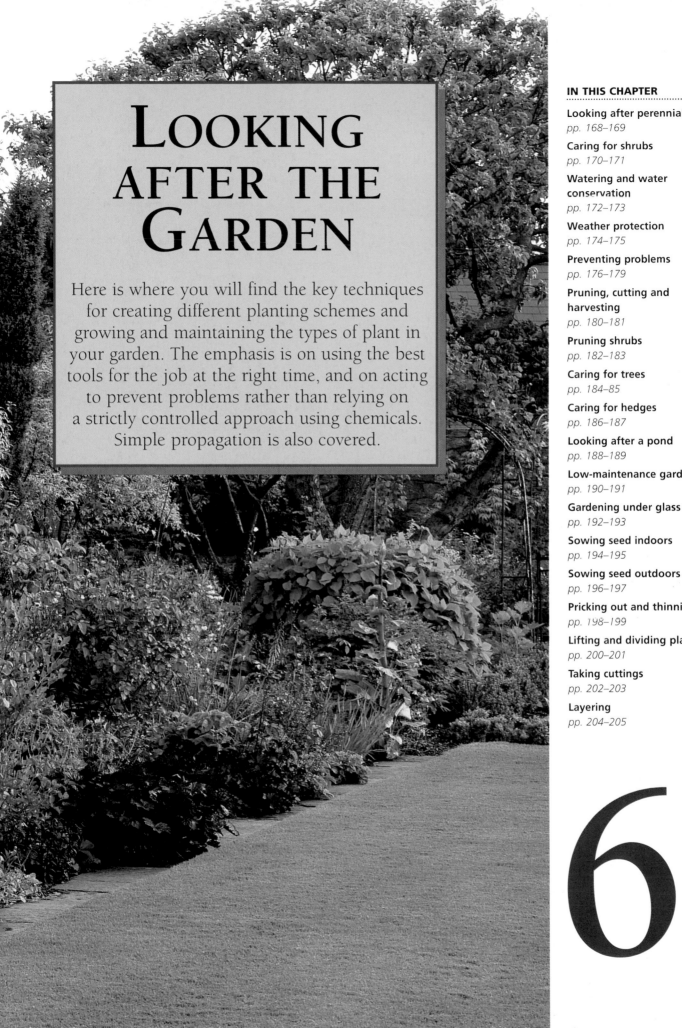

LOOKING AFTER THE GARDEN

Here is where you will find the key techniques for creating different planting schemes and growing and maintaining the types of plant in your garden. The emphasis is on using the best tools for the job at the right time, and on acting to prevent problems rather than relying on a strictly controlled approach using chemicals. Simple propagation is also covered.

LOOKING AFTER PERENNIALS

Perennials such as bergenias and other low-growing evergreen types need little care after planting, but highly bred or fast-growing herbaceous perennials often need attention. A border with fewer types of perennials correctly spaced will be far less work than one crammed full of different perennials competing with each other. If they flop over in summer, it is worth putting in supports in late spring for a better display.

To encourage more flowers to form on each plant, cut blooms for the house or snip off the faded flowers (deadheading). Cutting back promptly after flowering helps to prevent powdery mildew from spreading, but leave a few flowering stems if you want to collect the seed. Many, but not all, perennials come true from seed, so you might want to grow plants on and assess them before replanting them in a border.

Once the top growth of herbaceous perennials dies back after flowering, it can be cut down to the ground in autumn or left until the following spring.

Looking after full flower borders such as these is a matter of cutting back top growth at the end of the year and controlling the more invasive plants.

REPEAT FLOWERING

Cut back the first tall flowering spikes of delphinium as soon as the flowers have faded. Feed and water the plant and, with luck, you will have a second flowering spike for later colour in the border.

Shear off spent flowers and ragged foliage using garden shears or an electric trimmer. This pruning may look drastic on low-growing plants, but if you water them well, fresh mounds of foliage will soon appear, followed by a second flush of flowers.

SAVING YOUR OWN SEED

Cut off the seed heads from healthy plants and take them indoors. Put a clean sheet of paper on a flat surface and with your fingers remove the seeds from the surrounding petals. Clean up the seed by removing any surrounding chaff. You can use a sieve or blow the chaff away using a drinking straw.

To collect seeds from poppies and other perennials that eject fine seed rapidly, cut a stem with the seed head on the top, and put the whole stem into a paper bag with the seed head at the bottom.

If fleshy berries surround the seed, mash the berries up with some water and press them through a sieve. Allow the seeds to dry on paper towels.

Helpful hints

Wait until the seeds are ripe (usually mid- to late summer), but then collect them quickly before the seeds are dispersed – and take root where you may not want them – or begin to rot. Seed heads may split open when the seeds are ripe; the seed often changes colour, too. Label seed supplies with the name of the plant and when it was collected – this will be a great help when you come to sow the seed later on. Seeds can be sown fresh (perennials sown in late summer or early autumn will flower early the following year) or they can be stored until the weather begins to warm up in spring.

STAKING AND SUPPORT

The secret of using plant supports is to get them in place by late spring when the plant stems are still young and before flowering starts. The plant will then grow through and hide the supports. You can rig up supports using bamboo canes and twine or wooden sticks. Insert supports into moist ground or make holes first, otherwise the supports may break or buckle.

Support systems include circular grids to put over multi-stemmed clumped plants such as catmint (*Nepeta*) or peonies. Link stakes are L-shaped wires that interlock to form different shapes. Use them to encircle plants or to make a line to hold them back so they do not flop over a lawn or path. Cover any sharp tips on plant supports with inverted pots or caps to prevent eye injuries.

CARING FOR SHRUBS

Once a shrub has survived the first two years after its planting and has its roots firmly established in the soil, very little, if any, watering is needed. An annual application of mulch, such as bark chips or garden compost, each spring will keep down any weeds and help to retain moisture within the soil. Take care when mulching acid-loving shrubs that the material you are using is suitable: bark chips, pine needles, garden compost and leaf mould are fine, but avoid spent mushroom compost or many of the processed products.

Shrubs that need to be cut back hard each year to stimulate new growth will benefit from a handful of balanced general fertilizer, such as blood, fish and bone meal, during spring. Rose fertilizer is not only useful for roses but can be used for other flowering shrubs that produce large blooms.

Pruning, if needed, is usually carried out in spring, and any mulching and feeding can be done then too. Little else needs to be done to shrubs during the summer and autumn, although some of the tender or container-grown shrubs will need winter protection.

Shrubs that have been neglected and allowed to become overgrown can usually be rescued by a careful programme of renovation. However, if the plant shows any signs of disease or heavy pest damage, it is best to remove it completely and replace it with a new shrub.

Deciduous shrubs in an overgrown state are best tackled after flowering; evergreen shrubs should be renovated during spring. Try to avoid imposing shock tactics on the plant because it is unlikely to recover from severe pruning that is carried out all at once. Opt instead for a staggered renovation over one or two years, by cutting back one-third of the old, main stems to the ground each year. Remove all dead or damaged wood.

If shrubs are growing in the wrong place, it is worth moving them to a more suitable site. Perhaps they are not being displayed to their full advantage or no longer fit in with the planting scheme in a particular bed; maybe the soil in one part of the garden is too wet during the winter; or the early flowers might be caught by the frost each year. Often shrubs grow too big for their allotted space; if they are valuable to you it is worth moving them somewhere else. Move evergreens in spring and deciduous shrubs at any time in the dormant season.

DEADHEADING FADED FLOWERS

Small shrubs, such as heather, that have lots of small flower spikes can be cut back with shears after flowering, although flowers can be cut earlier for drying. It is worth removing faded flowers from shrubs such as rhododendrons and camellias. Nip off the dead heads with your finger and thumb but take care not to damage new shoots.

WALL-TRAINED SHRUBS

Wall shrubs will need regular pruning and tying in. Not only will a south- or west-facing wall be warmer, but the soil will be drier and hotter. A mulch of pebbles or gravel will help keep the roots cool. North and east walls are usually exposed to cold winds. Even shrubs that can survive when mature may need shelter or protection when young.

DEALING WITH A POTBOUND SHRUB

1 Container-grown shrubs often look attractive for many years then start to go downhill as they become potbound. If it is not possible to plant them in the garden or move them to a larger pot, repot them in spring after trimming their roots, and they should improve.

2 Remove the plant from its pot. Shrubs in simple-shaped pots that are wider at the top will come out easily. Where the roots have grown into the contours of a pot or where the pot is narrower at the rim, you may have to destroy the pot to get the shrub out.

3 Lay the plant gently on its side, with a sheet of newspapers underneath to catch the loose soil. If the roots have become heavily entangled, tease them out and remove any moss or weeds.

4 Using secateurs, cut away one-quarter to one-third of the thicker roots to encourage new, healthy roots to form.

5 Replant the shrub in a container that is the same size or slightly bigger. Place crocks over the drainage holes, line with a deep layer of gravel, then fill with fresh compost. Firm the soil down, water it well, and leave the container to drain.

Helpful hints

Most shrubs improve with age, but some look their best early on in their lives and it is better to replace them once they lose their shape or as flowering declines. Short-lived shrubs you might want to replace as the garden matures include: sage, thymes, heathers, smaller hebes, lavatera and brooms. Old woody lavenders that have not been regularly pruned are best replaced with very young plants. Many of these shrubs can be easily propagated by cuttings. For example, forsythia, deutzia and spirea can be propagated by hardwood cuttings; take semi-ripe cuttings for lavender, daphne and berberris.

WATERING AND WATER CONSERVATION

It is vital to give plants the amount of water they need for healthy growth. However, water is a scarce resource, particularly in summer when hosepipe bans or restrictions may be in operation, and it is important to use it wisely. Find out which plants are able to withstand drought and water these sparingly, and store water if possible (see below).

AN OUTSIDE TAP

It is well worth installing an outdoor tap if there isn't one already in place, since you will then be able to use better connectors and accessories than those available for indoor taps. Most modern taps are now fitted with a double-check valve that prevents contaminated water flowing back through the water system. You can buy a double-

check valve to screw on to the tap nozzle of older taps (in the UK it is now illegal to use a hose on a tap that has not been fitted with such a valve). Having an outdoor tap makes it not only easier and quicker to fill up watering cans but also allows you to attach a hose and a water timer to it as part of an automated watering system. Taps should be always be lagged in winter in cold climates to prevent them from freezing.

WATERING BY HAND

A watering can is an essential item, and if you have a pair you can carry one in each hand for more efficient watering. You may even want a third watering can (preferably in a different colour or design to make it easily recognizable) if you want to dilute and apply weedkillers.

It is safe to mix up liquid feeds in cans used for watering, but rinse them out afterwards to prevent algae from forming. Watering cans are made either of galvanized steel or plastic. Both types have their advantages and disadvantages: the metal ones are long lasting but heavy and noisy to use; the plastic ones are lighter and quieter but usually break after a few years.

Do buy a watering can with a detachable rose, since this will give you several watering options. When the rose is fitted with the holes facing upwards, a gentle spray of water droplets will come out and this is just right for watering seeds and seedlings without dislodging them. When the rose holes face downwards, the water will come out faster over a smaller area, ideal for watering in plants. Take the rose off if you want a steady

stream of water, for replenishing ponds or cleaning tools. Dribble bars can be fixed on to watering cans so the spray comes out along a bar. A watering jug with a long spout is useful for watering plants that are placed high up, like those in hanging baskets or pot plants placed on high shelves.

USING HOSEPIPES

Hosepipes save you from having to cart water around the garden. You can lay a permanent system of hoses unobtrusively, joining them together with snap-on connectors. Use hose guides so the hose does not kink when pulled around bends or get dragged over flower beds. An alternative is to have a hose neatly stored on a reel; this ensures that the hose does not get tangled. Reels can be freestanding

HOSE GUIDE

OUTSIDE TAP WITH DOUBLE-CHECK VALVE

WATER TIMER

WATER BUTT

SEEP HOSE

WATERING CAN WITH ROSE

or wall mounted. Most garden hoses are 12mm (½ in) in diameter and are sold in various lengths, typically 30 m (100 ft). It is worth getting a three-ply hose since they are stronger than two-ply ones and less likely to kink.

HOSEPIPE ATTACHMENTS

To join hosepipes together easily, use snap-on connectors that are the same make as the hose. In addition, there are a number of attachments that can be fitted to the end of a hose. One of the most useful is a watering lance, which allows you to reach up and water hanging baskets and window boxes without water trickling down your arm. Trigger gun attachments are also available, and some hoses can be fitted with fertilizer attachments for easy feeding of large areas.

AUTOMATED SYSTEMS

Where a garden has a lot of containers, particularly hanging baskets, or if there is a conservatory or greenhouse, watering can quickly become a chore. There are several systems available to automate watering so that plants can get enough water even if you are not around. Most systems comprise a timer that is fitted to an outdoor tap. At set times during the day, water flows down a series of pipes and tubing to the plants you want to water. Makes of timers vary in the number of times they turn the water on and off during a day, and some are easier to set up than others, so take a look at several makes before buying one.

You need to set up the network of pipes so that every container is supplied and the nozzle at the end of the pipe needs to be adjusted so the right amount of water is given to each plant. For watering a newly planted border or rows of vegetables, you can incorporate a seep hose into the system. A seep hose allows water to seep, or leak from its sides; it can be laid on either the surface of the soil or underneath a mulch.

STORING WATER

It is a sensible, as well as environmentally friendly, precaution to store water for use in the garden during dry spells. You can fit one or more water butts to collect water from the roof of the house, garage or other outbuilding. The rainwater collected is not only invaluable in a drought but can be used for acid-loving plants. Raise the water butt up on bricks so that it is easy to slip a watering can under the tap. Water butts should be covered with a lid and need to be cleaned out once a year with garden disinfectant.

Mulching the soil is a good way of conserving water since it keeps evaporation to a minimum, as well as reducing the growth of weeds, which will divert water away from your chosen plants.

INCREASING HUMIDITY

Hand-held misters with trigger sprays fitted are useful for wetting the soil surface when small seeds have been sown, or for keeping the humidity level high around individual plants in a greenhouse or conservatory. To increase the humidity level of the greenhouse itself, splash water on the floor and on staging. In a house where misting could result in staining soft furnishings or furniture, place a shallow tray of wetted pebbles, gravel or capilliary matting under pot plants to increase humidity.

WATERING JUG WITH
LONG SPOUT

SPRAY LANCE

AUTOMATIC WATERING SYSTEM
WITH NOZZLES

MISTER

HOSEPIPE
ON A REEL

WEATHER PROTECTION

YOU WILL NEED

Bark chippings,
evergreen prunings,
straw, or dried leaves

Netting

Stones

Lantern or bell cloches

Hessian

Garden fleece or other
insulating material

SEE ALSO

Assessing the elements
See *Microclimates,*
pp. 16–17

All kinds of weather
See *Gardens in different*
climates, pp. 18–19

Sun or shade?
See *Designs for different*
sites, pp. 26–27

Some deciduous shrubs and perennials may be on the borderline between being hardy and tender in your particular garden, and may get damaged during a hard winter. Rather than lifting them each autumn as you would with tender plants, provide some insulation around the base of each plant in late autumn (see opposite). The dead top growth of perennials can be left on until spring, or cut down before insulating.

It is often enough to provide a temporary windbreak to protect evergreens from cold winds in their early years. Enclose the foliage of more tender evergreens in a wrapping of hessian or garden fleece, stuffed with an insulating material such as straw. Prop pruned conifer branches, such as those from a Christmas tree, against any wall shrubs, tucking the ends under the training wires to keep them in place.

Hardy plants in containers can be at risk if the potting compost freezes; wrapping a double layer of insulating material around the container will help prevent this. In addition, rosette-type plants may rot over winter, particularly if cold water gets into the crown. They are best protected with a cloche or a piece of glass or polythene (see opposite). To prevent rot from entering the crown of red hot pokers (*Kniphofia*) gather the leaves to a point and tie with an elastic band.

SUMMER CONTAINERS

If plants in containers or hanging baskets dry out, move them to a shady place, then snip off dead flower heads and any brown foliage. Keep any growth that has new buds on it, but cut any plants that have finished flowering right back. Cut off trailing leaves if they have become tatty.

To re-wet very dry peat-based compost, half-fill a washing-up bowl with clean warm water, add a few drops of washing-up liquid and mix. Stand the basket or container in the water for 30 minutes, then allow it to drain before returning it to position.

A tall hedge of Portuguese laurel (Prunus lusitanica) forms a windbreak to protect border plants and provide a sheltered area.

PROVIDING INSULATION

Cover the bases of borderline hardy plants with 15 cm (6 in) of evergreen prunings, bark chippings, dry leaves, or straw. Place netting over the top and secure with stones. Remove in early spring to prevent the plant from putting up shoots too early. Spread bark chippings over the soil, but compost any straw, prunings or leaves.

USING CLOCHES

Small lantern or bell cloches can protect small borderline hardy plants from a few degrees of frost; they can also keep rain off rosette-type alpines. Push cloches into the ground, or place a stone on top to secure. Ventilate on warm days by placing a stone under the edge, or the plants will get too hot.

WRAPPING UP SPIKY EVERGREEN SHRUBS

1 Protect evergreens such as phormiums and cordylines by gathering up the foliage to a point. Wind strips of hessian around the leaves to secure them.

2 Cover the plant with insulating material, such as garden fleece. If the plants are in pots, wrap insulation, such as bubble wrap, around the pot to prevent the roots from freezing.

PROTECTING FROM WIND

To prevent a strong wind from damaging branches and stems, foliage and flowers, you need to reduce its speed before it hits the plants. For newly planted subjects, a windbreak of netting fixed to stakes or posts is sufficient protection. Erect the windbreak between the plant and the prevailing wind. In most cases, the windbreak is just a temporary structure and can be dismantled once the plant's roots become established. Use special windbreak netting that filters out 50 per cent of the wind – this is much more effective than solid barriers such as fencing or walls. If you need permanent protection from prevailing winds, a hedge or mixed shrub border is the best option. Make sure that any plants used as windbreaks are suitably hardy and sturdy; in coastal areas they will need to be tolerant of salt spray (see pp. 120–121). Put up a temporary windbreak to protect the hedge while it establishes itself.

PREVENTING PROBLEMS

YOU WILL NEED

Cloche

Garden pegs

Rubber gloves

Trap

Torch

Pesticide

SEE ALSO

Further problems
See *Natural prevention*,
pp. 178–179

Greenhouses
See *Gardening under
glass, pp.*

New plantings
See *Sowing seed outdoors*,
pp. 196–197

Sooner or later, some of your plants will fall prey to pests, diseases, viruses or lack of nutrients. There is little point in dosing plants with chemicals when such a course of action would be time consuming, expensive and environmentally unfriendly. There are several positive steps you can take. Always aim to grow strong, healthy plants in conditions they like so that they are able to shrug off pest and disease damage. Paying attention to garden hygiene and inspecting plants regularly, particularly in the greenhouse and vegetable plot, will also prevent many potential problems from becoming serious. Ways of preventing or controlling problems are outlined opposite and on pages 178–179.

Check young seedlings every day, new plantings every week, and mature shrubs and trees after a hard winter and halfway through the growing season. If you find a problem, first identify the cause. Note the appearance and time of year, and either look up the symptoms in a pest and disease book or take a sample of the plant to a local nursery expert. Once you know the cause you can read up on your options for control.

Hostas have beautiful foliage, but they are often shredded by slugs in late spring and early summer or eaten by deer later on. However, the plants usually survive and reemerge the following year.

USING CHEMICALS

There are times when a chemical control is the best option, usually when a problem is getting out of hand in one particular year. A few chemicals are derived from natural products and are accepted by organic gardeners. For example, derris, pyrethrum and insecticidal soaps will control insect pests, while Bordeaux mixture (based on copper sulphate) and sulphur, which are both derived from naturally occurring substances, control fungal diseases. Pesticides work either by contact or systemically. Contact pesticides need to make direct contact with the pests, so you must apply them thoroughly. They do work more or less instantly, although further applications may be necessary. They work well on soft-bodied pests such as caterpillars. Systemic sprays take longer to work because they first need to be absorbed into the plants' sap on which the pests then feed. Systemic pesticides provide longer-lasting protection and help to control tough-skinned insect pests. Whatever you use, always read the label on the packet carefully. It will tell you how much to use, which plants are suitable, when to apply the product, which pests it targets and how to store it safely.

USING BARRIERS

Protect juicy, young growth, such as emerging shoots or new plantings, with a mini-cloche (either bought or made out of a large plastic bottle). Cloches or fine netting work well to keep flying and crawling pests off plants. However, cloches can cause heat stress to the plants.

REMOVING BY HAND

Picking off pests such as caterpillars, vine weevil or slugs by hand is effective if numbers are small. Wear rubber gloves if handling hairy caterpillars, since some can cause skin irritation. Put collected pests on a bird table, throw them into water, or crush them underfoot. Slugs, vine weevils and snails tend to be nocturnal, so collect them at night using a torch.

GARDEN HYGIENE

There is not much you can do about pests and diseases flying or blowing into your garden, but you can make sure any plants you bring into the garden are healthy. The longer a pot-ready plant has been for sale, the more likely it is to have picked up a problem, so buy from outlets with a high turnover.

CHECKING NEW PLANTS

When obtaining plants, look at the young growing tips and underneath the leaves for small pests such as aphids. Check the foliage for white powder, or grey mould. Tip plants out of their pots before buying to look for grubs or, more likely, roots nibbled off the plant by grubs.

TRAPPING PESTS

Trapping pests can work well on a small scale. For whiteflies in a greenhouse, hang up sticky traps. In a cold frame, protect your plants with a mousetrap (but buy a humane one). A persistent mole problem may mean trapping, but this is time consuming to do on a large scale. Trapping is not practical for slugs and snails due to their high numbers.

Helpful hints

Hygiene is important, particularly in the greenhouse, where warm, enclosed conditions mean pests and diseases can build up rapidly. Start off each year with a scrupulously clean environment, including clean equipment and fresh compost. Use tap water for seedling stages, but stored water once your plants get older. Rain barrels should be covered and cleaned out once a year. To prevent soil-borne diseases, rotate crops in the vegetable plot. Certain plants, mainly roses and pansies, should not be planted where they grew previously, as they will succumb to pests or disease.

NATURAL PREVENTION

YOU WILL NEED

Biological controls

Virus-free plants

Liquid fertilizers

SEE ALSO

Feeding
See *Applying Fertilizers,*
pp. 98–99

Woods and hedgerows
See *Wildlife gardening,*
pp. 162–163

Natural settings
See *Wildlife meadows and*
ponds, pp. 164–165

Getting rid of pests
See *Natural prevention,*
pp. 178–179

There are some areas of the garden where you spend a lot of time and are likely to notice problems quickly, such as when they occur among container plants on the patio, frequently harvested crops, or plants in the greenhouse or conservatory. However, in a large garden with shrubberies and mature borders, a wild area and maybe a pond or a large hedge at the bottom of the garden, you will not be able to see problems in their early stages and therefore will not be able to deal with every outbreak. Do not worry too much about pests that appear in mature areas of the garden. They will build up, particularly at certain times of the year, but will rarely become a serious ongoing problem. Generally, once pest numbers reach a certain level, natural predators will be attracted to them as a food source. This will reduce their numbers to a manageable level again.

There are various things you can do in a garden to attract natural predators (see box opposite) but it is often more a case of not doing anything. For example, if you spray against insects that attack your plants, the chances are that you will also harm the predators that eat the pests. The ladybird is one well-known predator of aphids, but there are others too, such as lacewings, hoverfly larvae, parasitic wasps and small birds such as the blue tit. Encouraging these species into the garden means refraining from spraying, and allowing the aphid population to build up to a level that attracts the predators.

Most plants will stay problem-free, and practising good garden hygiene and removing unhealthy plants promptly will reduce the likelihood of any diseases taking hold.

BUYING BIOLOGICAL CONTROLS

Many garden pests can be controlled by the use of naturally occurring predators. You can buy the living organisms by mail order or there are powders of microorganisms that you activate by mixing with water. There are biological controls for whitefly (left), red spider mites, mealy bugs, aphids, vine weevil grubs and slugs.

APPLYING BIOLOGICAL CONTROLS

Use biological controls in a controlled environment, such as a greenhouse, or water on to a container plant. You need to introduce biological controls at the right time of year, and supplies must be fresh. Pesticides render these controls ineffective, so you cannot use them if you have already tried a chemical control.

DEALING WITH PROBLEMS

Viruses and some pests, such as eelworms, cause stunted growth, often with mottling, streaking or deformity on the foliage and flowers, as in this tulip. If one or two plants show these symptoms, pull them out and burn them straightaway.

INVESTIGATING CAUSES

Yellowing foliage can have a number of causes: lack of nutrients, physical damage to the roots or underwatering. Dig up the plant to see if the roots have been damaged or find out more about the soil (waterlogging and extremes of pH can also cause problems).

PREVENTING PROBLEMS

For long-lived cropping plants, seek out certified virus-free plants or buy from reputable suppliers. Some roses can be more susceptible to viruses than others – this one has mosiac virus – so it is worth seeking out a reputable rose specialist. Good garden hygiene and dealing with aphids promptly also helps to prevent viruses.

NUTRITIONAL PROBLEMS

Lack of nutrients is a major cause of yellowing foliage, dead patches or scorching. Adding nutrients to the soil will often rectify the problem, and using a liquid fertilizer will get nutrients to the plant quickly. The bergenias here are affected by lime-induced chlorosis, which mostly affects acid-lovers grown in alkaline soil.

ATTRACTING NATURAL PREDATORS

Don't be tidy if you want to attract predators – a pile of old logs may attract useful insects.

Besides not using pesticides, you can also be active in providing food and shelter for natural predators. Frogs and toads will eat slugs, as well as snails, caterpillars and woodlice, so it is worth building even a small pond to attract them. Birds of various sorts will tackle snails, caterpillars, other grubs and aphids. They are attracted to mature gardens with shrubby shelter where they can nest. Invite birds into a new, bare garden by putting out nesting boxes, baths or feeders. Leave piles of logs behind the shed or some other out-of-the-way shady place. Here they can slowly rot down and provide food and shelter for beetles that feed on slugs, as well as making hibernation sites for frogs and toads. Leave piles of dead leaves in place to provide shelter for overwintering insects.

PRUNING, CUTTING AND HARVESTING

PRUNING SHRUBS

A pair of secateurs is essential for the home gardener. To avoid misplacing them, buy a pair with brightly coloured handles or keep them in a sheath. It is worth paying more for secateurs with replaceable blades. You should also check that the safety catch is easy to work with one hand. Most models have blades that cut with a bypass action; if you are left-handed, it is worth getting a pair that is left-handed. For those who find the squeezing action painful, try a ratchet pair designed for people with a weak grip. Do not twist or strain your secateurs by using them on stems thicker than 1.2 cm (½ in) in diameter. To cut thicker branches, get a pair of long-handled loppers, and use them to cut back to the ground or a stump. There are now lighter-weight models and those designed so that you need to apply less force to make a cut. You may still find anvil cutting heads, where one blade cuts against an anvil as well as using a bypass action. For trimming hedges or individual shrubs, use garden shears. Size, weight and balance in shears vary greatly, so try several models before buying.

PRUNING TREES

Pole pruners can be up to 2–3 m (6–10 ft) or more in length. They consist of a cutting blade at the end of a pole and allow you to cut branches high up in trees while standing on the ground. You usually pull on a cord to make the cut, although there is also a type available that uses a lever system. Most pole pruners have telescopic handles so that you can tackle branches at different heights; however, they can deal only with branches up to 3 cm (1¼ in) in diameter. Some pole pruners have extra attachments for sawing or harvesting. To tackle thicker branches, up to 10 cm (4 in) in diameter, you will need a pruning saw. These are inexpensive, versatile tools with a curved blade and are easy to use in confined spaces. Apart from cutting branches, they can be used for root pruning or dividing up the roots of perennials. You should buy a pruning saw that folds up safely; remember to keep spare blades handy, since they often need replacing. Pruning saws cut only on the pull stroke, so when cutting up logs it is easier and quicker to use the larger, stronger bow saw, because it cuts on both the push and the pull strokes.

BYPASS LONG-HANDLED LOPPERS

ANVIL LONG-HANDLED LOPPERS

CLIPPING HEDGES AND TOPIARY

Garden shears will give hedges the best clipped finish. Choose a pair you find easy to hold and where the balance between the handles and blades feels right. Where there is a great deal of hedging, it is quicker to use a powered hedge trimmer (either electric or petrol, or ones with rechargeable batteries). Electric styles are lighter and easier to use than petrol ones, but you must keep the cord out of the way. Although a petrol version is heavier, you are not limited to plants within reach of the electricity source. Hedge trimmers using rechargeable batteries are light, easy and safe to use, but are better for smaller hedges that do not have stout stems. Although topiary can be clipped with the tips of pruning shears, it is worth getting a pair of sheep shears if you want a crisp outline. Sheep shears can also be used for cutting box edging, harvesting herbs or trimming aquatic plants.

CUTTING PERENNIALS

When cutting flowers for the house or deadheading, you can use a pair of flower shears, a cross between scissors and secateurs. They are lighter than secateurs and do not damage the sappy growth. Where flowers are just out of reach, try using long-handled, cut-and-hold cutters. Once perennials have finished flowering and have died back in the autumn, the top growth can be cut back with pruning shears, either to ground level or immediately above new growth.

TAKING CUTTINGS

A sharp, clean blade is vital for taking successful cuttings. Use an all-purpose garden knife or a scalpel with replaceable blades for taking softwood or semi-ripe cuttings during the growing season. However, for hardwood cuttings at the end of the growing season, use a pair of sharp secateurs. In order to limit the spread of viruses from one plant to another after you have taken cuttings, sterilize the blades by dipping them in turpentine, then holding them under a flame for a few seconds.

SHREDDING

Prunings from trees and shrubs, trimmings from hedges or vegetable debris (such as thick corn stalks) can occupy a great deal of space and will take a long time to compost. By shredding them into small pieces you will reduce their bulk, and they can be used as a woodland mulch or added to a compost heap. Shredders are available in both electric and petrol versions, but they vary in the ease with which they tackle thicker branches, how often they jam up, how noisy they are, and how safe they are to use, so it is worth seeing different models in action before you buy or rent one. When operating a shredder, you should always be sure to wear protective goggles and sturdy gloves.

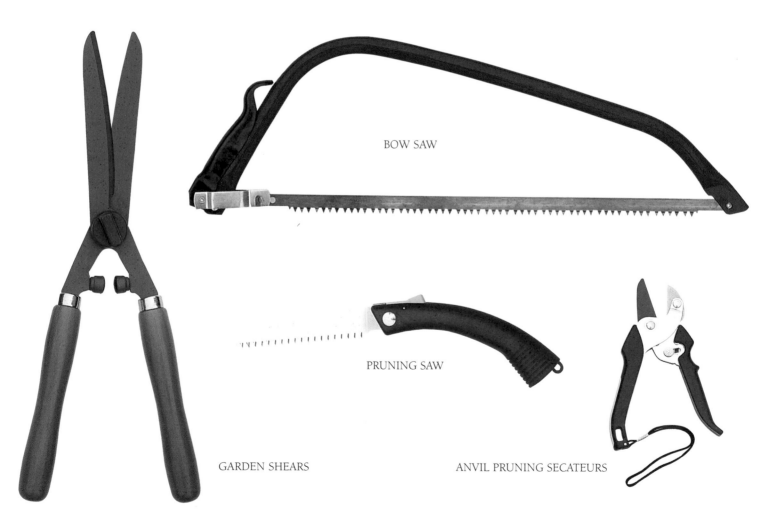

BOW SAW

PRUNING SAW

GARDEN SHEARS

ANVIL PRUNING SECATEURS

PRUNING SHRUBS

YOU WILL NEED

Secateurs

Long-handled loppers or pruning saw

Container for prunings

Shredder

SEE ALSO

All kinds of climbers
See *Choosing climbers and wall shrubs, pp. 126–127*

All kinds of shrubs
See *Choosing shrubs, pp. 136–137*

Which shrub?
See *Buying and planting shrubs, pp. 138–139*

Shrub maintenance
See *Caring for shrubs, pp. 170–171*

How to prune
See *Pruning, cutting and harvesting, pp. 180–181*

Most shrubs need pruning if problems arise, and some also benefit from a more regular and systematic pruning. These tend to be shrubs where the young growth is particularly attractive, and summer-flowering shrubs that bloom on new wood, such as a buddleja. The most widely used pruning technique is cutting out one stem in three (see below). This removes a proportion of the older wood each year, so giving young wood a chance to develop. A few shrubs can cope with harder pruning where all the stems are cut to the ground (see Cutting all stems down, opposite); this method stimulates new growth and is used where the new growth is a feature, such as coloured winter stems or attractive young foliage.

Some shrubs, mainly the short-lived ones, are reluctant to regrow from old wood, so hard cutting back is avoided. Instead, the new growth is clipped to keep them neat (see Shortening new growth, opposite).

Many grey-leaved shrubs, such as lavenders, are cut back hard only if there is new growth already emerging at the base. Start the first spring after planting, and cut back all the stems to where there is new growth; if there is no new growth, just trim off last year's growth lightly. You should be left with a stump 5–10 cm (2–4 in) high that will grow quickly to form new shoots. Older plants are unlikely to produce new growth from the base, and they may need to be replaced with younger plants.

The healthy cotoneaster in this easy-maintenance border is spilling out attractively on to the patio, but its growth has been kept in proportion by careful pruning in spring.

CUTTING OUT ONE STEM IN THREE

1 Start pruning when a shrub is about three years old and the stems are becoming over-crowded. First select any dead, diseased or damaged stems, and cut these back to the ground with secateurs. If the stems are thick, you can use loppers or a pruning saw.

2 Stand back and look at the shape. Select some other branches to take out to leave the shrub looking balanced and with an open centre. Take out no more than one stem in every three.

CUTTING ALL STEMS DOWN

1 Start pruning shrubs a year after planting, then repeat every one to two years thereafter. Prune all the stems down to 5 cm (2 in) from the ground or to a low stump.

2 Help the plant recover by watering, feeding and mulching. If you are growing two shrubs of the same type, cut down alternate shrubs each year, so that each shrub is hard-pruned only every other year.

PRUNING WALL-TRAINED SHRUBS

1 When pruning a shrub trained against a wall or fence, make sure that you keep any branches that can be trained flat. Remove any that grow outwards away from the wall.

2 Remember to tie in new growth to fill gaps while the shrub is young and flexible.

SHORTENING NEW GROWTH

Remove any dead, diseased or damaged shoots by cutting back to healthy growth, but keep drastic pruning to a minimum as many shrubs will not regrow readily from old wood. Start clipping when the shrubs are young. Once they are established, take off half to two-thirds of the new growth each year.

Helpful hints

If you cannot find out the name of the shrub you want to prune, opt for cutting out one stem in three in spring. Otherwise, use a shrub reference book to check which pruning method is the most suitable. Routine pruning is not essential for all shrubs and many are best left to develop their own natural shape – as long as you have given them the space they need. Make a note of what shrubs need pruning each season and hang it up with your secateurs. Collect up the prunings and pile them up. When you have enough, put them through a shredder before composting.

CARING FOR TREES

YOU WILL NEED

Pruning knife

Secateurs

Gloves

Tree loppers

Pruning saw

SEE ALSO

Tree shape and colour
See *Choosing trees,*
pp. 114–115

All kinds of trees
See *Styles of tree planting,*
pp. 116–117

Which tree?
See *Buying and planting*
trees, pp. 118–119

Newly planted trees should need little maintenance and will look after themselves if you have selected and planted carefully and appropriately for your garden and its microclimate. Make sure the tree has enough water in the growing season, and keep weeds and grass from its base so that nothing takes vital nutrients away from the tree. Research has shown that grass, in particular, can retard the growth of young trees. It is best to mulch the base of the tree in the early years; after that, it is worth underplanting with shade-tolerant ground cover, such as periwinkle (*Vinca*), comfrey (*Symphytum*), or the spreading evergreen perennial *Pachysandra terminalis*. You can carry out simple pruning on your tree, but do this only when strictly necessary.

Mature trees are an irreplaceable asset in a garden, although you may not think so if your garden is heavily shaded. However, it really is worth creating your garden around the tree, as far as possible – it will develop its own unique character in its own way.

An old tree may develop problems. These can pose safety risks, especially near your house, where the roots may damage foundations, and falling branches – or even the tree itself, if blown down by high winds – can cause quite extensive damage. If you are lucky enough to have a large amount of land, it may be worth allowing your tree to regain its health on its own, providing it poses no danger. A tree can decay naturally in parts but remain perfectly healthy in the rest of its framework, eventually producing new growth and surviving for many years.

If you are in any doubt about the tree's safety, or if your mature tree has developed problems, consult a tree surgeon (see panel opposite). But don't necessarily take the lowest quote. Poor-quality work will make the tree look dreadful and can cause problems in the future.

When a tree is young, undertake formative pruning. This pruning helps it to develop a beautiful form in maturity. The trunk and branches of a tropical tree grow quickly, so it is important to prune it correctly in the first few years. However, with evergreens, little pruning is needed, other than removing damaged, dead or crossing branches. There are various methods of pruning ornamental trees to achieve different effects.

REMOVING A SUCKER-ROOTSTOCK

Some trees are grafted on a strong-growing rootstock; occasionally, these roots will produce a sucker from below the graft. The sucker must be removed or it will grow more vigorously than the grafted tree, and eventually may take over. Trace the sucker right back to its source on a root and break it off or cut it with a knife.

REMOVING A RIVAL LEADER

If it is suited to its site, your tree should need no pruning. Sometimes a young tree will develop a leading side shoot that threatens to overtake the natural, central leader; this added leader will create a lopsided appearance. Shorten the rival leader to one-third of its length, pruning to an outward-pointing bud.

BASIC PRUNING TECHNIQUES

1 Crown thinning involves removing inside lateral branches to let light and air into the tree and to enhance its structure. Stand back and decide which branches must go. Begin thinning at the inside bottom, and work your way up and out. Be sure to remove any branches that cross each other, cutting them to the base.

2 Use loppers to cut through branches up to 2.5 cm (1 in) thick. Look for a swelling along the branch If you want to cut a branch back to a bud. You will stimulate growth from that bud, thus increasing the fullness of the tree or shrub. If you want to discourage additional growth, make a clean cut right back to a main branch or the trunk.

3 Large tree branches should be removed in three steps to prevent the heavy branch from breaking free and tearing off bark, thus leaving an opening for pests and diseases. Use a pruning saw to remove the main part of the branch, leaving a 30–45-cm (12–18-in) length on the tree. If the bark tears at this stage, it won't matter.

4 Make a second cut, starting underneath, where the branch meets the tree. Cut about halfway through the branch, staying just outside the slightly thickened area, called the branch collar.

5 Make the final cut from above, severing the limb stub completely. Avoid cutting too close to the tree; the unnecessarily large wound will be more vulnerable to pests and diseases. Ideally the clean cut should be just on the outside edge of the branch collar or ridge. It is not recommended to paint the cut with a wound dressing.

TREE SURGEONS

If you are in any doubt about safety, or if shade from your mature tree is causing problems, consult a tree surgeon who is properly qualified and the correct insurance. Obtain a list through your local government office or consult a landscaping association.

A tree surgeon will give advice on any essential work and also how to improve the visual appearance of the tree, making it more enjoyable in your garden. It is possible to thin out the top growth of the tree to reduce shade, either by removing some lower branches (crown lifting) or by selectively thinning the whole canopy (crown reduction).

CARING FOR HEDGES

YOU WILL NEED

Pruning saw

Gloves

Secateurs

Pruning knife

Garden shears

Loppers

Hedge trimmers

SEE ALSO

Hedging plants
See *Choosing a hedge,*
pp. 120–121

Hedge design
See *Styles of hedge,*
pp. 122–123

Laying hedges
See *Planting a hedge,*
pp. 124–125

How to prune
See *Pruning, cutting and*
harvesting, pp. 180–181

Hedges need to be regularly cared for if they are not to get overgrown and out of hand. The most important task is trimming, and for a formal hedge this should be done once a year in summer, remembering always to make the lower part of the hedge wider than the top. You can allow informal hedges to grow more naturally, depending on how much space they take up. It is worth finding out what your hedge consists of, because

plants have different needs and tendencies. Species such as privet (*Ligustrum ovalifolium*) and the shrubby honeysuckle (*Lonicera nitida*) need more frequent cutting, generally in early and late summer. Conifer hedges such as *Cupresso cyparis leylandii* will not grow from old wood; a few exceptions include *Thuja* spp. and yew. If the hedge becomes bare in places, you will have to remove whole plants. In this case it may be best to uproot the hedge and start again.

A hedge should be kept weed free at the base and mulched, especially in the first few years. During its first growing season, it will need plenty of water. A mature hedge needs lots of moisture and nutrients from the surrounding soil. Privet is particularly greedy, so neighbouring plants can suffer. It may be worth installing a barrier against the questing roots. Dig a trench 45 cm (18 in) from the outside edge of the hedge, sever the hedge's roots, and insert heavy plastic sheeting along its length. Hedges that are regularly trimmed benefit from a general fertiliser applied at the start of the growing season.

Hedges do not have to be clipped into straight lines or perfect domes. They can also be treated as green sculpture, and clipped into all sorts of mounds and curves.

Helpful hints

If the hedge in your garden looks boring and there is no room to plant in front of it, or if there are gaps to fill, you can replant the spaces with shrubs that have different foliage colour. Try yellow variegated privet and copper beech together, or use a dark green or gold variegated holly with beech, for instance. The hedge will probably not retain such a sharp outline with this treatment, because the plants may have different habits and speeds of growth, but the effect will be more lively. If you want to cut down on time spent keeping the hedge tidy, choose plants with a similar growth habit.

NOVEL WAYS OF USING HEDGES

Enliven your hedge with plants that have different foliage colour; use variegated yellows with copper and green, for example. Low-growing hedges can be laid out in a pattern to create an all-year-round feature. Such plantings are particularly effective when viewed from above.

REVIVING A HEDGE

1 First check the species to make sure it will grow from old wood. Cut the hedge back hard to about 15 cm (6 in) lower than the desired height, then shape it in slightly towards the top, so it looks roughly triangular. Hedges should never be wider at the top than at the bottom. If light cannot reach the lower branches, they will die, leaving a gappy hedge.

2 If you need to reduce the width of your hedge drastically, you must do this in two stages. Cut back one side hard the first year, trimming the other side normally. You can wait one or two years to cut the other side back, depending on how quickly your hedge regrows.

3 Cut dead branches back to their base, and remove dead plants within the hedge. Weed thoroughly at the base of the hedge and remove the top growth, especially the roots of weeds and plants such as ivy, elder or bramble that may be scrambling up inside the hedge. Replace tired soil with fresh soil-based compost or topsoil.

4 To fill gaps in the hedge, dig out and remove the dead plant, and prune back hard on either side of the gap to allow in as much light as possible. Plant the replacement in fresh soil-based compost and water it in well. Mulch the ground along the length of the hedge with compost, bark chips or well-rotted manure.

USING SHEARS OR HEDGE TRIMMERS

Try shears before you buy them, testing the weight and how they feel in your hands. Use one-handed shears for clipping small hedges or heathers. Always clean and oil shears after use and keep them well sharpened. For powered hedge trimmers, use a type with a single-sided blade; these are far safer than ones with double-sided blades. Always read the safety instructions before use. With an electric hedge trimmer, arrange the cord over your shoulder so that you don't sever it. Never operate electric tools either in or after rain and use a circuit breaker – a device that cuts the current if a problem occurs. If the hedge is high, rent a cutting platform – it is safer than a ladder. Cut away from yourself and always remove the clippings; never let them build up.

LOOKING AFTER A POND

YOU WILL NEED

Planters

Hessian or garden fleece

Bricks, aquatic compost

Knife or scissors

Gravel

Bamboo canes

Plant pots

Stiff netting

Pump or siphon

**Holding tank and net
(if fish)**

**Waders or Wellington
boots**

Plastic bucket

Hosepipe

Brush

SEE ALSO

Designing with water
See *Self-contained water
feature, pp. 64–65*

Making a pond
See *Flexible liner pond,
pp. 66–67*

Ponds and cascades
See *Styles of water garden,
pp. 68–69*

Once a pond has been built and filled with water, leave it to settle for a week before you add any plants. Aquatic centres will be able to advise you on what and how many plants you need for your size of pond,

Spending a little time on basic maintenance keeps a pond and any water features looking good, and means that they will need major attention only once every few years.

but it is usual to have some oxygenating and floating plants, together with some marginal plants in planting baskets. Give the plants several weeks to start establishing themselves before you introduce any fish – it can take several years for a pond to settle down and achieve a natural balance.

Caring for an established pond is mostly a case of cutting back and removing faded or dying foliage promptly, and netting the pond in early autumn to keep out falling leaves. In spring and summer, keep your eyes open for green water (see box opposite). If you have fish in the pond, or it includes any extra features, such as fountains and lights, they will need to be cared for as well.

As long as you keep debris out of the pond, a full-scale cleanup is needed only once every few years. Late spring is a good time to clean out a pond and to plant or repot any water plants in baskets. In winter, float a plastic ball on the pond to prevent the pond freezing. If a pond freezes over, gently pour boiling water to make a hole. The hole allows methane to escape from the pond, preventing a dangerous build-up of gas in the water that can be lethal to fish.

PLANTING MARGINALS

1 Wash the plants to remove any pests or threads of blanket weed. Fine-mesh or fleece-type planters do not need a liner, but those with large mesh sides need lining with a hessian square or garden fleece. Put a brick or large stone in the bottom of planters if using top-heavy plants like irises. Half-fill the container with an aquatic compost.

2 Take the plant out of its pot and cut away any dead foliage or overlong roots. Place it in the container, add more compost and firm it down. Spread a 2.5-cm (1-in) deep layer of gravel over the surface of the compost to prevent it from muddying the water and to keep fish from disturbing the plants. Lower the basket slowly into the pond.

NETTING A POND

1 To cover a small pond, you can make a wooden frame and nail stiff plastic or wire netting to it. For medium to large ponds, put a series of bamboo canes sunk in the ground around the pond. Put upturned pots over the top of the canes and drape loose netting over the top.

2 The weight of fallen leaves, especially when wet, will cause the netting to sag, so pull it fairly taut. The edges should touch the ground and be secured with bricks. Remove the leaves regularly or the whole structure could collapse. Remove the netting in early spring, check the net for holes and repair, if necessary; then store until the following year.

POND CLEANING

1 Use a pump or siphon to remove as much water as you need to in order to stand in the pond safely. Take out the pond pump, if used, then catch any fish and transfer them to a holding tank of pond water. Remove any stones from the bottom of your waders before getting into the pond, and tread carefully so as not to damage the liner.

2 Take out any excess invasive floating plants. Use a plastic bucket to scoop up silt and place it on soil borders. Clean the sides of the pond with a hose and brush, or with a pressure sprayer. Repair the pond if necessary. Refill the pond half way. Replace the plants, pump and fish. Then finish refilling the pond.

GREEN WATER PROBLEMS

All new ponds develop green water, which is caused by algae. This is nothing to worry about as long as you have put in oxygenating plants. Green water in an established pond needs addressing. The water may develop a "pea soup" appearance in spring before the floating plants, such as waterlilies, have covered the surface. You can add chemical treatments or, if you have fish, install a filtration system fitted with an ultraviolet clarifier. Blanket weed, which is also an alga and looks like handfuls of green cotton balls, is a major cause of green water. It thrives when the pond is full of nutrients, so make sure you do not increase them by using tap water or overfeeding the garden nearby. Check that you have enough oxygenators since they compete with the weed for nutrients. Take out blanket weed before it dies and sinks to the bottom of the pond – use a wire rake to skim the surface and pull sheets of it out. Small creatures can get caught up in the weed, so leave it by the side of the pond for a while so that they can make their way back to the water.

LOW-MAINTENANCE GARDENING

PLANTING SUGGESTIONS

As a general principle, aim for simple planting designs with broad drifts or blocks of just a few types of plant. This approach looks more cohesive than many single plants, and will be less work. Too much variety means too many care requirements. You will have a constant battle controlling the vigorous plants so that they do not encroach on the slower-growing ones.

Bedding plants need a great deal of work if used on a large scale to fill whole beds or lots of pots; new plants have to be grown and planted out each year. Fill beds or large pots with long-term plants (such as small shrubs, evergreen ground-cover perennials or alpines). To add seasonal highlights, use spring bulbs or a few bedding plants.

Highly bred plants with large or double flowers cause stems to flop and will need staking. You will also have to water, feed and deadhead to keep them looking good. So choose noninvasive native or species plants that bear many small, single flowers.

Even if you enjoy plants and gardening, you might want to reduce the amount of time you spend on certain tasks such as weeding, watering, mowing or staking. The secret is to plan the design of the garden and the plants grown to meet your needs. So whether you hire a garden designer or design the garden yourself, consider how easy various features and plants will be to maintain before introducing them into your garden. Lawns can be replaced with paving stones, bricks, wood decking, cobblestones or gravel, which need only weeding between the cracks, sweeping or raking. Use flowering shrubs, ground-cover plants and small trees rather than bedding.

▶ LONG-TERM CONTAINERS
A stone trough filled with easy-to-care-for, slow-growing alpines, which include *Sempervivum*, *Echeveria*, *Acaena* and dwarf conifers, provides a longer-lasting planting than a pot of bedding plants.

▲ CONTAINER GARDENING
Pot-grown herbs, such as purple-leaved basil, are less prone to slugs and can also be moved under cover before cold spells.

◀ GRAVEL BEDS
Gravel over a sheet mulch can double up as a path and a planting area; it remains free from weeds and does not need mowing.

▲ WOODLAND GARDENS
Graceful silver birches needing little maintenance, underplanted with evergreen shrubs and colourful flowers such as poppies, create a lovely woodland area.

◄ SIMPLE PLANTING
A "river" of ornamental grass is a dramatic solution to suppressing weeds and less work than many different rock garden plants.

► FLOWERING SPIRES
Not all perennials with long flowering spikes need staking. Here, the clump-forming *Sisyrinchium striatum* and the grey, velvety *Verbascum olympicum* provide strong vertical shapes. There is not a bamboo cane or plant support in sight.

▼ RIGHT PLANT, RIGHT PLACE
Bog-loving perennials with large lush foliage, here *Rheum palmatum* and *Ligularia dentata*, thrive in wet soils, but need extra watering in average or dry soil.

GARDENING UNDER GLASS

YOU WILL NEED

Shading paint or film

Roller or large brush to apply shading paint

Scissors to cut and trim shading film

Bubble polythene

Heated propagator

Max-min thermometer

SEE ALSO

Automated systems
See *Watering and water conservation, pp. 172–173*

Indoor germination
See *Sowing seed indoors, pp. 194–195*

A greenhouse will provide shelter and warmth through the colder months of the year. And by heating it, at least for part of the year, you will get more use out of it during the winter and early spring. As the weather gets warmer, it will get even hotter under glass, so adequate ventilation and shading will be needed. Shading will protect plants from excessive heat and sun scorch. It is most effective at reducing heat stress when applied to the outside of the glass. The greenhouse should be ventilated to avoid the build-up of damp, stuffy air. And, of course, watering the plants is a priority, so you might want to set up an automatic watering system to make this chore easier, or else make full use of a well-mulched soil border.

It is not only plants that thrive in the shelter and warmth: pests and diseases can soon take hold. Basic hygiene and good air circulation can help prevent diseases, although you may need to resort to some chemical control. For pest problems, it is worth trying a suitable biological control as an alternative to spraying.

Clear out the greenhouse once a year, in late autumn or winter, and give it a thorough cleaning. Scrub the frame and glass (including the gaps between the glass sheets) with a greenhouse disinfectant or hot soapy water to remove algae and grime. Clean and sterilize all pots and trays used for seedlings, as well as the propagator and benches.

Despite the initial outlay, a greenhouse will more than pay for itself. Its all-weather environment will allow you to propagate and develop plants before moving them outside.

PROVIDING VENTILATION AND SHADING

1 When you buy your greenhouse, make sure that it has several opening vents. These should preferably be both on the roof and at floor level (called louvre vents) so that you get a through draught. The vent area should be 20 per cent of the floor area. You could also fit automatic vent openers, which open and close vents in response to temperature changes.

2 Paint on a shading "whitewash" using a roller or large brush. One of the best shading paints changes from white to clear when the weather turns cloudy. A newer idea is a shading film made of perforated plastic. This clings to the glass by static electricity. It will last two years if used outside, more if used inside, but it reduces heat more if used outside.

ADDING INSULATION AND HEATING

1 Get a professional electrician to install an electricity supply to your greenhouse. You will then be able to fit a heated propagator to germinate seeds and an electric fan heater to generate background heat. Max-min and soil thermometers will help you to ensure the propagator is kept at the right settings.

2 Fix large-bubble polythene to the inside frame of the greenhouse in autumn. Use special fixings for aluminium frames and drawing pins for wooden frames. Only heat the space you need to use: drape the insulation over the door and run it across the roof space at head height. You can also screen off an area with a curtain of insulation.

USING SOIL BORDERS

When putting down a hard surface on the greenhouse floor, leave a soil border to plant into. A soil border needs less watering than pots and there is more headroom for taller plants. Mulch with garden compost or manure each spring and alternate unrelated crops, such as tomatoes and cucumbers, each year to stop soil diseases developing.

WATERING

Instead of long and tedious routines of hand watering, you can install watering systems (see pp. 172–173). Capillary matting on trays can move water from a reservoir up to the base of pots or you can use a network of tubing and nozzles to supply water to each pot. Some fine-tuning is needed to make sure each plant receives the right amount of water.

USING A COLD FRAME

As well as brick and wood, cold frames are commonly made of aluminium.

A cold frame is a large box with glass (or clear plastic), timber or brick sides and a glass lid. It provides an environment half-way between a greenhouse and the outdoors. Move young plants, raised under glass, into a cold frame about a week or so before planting out. First keep the cold frame lid closed for a day, then open the lid slightly the second day but close it at night. Repeat this, opening the lid wider each day until it is wide open during the day. Then start opening the lid slightly at night, increasing this until the plants are fully acclimatized to outdoor conditions. If you wish to grow plants directly in the cold frame, make sure you lay a suitable drainage material (broken pots or coarse gravel) before putting down a 15-cm (6-in) layer of compost.

SOWING SEED INDOORS

YOU WILL NEED

Packets of assorted seeds

Heated propagator with a clear plastic lid

Pots and seed trays

Sieve

Seed or multipurpose compost

Vermiculite

Plant labels

Thermometer

Watering can with a finely perforated nozzle or spray bottle

SEE ALSO

Growing in a greenhouse
See *Gardening under glass, pp. 192–193*

Outdoor sowing
See *Sowing seed outdoors, pp. 196–197*

Planting out
See *Pricking out and thinning, pp. 198–199*

To germinate successfully, tender plants such as some vegetables and bedding plants, need a steady temperature of 18–20°C (64–68°F). To provide warmth, cocoon seeds in an electric propagator. The plastic tray has a built-in heating element to provide gentle heat from below and a transparent top to let in light and keep the atmosphere moist. Various sizes of propagator are available. Choose one with a built-in thermostat so it will turn itself off if it gets too hot. To raise seeds without a propagator, use clear plastic

bags over pots and trays to keep the humidity high. To sow just a few seeds, use 7-cm (3-in) diameter pots. Seed trays or half-trays will hold more seed than small pots, but the seedling roots may get tangled. Keep the roots separate by using plastic plug trays that are divided into compartments. Use a good-quality compost that has been recently bought – either a seed or multipurpose type. When seeds require light to germinate, sprinkle fine-grade vermiculite over them. This will absorb moisture and let in light.

Pumpkins, squashes and ornamental gourds are great subjects to raise from seed. The seeds are large and easy to handle and a good crop can be produced from only a few plants.

TIMING SEED SOWING

To ensure you sow seeds at the right time, you need a sturdy box with dividers for each month. As you buy the seed, file the bags according to the sowing month. Each month check your box and sow the appropriate seeds. If you do not get around to sowing them, move the bag into next month's slot; a few weeks' delay will not cause a problem. Once the sowing date has passed, take the unopened seed bag out of your box and store it correctly for use next year. Put some silica gel in your seed box to absorb moisture from the air; to reuse the gel, dry it in an oven on the lowest setting.

Helpful hints

To prevent seeds and seedlings from rotting or being infected with fungal diseases, use a good-quality, fresh compost (either a seed or multipurpose type) that has been purchased within the past year and stored under cover. Wash containers and propagators in hot, soapy water and rinse well before use. If you have had disease problems in previous years, use a garden disinfectant first, rinsing well afterwards using tap water (rather than water from a water butt). These steps will prevent damping-off, but if it strikes and seedlings collapse, water with a copper-based fungicide.

SOWING SEED IN TRAYS

1 Loosen up fresh compost by running it through your fingers and then breaking up any lumps.

2 Fill the seed trays with compost up to the level of the rim. Press the surface down gently with your hand or an empty seed tray. The soil surface should be about 1–2 cm (½–¾ in) below the rim.

3 Stand seed trays in a sink or larger tray containing a small depth of water until the surface of the compost feels moist. Then lift the trays out and allow any excess water to drain away. Alternatively, water the compost gently from above, using tap water in a watering can fitted with a finely perforated nozzle.

4 To sow small, fine seeds, take a pinch of seed and sow thinly. For medium-sized and large seeds, press them individually into the compost.

5 Cover the seeds with sieved compost to the depth stated on the packet. Use fine-grade vermiculite for seeds that need light for germination. This will absorb moisture and let in light.

6 Label pots and trays with the variety of the plant as well as the sowing date. If you have used vermiculite, spray the surface with water. Most seeds will germinate within 7 to 20 days; check them daily. If you do not have a propagator, cover the container with clear a plastic bag to prevent the soil from drying out. Set the tray on a warm windowsill.

SOWING SEED OUTDOORS

YOU WILL NEED

Garden rake or spade

Garden line (or two pegs
and a length of string
for straight rows)

Pointing trowel, cane,
stick or draw hoe (for
making seed drills)

Soil thermometer

Sand

Plant labels

Bamboo canes

SEE ALSO

Indoor germination
See *Sowing seed indoors,
pp. 194–195*

Planting out
See *Pricking out and
thinning, pp. 198–199*

The best vegetables
See *Successful vegetable
techniques, pp. 212–213*

Most plants can either be sown directly outdoors or started off in pots. Some do not transplant well from pots, so these are best sown directly into the ground. Examples include flowering plants such as borage, cornflower and poppy, and vegetables such as carrot, parsnip, radish and spring onion.

Seed sown directly into the soil is more vulnerable to the weather and to pests and diseases. To assess whether it is time to sow, take the temperature early in the morning, using a special soil thermometer with a metal tip. Push the tip into the soil the same depth as you will sow the seed. Refer to the minimum temperature on the seed packet. When the thermometer registers this temperature daily over a period of a week, it is safe to sow.

Very hardy plants can be sown outdoors in early spring, but those that are susceptible to frost should not be sown until later in the season. Allowing attractive plants to self-seed is an easy and inexpensive way to fill a large garden.

SOWING STYLES

Vegetables and cut flowers are usually sown in straight rows (seed drills) for easier picking. This also helps when weeding, since you can more easily identify weed seedlings from sown seedlings. For the greatest choice of seed varieties, order from mail-order suppliers during the winter before sowing. Some seed is very inexpensive; this is usually open-pollinated and can be quite a mixture of different heights and colours. These seeds are ideal for creating informal drifts or for covering large areas. Highly bred seed, such as F_1 hybrids, are produced under controlled conditions to give a uniform display or high yield. They produce more impact in small spaces, but they are expensive, and any seed you save will not come true.

MAKING A SEED BED

1 Remove any plant debris and weeds from the area to be sown. Use a hand fork to dislodge any large stones or to dig out the roots of weeds.

2 Break up any large lumps of soil with the back of a garden fork or use a chopping action with a garden rake or spade.

3 Using a garden rake with a steady but gentle push-pull action, work the surface of the soil until it has a fine even texture and is flat and level.

4 Mark the position of the rows. Use the correct row spacing and depth for each plant. To take out a seed drill, use a pointing trowel, a cane or stick, the corner of a draw hoe, or even the corner of a soil rake. If the soil is very dry, water the bottom of the drill.

5 Take a pinch of seed and sow along the bottom of the drill. Try to keep an even spacing between the seeds, or keep to the intervals recommended in the sowing instructions.

6 Draw soil over the seed drill. To sow radish, spring onions and peas in bands rather than single rows, use a trowel to make a shallow trough. Sow the seed thinly across the width of the band.

PRICKING OUT AND THINNING

YOU WILL NEED

Compost (multipurpose or potting)

Pots or modular trays

Dibber or plant label

SEE ALSO

Growing in a greenhouse
See *Gardening under glass, pp. 192–193*

Indoor germination
See *Sowing seed indoors, pp. 194–195*

Outdoor sowing
See *Sowing seed outdoors, pp. 196–197*

Growing in
See *Taking cuttings, pp. 202–203*

Once seeds have germinated, the seedlings start to grow quickly. They are quite vulnerable at this stage. A sudden change in temperature, dryness, pests, or disease can kill them, so they need daily attention. Where light comes from one direction, such as on a windowsill, the seedlings will bend towards it. To keep the

stems straight, turn the pots daily. Strong sunlight can scorch seedlings, so lightly shade them during the hottest part of the day.

To prevent overcrowding you need to space out the seedlings by selecting the strongest-growing ones and discarding the weaker ones. For seedlings raised in pots or trays, move the strongest to new containers, a technique known as pricking out. For those grown in the ground, leave the strongest ones and pull up the weaker ones, a technique known as thinning. Look at the growth of the seedling to judge when it is time to prick out or thin. When a seed germinates, the first pair of leaves are part of the seed and it is the next pair to appear that are the first true leaves and are more characteristic of the plant. Large seeds produce very large seed leaves and can be handled as soon as they have fully opened. Where the seed leaves are smaller, wait until at least one pair of true leaves has fully opened before pricking out or thinning. Young plants need to be transplanted to their final positions.

Seedlings and young plants need enough space to grow on to become healthy mature plants. Remove any weak seedlings to prevent them from crowding out stronger ones.

THINNING OUT PLANTS

As soon as the seedlings are large enough to identify, start to pull out any surplus ones. Choose a day when the soil is moist, or water the soil before thinning. Start by thinning larger clumps to leave one or two strong seedlings. A couple of weeks later, remove all but one plant at about one-half or one-third of the final spacing.

TRANSPLANTING

A 10-cm (4-in) pot is large enough to sustain two or three sown seedlings, making it unnecessary to prick out any of the seedlings. When time comes to transplant, use a knife so as to keep ample soil around each plant's root.

PRICKING OUT SEEDLINGS

1 Hand-fill pots with moistened compost. You can use multipurpose or potting compost. Shake the pot and gently firm down to remove any air pockets.

2 Use a dibber or a plastic plant label to gently ease individual seedlings out of the soil mix keeping as much root intact as possible.

3 Make a hole in the compost in the new pot, and holding the seedling carefully by the tip of a leaf, never the stem, drop the root into the hole.

4 The seedling should end up at the same depth as it was in the original pot. Firm the compost around the seedling with your fingers. Return the seedlings to a propagator to recover for a few days, then gradually get them used to drier, cooler air.

TRANSPLANTING

Once plants have been acclimatized to outdoor conditions, they are ready for planting out. Tender plants should be planted out only after all danger of frost has passed. Water the plants thoroughly and space them out in their final positions. Use a trowel to make a planting hole twice the size of the rootball. Take the plant out of its pot and insert it into the ground. Firm the soil and water.

Sometimes there is a delay of more than four weeks in transplanting plants into their final growing positions, perhaps due to poor weather or to the space where you want to grow them being occupied by a previous crop or spring bedding. Plants growing vigorously for more than four weeks need either liquid feeding or transferring into a larger pot. If the

larger pot is also deeper, put a layer of compost in the bottom. Remove the plant from the smaller pot with the ball of soil intact. Do not pull the stem but put your hand over the top of the pot, with the plant stem between your two middle fingers. Tap firmly on the bottom of the pot. Drop the plant plus compost into the larger pot and fill around it with fresh compost.

LIFTING AND DIVIDING PLANTS

YOU WILL NEED

Garden fork

Trowel

Clean, sharp knife

Damp sacking or compost

Bucket of water

Manure or garden compost

SEE ALSO

Specially prepared bulbs
See *Planting bulbs, corms and tubers, pp. 152–153*

Caring for perennials
See *Looking after perennials, pp. 168–169*

Growing on
See *Taking cuttings, pp. 202–203*

After a perennial has been growing in the same place for several years, it tends to become a congested clump of roots and stems. This is often seen in a border about five years or so after planting. By this time, each plant takes up a considerable amount of

space, and young growth and flowering take place only at the outer edges. These plants can be rejuvenated very easily. Lift them up out of the ground, divide the clump, and replant the younger sections into fresh compost. The same technique can be used to obtain more plants either for other parts of the garden or for swapping with friends.

Dividing perennials is usually done in autumn or spring, but most can be divided any time during the growing season if they are kept well watered when replanted. Choose a day when the soil is warm and moist, but which is not too hot or windy. There are various ways of dividing perennials depending on what types of roots they have.

Most have fibrous roots that can be pulled or prized apart, but some, such as bearded iris and bergenia, have fleshy underground stems, called rhizomes, that need to be cut up. Clumps of bulbs can also become congested. If flowering ceases after several years, it is certainly worth lifting the bulbs and gently separating the young offsets from the parent bulbs.

Daffodils will flower each spring, year after year, but in time the bulbs will become congested and need separating. If they are not separated, flowering will fail.

BULBS AND TUBERS

Dig up mature clumps of bulbs that have failed to flower – the best time is just after the foliage has died down when the bulbs are becoming dormant. You should see a congested clump of parent bulbs with smaller bulbs, called offsets, attached to them. Pull the bulbs apart from one another with your fingers and thumbs; be gentle or you could damage the root system.

Large healthy offsets can be separated from their parent bulb and replanted in the ground. Small offsets are best potted up and grown on for a couple of years. Healthy parent bulbs can also be replanted after rubbing off any loose papery skin. Discard any bulbs that are soft, shrivelled or damaged. A few plants, such as dahlias, have tubers that form

clumps as they grow older. These clumps can be divided in spring before the tubers are planted. Use a clean, sharp knife to divide the clump into sections; each one should have a tuber and a dormant bud. Dust the cut surfaces with a fungicide – this is optional – and plant the sections 10–15 cm (4–6 in) deep where you want them to flower.

DIVIDING PERENNIALS WITH FIBROUS ROOTS

1 Ease a garden fork under the plant's roots. Where the plant has grown to form a large clump, loosen the soil all around the plant first before lifting out the clump to some spare ground nearby.

2 Discard any old or diseased portions of the plant, retaining young healthy sections. While dividing up a section, protect the roots of the other divisions with a cover of moist compost or damp sacking.

3 To be viable, each division needs a fistful of roots and growing points, such as buds or shoots. To divide the sections, pull them apart with your hands, or use a pair of forks back to back to prise the roots apart. Where there is a great deal of foliage, remove some of the older leaves.

4 Replant the best sections either in a new site or, with the addition of some organic matter, in the same site. Space between three and five plant sections about 30 cm (12 in) away from each other; they will soon grow together to form a drift.

TRIMMING TOP GROWTH

S ome tall plants, such as many of the irises, tend to be top-heavy, particularly until the roots have had a chance to anchor the plant, so it is worth trimming the top growth. Use a clean knife to trim the leaves so that only 15 cm (6 in) or so of the foliage remains.

Helpful hints

Small divisions or small offsets are going to struggle if planted straight out into the ground; they will not reach flowering size for several years. These are best potted up and grown on as you would a container plant; they can be planted out once they have a fair-sized rootball. Young sections may wilt straight after planting, but they should recover. Regularly water the soil if it is dry until you see new growth appearing. Potbound perennials can be divided up into smaller sections before planting out. These will soon grow together to form a drift that will not need lifting and dividing for several years.

TAKING CUTTINGS

YOU WILL NEED

Clean, sharp knife

Small pots

Sharp sand

Potting compost

Plastic bags

Dibber pencil

Labels

Secateurs

SEE ALSO

Planting out
See *Pricking out and thinning, pp. 198–199*

Dividing perennials
See *Lifting and dividing plants, pp. 200–201*

How to layer climbers, heathers and shrubs
See *Layering, pp. 204–205*

Taking cuttings from shrubs and perennials is a popular and inexpensive way of getting large numbers of plants for hedging, edging or ground cover. In gardens where many tender plants are used, taking cuttings in summer is a worthwhile precaution against the potential loss of the parent plant during the winter.

Cuttings can be taken throughout the year, but for any particular species there is often an ideal time, when the stems are at the right stage of maturity. Softwood cuttings are taken while the stem is young and sappy, usually from late spring to early summer. These cuttings need a constant supply of moisture and often warmth at the roots. Semi-ripe cuttings are taken as the current season's wood starts to harden at the base; between early summer and late summer for deciduous shrubs or early autumn for evergreens.

Hardwood cuttings are prepared from well-ripened stems and can be taken at any time between late autumn and winter. Deciduous hardwood cuttings can be planted in a cold frame. Alternatively, they can be inserted into a V-shaped trench lined with sharp sand in a sheltered, well-drained spot in the open garden. Cuttings of hardwood evergreens, however, do best in a greenhouse.

Honeysuckle (Lonicera) is one of the many popular climbers that can be grown from cuttings. Take cuttings from late spring until winter – plants should flower in three years.

RECOMMENDED CUTTINGS LIST

The following are some of the easiest plants to root from cuttings. In most cases you will have more success if you dip the cutting in rooting hormone powder before you plant it. Keep cuttings evenly moist until they have rooted. Semi-hardwood cuttings benefit from bottom heat during the rooting period.

Softwood cuttings:
Bottlebrush (*Callistemon*); broom (*Cytisus*); buddleja; cotoneaster; daphne; deutzia; dogwood (*Cornus florida*); holly (*Ilex*); honeysuckle (*Lonicera*); *Hydrangea grandiflora*; jasmine; weigelia. If possible, take cuttings 15–25 cm (6–10 in) long.

Compost with vermiculite-added generally works best.
Semi-ripe cuttings:
Camellia japonica; evergreen holly (*Ilex*); St-John's- wort (*Hypericum*)
Hardwood cuttings:
Bougainvillea; box; forsythia; gardenia; shrub roses; Siberian dogwood (*Cornus alba*)

TAKING SOFTWOOD CUTTINGS

1 Select a healthy plant free from pests and disease. Take cuttings either by pinching out 2.5cm (1 in) of a growing tip or by using a clean sharp blade to cut stems into 2.5-cm (1-in) sections with the leaf joint in the middle (this is known as an internodal cutting).

2 Fill some small pots with a free-draining potting compost with sharp sand added, water the soil and allow it to drain.

3 Make holes in the compost with a dibber pencil, or plant label. Drop a cutting in each one and close up the hole. Label the pot with the date and name of the plant.

4 Cover the pot with a clear plastic bag, and place in indirect light at a temperature of 15°C (59°F). Cuttings should root within 2–3 weeks. Pot up each one in its own pot.

OTHER TYPES OF CUTTINGS

To take semi-ripe cuttings, cut off a healthy shoot of the current season's growth in early to late summer. The wood should be ripening but not fully hardened. Use a clean, sharp knife to remove any side shoots; cut just below a leaf joint (a nodal cutting) to leave a cutting 10 cm (4 in) long. Remove the lower leaves. Dip the base of the cutting in rooting powder. Insert into a pot of compost and leave in a coldframe or greenhouse; these cuttings take several months to root.

To take hardwood cuttings of deciduous shrubs, wait until after leaf fall and use secateurs to take pencil-thick stem cuttings of at least 20 cm (8 in). To be sure which is the top of the cutting, make a horizontal cut just below a node at the base of the cutting and a sloping cut away from a bud at the top. Dip the base in rooting powder. If you have a well-drained, sheltered site, prepare a 15-cm (6-in) deep V-shaped trench and line it with 2-cm (1-in) of sharp sand; otherwise plant into compost in a coldframe. Insert the cuttings into the trench 30 cm (12 in) apart with only 5 cm (2 in) visible above ground. Backfill the trench, firm the soil and water if dry. Lift and transplant the following autumn.

LAYERING

YOU WILL NEED

Sharp knife

U-shaped metal peg or wire coathanger

Small stake

Tie

Hammer

Secateurs

SEE ALSO

Planting out
See *Pricking and thinning, pp. 198–199*

Dividing perennials
See *Lifting and dividing plants, pp. 200–201*

Growing on
See *Taking cuttings, pp. 202–203*

Many shrubs and climbers have stems that can be encouraged to root while they are still attached to the parent plant. This technique is called layering. The advantages of layering are that you need little equipment and there is little aftercare. Layered plants take many months, even a year or more, to root, but they can be started at any time in autumn or early spring.

The easiest shrubs to layer are those with low-growing branches that can be simply

pegged into the ground, but to tackle a shrub with more upright branches you can try air layering. With most shrubs, you will probably get only one or two new plants. Heathers are an exception because most of their stems layer particularly well. Layering climbers will produce more new plants than layering shrubs; some, such as ivy, even layer themselves naturally.

The best material for layering is young, flexible shoots growing near the surface of the soil. If no suitable shoots occur naturally, prune the shrub back hard (usually in early spring) to encourage new vigorous shoots; one of these can then be layered. You can root layers in most garden soils, but if your soil is very dry or very wet, fork in some garden compost or fresh topsoil before layering.

Once you have prepared the branch for layering, it needs very little aftercare. Apart from watering the soil during dry spells, you can leave the plant and let nature do the rest. After six months to two years, sever the new plant from the parent and pot it up.

Variegated ivy carpets the ground between a pollarded willow and a flowering witch hazel.

Helpful hints

If you want to create a lot of new plants quickly from one parent, try serpentine layering. This works best on plants that produce long shoots of new growth each year, such as clematis, wisteria and golden hop (*Humulus lupulus* 'Aureus'). In early spring, prepare the ground as described opposite. Bring a shoot at least 60–75 cm (24–30 in) down to ground level. If the stem is thin, you do not need to wound it; for a thicker stem, nick the stem with a sharp knife and peg it to the ground with the wound below soil level. Repeat at intervals along the stem. You should get new plants within 12 months.

ROOTING CLIMBERS

A single stem can root in many places and make several plants. In early spring, gently lift the stem off the ground and cut it just above a node. Cut the rooted stem into sections, each with some roots and some new top growth. Well-rooted sections can be replanted, or the sections can be potted up and grown on.

LAYERING HEATHERS

1 Heathers can be layered by pegging down the stems, but it is easier to mound rooting medium around the whole plant. In spring or autumn, mix together equal parts of sharp sand and peat. Work this around the stems of the heather so that the stems are not touching each other and only 5 cm (2 in) of the stem tips are visible.

2 Water the mound gently in dry spells. Replenish the rooting mix if it is disturbed or washed away by heavy rain. The stems will have rooted by late summer. Detach the rooted stems from the parent plant and either plant them in a new site or pot them up and grow them on for spring planting.

LAYERING A SHRUB

1 Take a low-growing healthy branch and strip off the leaves, starting about 20 cm (8 in) in from the tip. Remove the foliage from the section you plan to root. Gently scrape away the outside layer of bark on the underside of the stem that will touch the ground.

2 Anchor the branch to the soil (bent wire coathangers make good pegs) with the scraped side touching the ground. Cover the pinned section of the branch with soil and water in well.

AIR LAYERING

Often used indoors, air layering can also be used on shrubs such as rhododendrons and daphne.

In spring, select a healthy shoot and trim off any side shoots to leave a clear length of stem. Use a sharp knife to make a slanting cut halfway through the stem. Take a pinch of moist sphagnum moss, dip it in rooting powder and insert it into the cut. Make a sleeve of black plastic about 10–15 cm (4–6 in) long, stick one end to the stem with tape and pack more moist moss into it. Seal the other end. Leave in place until the following spring.

When you peel back the plastic there should be roots in the moss. Cut the stem below the rootball. Pot up the new plant.

PLANTS FOR LAYERING

Among the many plants that respond well to layering are: *Amelanchier*, *Actinidia*, bougainvillea, spotted laurel (*Aucuba japonica*), trumpet vine (*Campsis radicans*), camellia, flowering quince (*Chaenomeles*), clematis, dogwood, smoke bush (*Cotinus*), cotoneaster, forsythia, fothergilla, heather, holly, hydrangea, ivy, mountain laurel (*Kalmia latifolica*), evergreen honeysuckle (*Lonicera japonica*), *Potentilla fructicosa*, rhododendron, spiraea and thyme.

THE EDIBLE GARDEN

Grow your own food and not only will you harvest and enjoy far fresher vegetables, fruits and herbs than you can purchase in the shops but you will have the reassurance of knowing how they were grown and whether or not they were sprayed with synthetic chemicals. This chapter covers the basic techniques to get you started with vegetables, fruits and herbs.

PLANNING WHERE TO GROW VEGETABLES

BEST PLANTS

Cabbage family

Root crops

Onion family

Pea family

Potato family

SEE ALSO

All kinds of vegetables
See *Styles of vegetable garden, pp. 210–211*

The best vegetables
See *Successful vegetable techniques, pp. 212–213*

Types of vegetable
See *Leafy crops; Roots and tubers; Fruiting crops and bulbous vegetables, pp. 214–219*

This formal vegetable garden still adheres to the rules of crop separation and rotation. Crops have also been chosen according to a general colour scheme.

Vegetables prefer a sunny site, although there are plants that will crop reasonably well in light shade. Most vegetables crop better if sheltered from strong winds. The ideal soil is moist but well drained. Remember, however, you can improve most sites by adding plenty of well-rotted organic matter each year, and you can also grow small amounts of produce in tubs of potting compost. A "proper" vegetable plot is not essential, and on the next page there are plenty of ideas for growing vegetables to suit the style of your garden and to fit into the smallest place. But for produce in quantity and variety, year after year, it makes sense to have a dedicated area divided into beds separated by paths for easy access.

Most vegetables are annuals, the handful of perennial vegetables is discussed on pages 220–221. Annuals need to be sown and raised afresh each year. Rather than sowing or planting the same crop in the same place each year, it is better to move them around

An informal planting of crops does not have to look out of style in a leisure garden. Here, vegetables and ornamental plants are carefully interwoven in a seamless design.

to prevent soil pest and disease levels from building up. You could simply write down where each crop was grown and grow it in a different place or even in a container the following year. At the very least, members of the potato, onion and cabbage families should be grown in a different area each year and other crops fitted in around them.

A proper crop rotation system moves crops around from year to year but also groups them into families with similar nutrient requirements. This means that the soil can be cared for more easily with the minimum amount of chemicals and fertilizers. For example, where the amount of organic matter available is limited, you can make sure it goes to the hungriest crops like beans. And from a timesaving and cost-reduction point of view, you need only apply the manure to a third of the whole vegetable area in any one year.

CROP ROTATION

To practise crop rotation, divide the vegetable-growing area into three or four equal areas with paths in between, or build three or four raised beds. Each bed will be home to one family of vegetables each year. The following year, move each crop to another bed, leaving as long a time gap as possible before a crop returns to the same bed.

THREE-YEAR ROTATION

1st year

Bed 1	Potatoes and roots
Bed 2	Pea and onion families
Bed 3	Cabbage family

2nd year

Bed 1	Pea and onion families
Bed 2	Cabbage family
Bed 3	Potatoes and roots

3rd year

Bed 1	Cabbage family
Bed 2	Potatoes and roots
Bed 3	Pea and onion families

FOUR-YEAR ROTATION

1st year

Bed 1	Potatoes
Bed 2	Pea family
Bed 3	Cabbage family
Bed 4	Roots and onions

2nd year

Bed 1	Pea family
Bed 2	Cabbage family
Bed 3	Roots and onions
Bed 4	Potatoes

3rd year

Bed 1	Cabbage family
Bed 2	Roots and onions
Bed 3	Potatoes
Bed 4	Pea family

4th year

Bed 1	Roots and onions
Bed 2	Potatoes
Bed 3	Pea family
Bed 4	Cabbage family

Cabbage family
Broccoli, Brussels sprouts, cabbage, cauliflower, oriental greens, kale, kohl rabi, radishes, swede and turnip. Wallflowers and Sweet Williams are also related.

Root crops
Carrots and parsnips (also parsley – although this is a leafy herb, it suffers from carrot fly).

Onion family
All types of onion, chives, garlic, leek and shallot.

Pea family
Garden and mangetout peas, broad beans, french and runner beans.

Potato family
Potatoes, tomatoes, aubergines and peppers.

Fit-in-anywhere vegetables
The following crops can be fitted anywhere in the rotation: beetroot; spinach, including leaf beet and chard; lettuce; courgettes; cucumbers; pumpkins; squash and sweet corn.

STYLES OF VEGETABLE GARDEN

PLANTING SUGGESTIONS

When planning an ornamental vegetable garden, remember that it may look bleak in winter or after harvesting. It's a good idea to include some strong structural elements, such as clipped box or another evergreen edging, good-quality cloches and forcing pots, or attractive landscaped paths. Grow winter vegetables in an interesting way: for example, use varieties of brassica that have coloured or textured foliage, such as red Brussels sprouts or blue-black curly kale.

Colourful vegetables for edging beds include Swiss ruby chard, beetroot and purple varieties of kohlrabi. Lettuce is available in various greens and red-bronze.

Keep perennial vegetables such as rhubarb, asparagus and artichokes separate from annual vegetables used in crop rotation. You could grow them in large borders.

In a traditional vegetable garden, you can grow a wide range of crops by planting in long rows. This is functional vegetable growing: efficient, but not particularly attractive. However, you can grow just a few vegetables by fitting them into existing flower borders, by using pots on the patio, or by having a small patch just for salad crops. The increasing popularity of raised beds has led to more planting in short rows or in blocks because this has more scope for making patterns using the colour and texture contrasts of foliage plants. On a large scale, patterns of beds can be created to form a *potager*, where vegetables are planted in patterns, often rubbing shoulders with fruit and herbs. On a smaller scale, even a small patio or balcony can yield some choice vegetable treats for a city gardener. When planning your vegetable garden, note the soil's fertility, the climate (how altitude and amounts of wind, sun and rain will affect the site), and decide whether to rotate crops or to put fast- or slow-growing plants in the same bed.

▲ IN BORDERS

In a narrow border there is still room for some vegetables. Leafy crops and herbs such as curly parsley and thyme fill gaps around runner beans growing up a tripod. A path beside the border makes harvesting easier.

▶ FORMAL *POTAGER*

Green or yellow box (as edging or clipped specimens) adds structure and colour all year. Interplant cabbages with lettuces that have red and lime-green leaves.

▼ COTTAGE STYLE
This informal cottage-garden style is ideal for rural areas. The vegetables are grown in short rows beside flowers and herbs, while the paths between the beds are covered with straw. Plant supports and screens are made of woven willow and blend in well with this country scene.

▲ SIMPLE BEDS
Here, square beds are marked out by brick paths. At the front are easy crops such as lettuce and courgettes; perennial vegetables are used as screenings at the back. An easy-to-care-for garden to suit busy gardeners.

▲ FLOWERING BEDS
Although more expensive than plastic, glass is an excellent material for cloches, since it quickly warms up in the sun and transmits light well. These pyramid-shaped cloches add interest to a bed of nasturtiums.

SUCCESSFUL VEGETABLE TECHNIQUES

YOU WILL NEED

Pegs and string

Split poles and timber

Posts and nails

Spirit level

Topsoil, organic matter

Sheet mulch

PVC pipe

Crop covers

Hammer, shovel

SEE ALSO

Sowing from seed
See *Sowing seed: indoors/ outdoors, pp. 194–197*

Designs for vegetable gardens
See *Planning where to grow vegetables, pp. 208–209*

All kinds of vegetables
See *Styles of vegetable garden, pp. 210–211*

Types of vegetables
See *Leafy crops; Roots and tubers; Fruiting crops and bulbous vegetables, pp. 214–219*

Artichokes, asparagus and rhubarb
See *Perennial vegetables, pp. 220–221*

An efficient way to grow vegetables is to build raised beds, where the depth of topsoil is increased by adding organic matter so the bed is higher than nearby paths. Raised beds warm up earlier in spring than the surrounding soil and drain more quickly after rain. They are also easy to cover and protect: horticultural fabric guards against late frosts, and fine mesh covers keep out pests. If you do all your planting and weeding from the paths, the soil will remain in peak condition and not need digging each year. Apply well-rotted organic matter to the surface of the beds every year, to suppress weeds and, once the earthworms have dragged it down, to improve the soil.

A simple, rectangular bed approximately 3 m (10 ft) long and 1.2 m (4 ft) wide is easy to build and maintain. The narrow width allows you to reach the centre of the bed from the path on either side. Paths should be about 45 cm (18 in) wide, 30 cm (12 in) wide at minimum; but wider than 60 cm (24 in) wastes valuable growing space.

Catch crops are small, fast-growing plants that fill the space between slower crops or are sown before planting or after harvesting the main crop. Beetroot, carrots, lettuce and spinach are good catch crops because they can be eaten while immature.

This maturing vegetable garden features a variety of shades of green foliage as well as a combination of leaf shape and texture, making an attractive and edible garden.

INTENSIVE GARDENING TO SAVE SPACE

Use the space between slow-growing brassicas, such as Brussels sprouts, broccoli, kale and cauliflower, to sow a quick-maturing crop of smaller vegetables such as radish, turnip or lettuce. As summer heat intensifies, cool-season vegetables such as lettuce, spinach and radishes appreciate the shade cast by a stand of corn. The shade will help to extend their growing season.

Grow small plants, such as mizuna greens or oriental mustards, as decorative edging around the borders of your vegetable patch. The various leaf shapes and colours are attractive, as well as nutritious.

Vining crops, such as peas, runner beans, cucumbers and some melons, thrive on trellises or tied to stakes. This vertical gardening leaves ground space for other plants.

MAKING AND USING RAISED BEDS

1 Mark out the shape of the beds on prepared ground. Hammer posts in at the corners, leaving them about 13 cm (5 in) above ground level. Cut the split poles to size and fix them to the posts with galvanized nails. Check the tops with a level. Cover the paths with woven polypropylene sheeting topped with bark chips.

2 Dig the soil inside the bed and add well-rotted organic matter to raise the level. Sow or plant across the width of the beds. These rows are shorter than in a normal plot, but this makes it easier to sow little and often to avoid having a glut of one type of crop at any one time.

3 Make some supports over the raised beds to hold up crop covers. Insert hoops of PVC pipe (bought from a hardware shop) or stiff wire hoops over the width of the beds at 60-cm (24-in) intervals. Drape the crop cover (horticultural fleece or fine mesh) over the hoops, securing the edges and ends with suitably sized stones.

4 In early summer, replace the horticultural fleece with very fine plastic mesh, weighing down the edges and ends so pests cannot get in. Crop covers will keep out flying and crawling pests and can be left in place while watering. In winter, remove the crop cover and replace it with clear plastic sheeting to protect overwintering crops.

5 To edge raised beds, use lengths of untreated timber or set paving slabs on edge, with 30 cm (12 in) showing above soil level. Alternatively, use bricks or paving blocks, either laid loose or cemented in. Railway sleepers are heavy and hard to cut, but provide solid edges for larger raised beds. Choose an edge whose style complements your overall garden design.

Helpful hints

A double layer of horticultural fleece will protect seedlings and plants from frost if you live in an area where the average outside temperature falls to -4°C (25°F) or below. Remove the fleece once the weather gets warmer in the spring or the crops may scorch and die. Horticultural fleece is reusable; simply wash it in the washing machine, dry and store then reuse it the following year.

If the soil around your flowering vegetable plants dries out, water the crop well, then fork in a mulch to prevent moisture from evaporating; a mulch also suppresses weeds that might take nutrients needed by your crop.

LEAFY CROPS

YOU WILL NEED

Trowel

Scissors

Liquid feed

Plant pots

Garden fleece

Slug repellent

Bird netting

SEE ALSO

Vegetable gardens
See *Planning where to grow vegetables,*
pp. 208–209

All kinds of vegetables
See *Styles of vegetable garden, pp. 210–211*

The best vegetables
See *Successful vegetable techniques, pp. 212–213*

Types of vegetables
See *Roots and tubers; Fruiting crops and bulbous vegetables; Perennial vegetables, pp. 216–221*

Leafy crops are best eaten when they are fresh, so they are worth growing yourself. Lettuce plants are quick growing and can be grown in the smallest of spaces including borders or containers such as window boxes. As well as the lettuce varieties that have firm

This 'Black Tuscany' kale is ready for harvesting. By planting through spring and summer, you can achieve an almost constant supply of leafy crops throughout the year.

hearts, there are also the "cut-and-come-again" types. These salad plants regrow from the stump that is left when the leaves are cut.

You can either buy seed packets of ready-mixed lettuce or mixtures of edible leaves, such as 'Saladini', which usually include lettuce, endive, chicory and other species. An interesting idea is to buy separate packets of lettuce, rocket, endive, spinach and chervil, sow them in separate rows, then mix them together after harvesting. For a supply of fresh greens in the winter or early spring, plant a leafy member of the brassica family. Some of them can be tricky to grow, but kale is one of the easiest.

BOLTING

For tasty leafy crops, you want the plant to remain immature and not run to seed (bolt). Bolting happens very quickly in a fast-growing season (one that is sunny early on) and there is nothing you can do once a plant has bolted. Keeping plants well supplied with moisture and growing the later sowings in light shade will make bolting less likely.

CUT-AND-COME-AGAIN SALADS

1 Mixed packets of seed are usually scattered. If you have separate packets, sow each ingredient in single rows with each row 10 cm (4 in) apart. Aim for roughly 1 cm (½ in) between seeds. When the seedlings reach about 10 cm (4 in), cut the leaves with scissors about 2 cm (¾ in) above the soil, leaving the cut stumps to grow again.

2 Apply a high-nitrogen liquid feed and keep the plants well watered. Within three or four weeks a flush of new leaves will grow from the cut stumps. These can be cut as before – you should get at least two pickings and possibly up to four from one sowing. Ideally, you should sow a batch every two weeks for a continual supply.

GROWING KALE

1 Kale is started off in a seed bed (limed if the soil is acid) or in pots in late spring, then transplanted to the final growing position in early summer. When the soil temperature is at least 5°C (41°F) sow the seed. Draw a shallow seed drill, water the bottom well and sow the seed thinly, aiming for one every 5 cm (2 in) or so. Cover the seed with soil.

2 Cover the seed bed with garden fleece to protect young plants from flea beetles (which riddle the leaves with tiny holes) and aphids. Slugs might also be a problem; a 5-cm (2-in) strip of organic repellent or wood ash spread around the plant will keep them at bay. If the leaves start to change colour, the plants may need nutrients, so water in a liquid feed.

3 Plant the kale out into its final position in early summer. Water the pot or the seed bed well, then lift the young plants carefully using a hand fork or trowel and taking as much root as possible. Plants may well flop after planting, even if adequately watered, but should soon recover. Space plants 15–45 cm (5–20 in) apart depending on the variety used.

4 Pick individual younger leaves as required through the winter. Wash them carefully to remove any aphids or whiteflies lurking in the wrinkles. Cover the crops with bird netting or install bird scarers if pigeons start to damage the young leaves. In spring, the immature flower shoots can be picked (left) and eaten like sprouting broccoli.

LETTUCE WITH A HEART

You need to use a variety that will produce a heart and provide enough space between plants for the heart to develop. Space plants 30 cm (10 in) apart each way. Some small varieties such as 'Little Gem' can be grown 23 cm (9 in) apart. For large heads of crisphead varieties, increase the spacing to 38 cm (15 in).

Helpful hints

If you want only a few plants for a container or border, start seeds off in pots. Kale seed is large and easy to handle – sow two seeds per 7-cm (3-in) pot and pull out the weaker one if both germinate. A cool but frost-free place in the garden or an unheated room is fine, as long as it has a minimum temperature of 5°C (41°F). For lettuce, sow two or three seeds in pots or modular seed trays. These will germinate at low temperatures but not above 20°C (68°F), so make summer sowings in the evening. For a year-round supply in cool climates sow at two-week intervals from spring to summer.

ROOTS AND TUBERS

Vegetables grown for their roots or tubers are a staple feature of the vegetable garden and many can be lifted and stored. Maincrop varieties of potatoes can be grown for use throughout the winter, while early varieties provide tasty new potatoes. Beetroot

Root vegetables are among the most versatile of crops: some are best when young and fresh, others can be stored.

and carrots are both ideal for small spaces, and have the added advantages of growing quickly and having very attractive foliage. For small baby carrots, choose an early variety and sow little and often; if you want to store carrots over winter, opt for a single sowing of a maincrop variety.

A well-cultivated soil is needed for root crops, and it is worth following a crop rotation to keep soil pests and diseases to a minimum (see pp. 208–209). If this is not possible, try growing vegetables in deep containers. Potatoes and beetroot like a well-dug soil with plenty of well-rotted manure incorporated, plus a general fertilizer. Carrots like a deep but well-drained soil they can penetrate easily, so a heavy soil needs to be dug well if it is compacted – but do not add any organic matter or additional fertilizer.

Multi-seeding works really well with beetroot because each of the large corky seed capsules contains up to four seeds. The idea is that you grow between six and eight seedlings in a small pot and plant the whole clump out together. As the plants grow, the roots will push each other apart to produce a clump of small but perfectly round roots.

SOWING CARROTS

Sow carrot seed as thinly as you can to avoid having to thin the young plants later – aim for a seed every 2.5 cm (1 in). If you find handling carrot seed difficult, buy seed tape (seed sandwiched between long paper ribbons) and lay these onto a prepared drill. Cover the drill with dry soil. Do not water since this disturbs the seeds.

MULTI-SEEDING BEETROOT

Sow two seed clusters per 7-cm (2¾-in) pot. Place the pots in a cool but frost-free place and keep the compost moist. When seedlings develop the first leaves, plant each clump out. Dig a hole with a trowel, then tap the rootball out of the pot and plant it level with the soil surface. Space the clumps so that they are 15 cm (6 in) apart.

GROWING POTATOES

1 Lay the tubers out in empty trays so the ends with the greatest number of eyes are uppermost. Place the trays in a cool, dry place with good light, but not direct sunlight. After a few weeks, sprouts will start to grow. Rub off all but the four strongest sprouts. This is "chitting" and starts tubers off while the soil is too cold for them to grow outdoors.

2 Dig the ground over and work in well-rotted manure. You can leave the surface fairly rough, but scatter over a little balanced fertilizer. Plant tubers in mid- to late spring. Plant tubers about 15 cm (6 in) deep and 40 cm (16 in) apart. Allow 75 cm (30 in) between rows of maincrops and 45 cm (18 in) between rows of early varieties.

3 When the first shoots appear above the surface, start to draw earth from between the rows over the centre of the row, to cover the shoots. This is called "earthing up" and encourages tubers to grow, prevents them from turning green, and protects young shoots from frost. Aim for a flat-topped ridge about 30 cm (12 in) across and 25 cm (10 in) high.

4 Cover foliage with fleece if frost is likely; otherwise yield may be affected. Water only when the tubers start forming. Dig up early potatoes as soon as you can feel egg-sized tubers. To harvest maincrop potatoes, leave the plants to die down completely, then push a garden fork in about 30 cm (12 in) from the dead tops and under the plant.

STORING ROOTS

To store potatoes, dry them off for a few days, then pack in double paper sacks. Store in a place that is dark and cool but above 4°C (39°F) – an outbuilding, cellar, garage or a cupboard under the stairs is usually suitable. Root vegetables such as carrots and beetroot can be left in well-drained soil until needed. Mark crops so you can find them once the foliage has died down. Cover the soil with a layer of straw, then black plastic to stop the soil freezing; this makes the vegetables easier to dig up. Pests and diseases may affect crops left in the ground and harvesting in midwinter is not pleasant, so put some of the crop in boxes of sand and keep in a shed, cellar or garage. Remove foliage and lay roots on a layer of moist sand then cover with more sand. Put the large roots at the bottom as they will store for longer than smaller ones.

Carrots store well if covered in sand and kept dry, but check regularly for signs of rotting.

FRUITING CROPS AND BULBOUS VEGETABLES

YOU WILL NEED

Peasticks

Plant pots

Trowel

Manure or compost

Cane supports

String

General fertilizer

SEE ALSO

Vegetable gardens
See *Planning where to grow vegetables,* pp. 208–209

All kinds of vegetables
See *Styles of vegetable garden,* pp. 210–211

The best vegetables
See *Successful vegetable techniques,* pp. 212–213

Types of vegetables
See *Leafy crops; Roots and tubers; Perennial vegetables,* pp. 214–215, 216–217, 220–221

Tomatoes and runner beans are such productive fruiting crops that even a couple of plants will supply enough produce over the summer for a family. You do not need a vegetable plot to grow them since tomatoes can be grown in a large container, and runner beans make attractive climbers for a sunny border. Both tomato plants and runner beans are tender and will need protecting from frost. Tomato seeds need a high germination temperature early in the year, so if you only need a couple of tomato plants it is better to buy them as young plants from a garden centre – these can be grown outside as well as in the greenhouse. Tomatoes are greedy feeders and you will need to keep them well supplied with a liquid tomato feed throughout the season.

If you have more space, other fruiting crops to consider include courgettes, squashes, other types of beans and peas. All like a soil enriched with organic material. Beans and peas are legumes that manufacture their own nitrogen fertilizer from the air through the nodules on their roots, so need little feeding. The secret of high yield with all fruiting crops is to grow them where they get plenty of sun,

and to pick the crop frequently. This ensures that the plants will continue to flower and fruit for many months. Bulbous vegetables, such as onions, garlic and shallots, are generally easy to grow. Unlike fruiting crops, they can be picked as they are needed or lifted all at once. If dried off in the sun, they store throughout the winter.

Fruiting crops are an essential and popular feature of the well-stocked kitchen garden – and are simple to grow.

ONIONS

The easiest way to grow onions is from immature onion bulbs (sets). In spring, push the sets gently into the soil so the tip is level with the surface. For lots of small bulbs, plant the sets 2.5 cm (1 in) apart in rows 15 cm (6 in) apart – onions cannot compete with weeds and you will need to hoe between the rows with an onion hoe or weed by hand.

PEAS

Peas will germinate at 4°C (39°F), but nearer 10°C (50°F) is better, since there is less chance of rotting. Seeds are sown in 10-cm (4-in) wide drills about 2.5–5 cm (1–2 in) deep. Sow thinly, aiming for a seed every 5 cm (2 in). Allow 60 cm (24 in) between rows, and slightly more for taller varieties. All but the smallest varieties need support with peasticks.

GROWING TOMATOES IN A GREENHOUSE

1 Plant young plants in a soil border, large pot of compost or a growing bag. Allow one plant to a pot, or two to three plants to a growing bag. Most greenhouse tomatoes are trained up supports. Place a cane next to each plant and tie the top to the greenhouse. Tie the main stem loosely to the support as the plant grows.

2 Pinch out any side shoots that form, but be careful not to damage the tiny clusters of yellow flowers. Water the plants frequently, which may mean twice a day if you use growing bags or pots. Feed plants regularly with a tomato feed. Leave the door open on sunny days, to ventilate the greenhouse.

GROWING RUNNER BEANS

1 Sow two seeds to a 12-cm (4½-in) pot and keep at 10–12°C (50-54°F). Grow on the seedlings at 7°C (45°F) until they are 15–20 cm (6–8 in) tall. Dig well-rotted manure into the site. Make a wigwam of 2-m (6 ft 6-in) canes. Make the base 60 cm (24 in) in diameter and space the canes 15 cm (6 in) apart. Tie securely or use a plastic grip.

2 Scatter a little general-purpose fertilizer over the site about two weeks before planting. Gradually harden off the young plants, and plant two to each support at 15-cm (6-in) intervals.

3 Water well and protect young plants from slugs and wind. Mulch around the plants with well-rotted manure, grass cuttings or compost to retain moisture and suppress weeds.

Helpful hints

Watering encourages flowering and increases the size of the pods and fruits, so water fruiting crops regularly, especially during dry weather spells. Give a generous soaking – using about 10 litres of water per sq m (around 2 gallons per 10 sq ft) once a week. When the plants reach the top of their supports, pinch out their growing tips, to encourage the formation of side shoots. Pick all fruiting crops frequently and start picking beans when they reach about 17–18 cm (6½–7 in) in length to encourage continued cropping.

PERENNIAL VEGETABLES

YOU WILL NEED

Trowel

Fertilizer or organic matter

Knife

Spade

Rhubarb pot

Large container

SEE ALSO

Vegetable gardens
See *Planning where to grow vegetables,* pp. 208–209

All kinds of vegetables
See *Styles of vegetable garden,* pp. 210–211

The best vegetables
See *Successful vegetable techniques,* pp. 212–213

Types of vegetable
See *Leafy crops; Roots and tubers; Fruiting crops and bulbous vegetables,* pp. 214–219,

Most vegetables are annuals and are raised from seed each year, but there are a few perennials, such as asparagus, artichokes and rhubarb, that will crop year after year. These are not grown as part of a crop rotation but are given their own spot in the vegetable plot or are incorporated into the ornamental garden. All need a reasonable amount of space and it may take several years before you get a decent crop; on the other hand, once you have them they will crop each year and require very little effort.

Asparagus is usually grown in its own bed of at least 10 plants. The ideal site is well-drained, with neutral or slightly alkaline soil and free of perennial weeds. On wet soils you will need to raise up the soil level to improve drainage. In early spring, dig in plenty of well-rotted organic matter – spent mushroom compost is ideal. Asparagus can be grown from crowns or pot plants (see below). Allow 45 cm (18 in) between plants and 90 cm (3 ft) between the rows.

Globe artichokes like a sunny but sheltered site and a very rich soil, while Jerusalem artichokes are not fussy about soil and will tolerate partial shade; the latter act as a temporary windbreak to protect more tender

vegetables, but in exposed sites you may need to provide support by staking the stem. Rhubarb plants prefer a sunny position and a moist, but not waterlogged, soil. They can also tolerate light shade.

Globe artichokes are striking plants that make impressive focal points for the back of an ornamental border.

GROWING ASPARAGUS

1 Plant dormant crowns. Lay them on a ridge in the centre of a trench, with the roots spread on either side. Keep the tops of the crowns 10 cm (4 in) below the soil surface and cover with soil. Plant pot-grown plants in early summer, at container level. In spring, scatter a balanced fertilizer on the bed or mulch with organic matter.

2 You will get a crop two years after planting. In mid- to late spring, cut 5–7-cm (2–2¾-in) high spears with tight buds, cutting 2.5–5 cm (1–2 in) below the soil. Harvest twice a week but stop cutting after six weeks. Apply a high-nitrogen fertilizer and weed by hand regularly. Cut dead ferns to the ground in the autumn.

GLOBE ARTICHOKES

Dig garden compost into the site before planting in spring. Allow 75 cm (30 in) per plant and water well. Remove any flowers that form on new plants. A mature plant yields about 12 flowers in summer – cut the heads with a little stalk when the outer scales have opened flat. Cut dead stems down in late autumn and protect the crowns with straw.

JERUSALEM ARTICHOKES

Plant the tubers 10–15 cm (4–6 in) deep and 30 cm (12 in) apart in spring. When the plants reach 1.5–1.8 m (5–6 ft) in height, pinch out the tops. Cut the blackened stems to ground level, but mark the position so you can dig the tubers up over the winter. In cold areas protect the crowns with straw. Remove all but one egg-sized tuber as the plants are invasive.

GROWING RHUBARB

1 The best time to plant new crowns is during the winter, planting into well-manured ground. Bury the crown so that the top bud is just below the soil surface. Plant a pot-grown plant in the spring. Do not harvest any stems for two years after planting.

2 Harvest the sticks regularly from spring onwards when they are tender. Pull the stems rather than cut them. The leaves are poisonous and should be cut off. Leaf stalks contain low levels of poisons. They should not be eaten raw but they can be composted. Feed established clumps with a general fertilizer and mulch to increase next year's crop.

BLANCHING RHUBARB

1 For an early crop of blanched rhubarb, cover the dormant clumps to exclude light just before Christmas. You can use a terracotta rhubarb pot or a large flower pot or bucket. Place a stone on top to stop light from entering the drainage hole.

2 Early varieties covered before Christmas should be ready for harvesting in late winter or early spring. Early rhubarb varieties left uncovered should be ready to pull in early to mid-spring.

TYPES OF FRUIT GROWING

PLANTING SUGGESTIONS

In a large garden, where space is not a problem, you can have an area that is strictly devoted to fruit, with formal rows of fruit trees such as apple, cherry or pear, as well as soft fruits, such as blueberries, blackberries and raspberries. If trees and bushes are planted in one particular area, it is easier to protect them from birds or early frosts. When blossom time arrives, you will delight in the fragrance wafting from the fruit site.

You can grow trained fruit trees on a wooden fence, the house wall or the garden shed. Choose from a variety of shapes, such as cordon, espalier or fan. Alternatively, you can opt to let your fruit grow in a more unrestricted way to form a bush tree or a dwarf pyramid shape. The latter will require less pruning.

If you have a sunny, open space in your garden, you might consider growing nut-bearing trees or bushes: walnut or sweet chestnut on a large site, almond in a smaller area.

Growing fruit in a greenhouse may be the answer if you live in a cool climate. Grapes and peaches do well under cover, but make sure that you provide enough side and top vents to let air flow freely. Pot-grown strawberries can sit on a sunny, sheltered patio in the summer, then be brought into the greenhouse for the winter.

If you do not have room for a large, dedicated fruit garden, you can still grow one or two of your favourite fruits by using them around the rest of the garden either in shrub borders or as screens or container plants. Most fruits are grown on long-term plants, such as shrubs, trees or vines. They take a fair amount of space so you will need to consider carefully where to put them, particularly as most fruits need sun to ripen them and a moist but well-drained soil. Once planted and established, all fruits will continue to crop for many years, so they are a long-term investment for any garden. One exception is the strawberry; it crops well for only a few years before deteriorating, so aim to replace all your strawberries every two to three years with new stock.

▲ DWARF FRUIT TREES
A row of a dozen apple trees on a dwarfing rootstock gives a screen of blossom in spring, as well as high yields of fruit in autumn. Dwarfing rootstocks allow easier picking, but they need good growing conditions. Here, the turf has been removed to help the trees get established without having to compete with the grass.

◄ WALL-TRAINED FRUIT
A warm wall of a house provides an ideal site for fruit. Here, a young apple tree has been trained into a formal espalier, to make a decorative and productive feature that will last for many years to come.

▼ TRAINED SOFT FRUIT
This gooseberry, trained to form a vertical cordon, takes up very little ground space compared to a gooseberry bush. Red currants can also be trained as cordons.

► PATIO FRUIT
A well-established citrus plant, such as an orange or lemon, can spend the summer in a terracotta pot on the patio, but in cold climates it should be inside, ideally in a heated greenhouse, during the winter.

◄ GREENHOUSE FRUIT
Train a grapevine on wires up a wall and the roof of a greenhouse. The leaf canopy provides shade in summer.

► POTS OF STRAWBERRIES
In a very small garden, these pots save space and may be brought inside to ripen fruit faster.

GROWING FRUIT TREES

YOU WILL NEED

Wires and posts

Spade

Secateurs

Bamboo canes

Adjustable plastic ties

Stakes

SEE ALSO

Which tree?
See *Buying and planting trees, pp. 118–119*

All kinds of fruit
See *Types of fruit growing, pp. 222–223*

Apples and pears
See *Training and pruning fruit trees, pp. 226–227*

An apple tree growing at the bottom of a garden is a worthwhile, easy-to-care-for fruit tree that will last for many decades. Where space is limited or you want a more formal effect, consider "restricted" forms such as cordons and espaliers. However, make sure you will have time to train and prune them in summer and winter.

Cordons are trees trained as single stems, growing either vertically, horizontally, diagonally or in a serpentine pattern. They are often grown in rows. Diagonal cordons planted at an angle of 45° to the ground give the maximum amount of fruit per ground area. Apples, pears and red currants are popular subjects for cordons. A fruit tree can also be trained as an espalier, with a central vertical stem and tiered horizontals. This needs more space than a cordon, but makes a living sculpture for a sunny wall or fence.

To choose from the vast array of apple varieties, go to a few apple tastings in autumn. Ask about storing qualities if you want to store surplus fruit. For a tree to bear fruit, its blossom needs to be pollinated, either with its own pollen or that from another variety of the same species. Apples and pears and some varieties of cherry and plum need different pollen from a compatible variety, so you may have to buy more than one. Most fruit catalogues will list which varieties are compatible with each other. Finally, check with your fruit supplier that the rootstock of the plant is suitable for your site and how the tree will be grown.

Apples are some of the most popular fruits to grow and there is a huge number of varieties to choose from.

TRAINING A DIAGONAL CORDON

1 Set up three or four horizontal wires at 45 cm (18 in) intervals, securing them on posts driven into the ground. Plant maidens, or whips, (young, single-stemmed trees) so that they are 75 cm (30 in) apart and 20–25 cm (8–10 in) away from the wires. Plant the trees at an angle of 45° to the ground, making sure the graft union is well above the soil.

2 Each cordon needs a bamboo cane for support. Attach the cane to the wires, and use an adjustable plastic tie to secure the tree to the cane. After planting, prune side shoots that are more than 10 cm (4 in) long back to three buds. Do not prune the central leading shoot. Continue pruning as necessary to encourage compact growth along the main stem. (See also p. 226.)

TRAINING A YOUNG TREE

1 Choose a young tree that has three strong, well-balanced shoots. Plant and secure to a stake with an adjustable plastic tie. Prune back the leader to just above the strong shoots. Shorten each shoot by two-thirds. Cut to an outward-facing bud if the shoots are upright to encourage the tree into an open-centred shape.

2 The second winter (or if the tree is two years old), select about five well-spaced, strong branches to form the framework of the tree. Cut back each one by one-half to two-thirds their length, cutting to an outward-facing bud if possible. Any other shoots can be cut back to four buds. Remove any growth on the main stem that is below the selected branches.

TRAINING AN ESPALIER

1 Plant a maiden, or whip, (you will need horizontal wires as described for cordons opposite). The first winter after planting, cut it back to the point there are two buds, one on each side. The cut should be about 5 cm (2 in) above the first wire, since the shoots arising from these buds will create the first tier of the espalier.

2 In summer, tie the shoots that will form the first tier to canes at an angle of 45° to the ground. Tie the leading shoot to a vertical cane. At the end of the growing season, attach the canes with the shoots for the first tier to the lower wire. Cut back other shoots from the main stem to three leaves. Train the higher tiers in the same way. (See also p. 227.)

BUYING FRUIT TREES

For the greatest choice of varieties it is worth using a fruit specialist. They tend to sell young, bare-rooted trees that need some initial training; such trees are not only less expensive than the ready-trained container-grown ones but will establish more quickly. You may be offered one- or two-year-old trees or a "feathered maiden" (a one-year-old tree with side shoots ready for training). The types of rootstock a nursery uses will affect the vigour and final size of the tree, so ask which one is best for your situation. For example, very dwarf rootstocks sound tempting but they need top-quality soil and conditions.

Helpful hints

A sunny sheltered site and a moist, slightly acid soil are ideal for most fruit, but apples are more tolerant than other fruit trees. A sunny fence or wall provides a promising site for cordons or espaliers. Spring frosts can damage blossom, which reduces cropping, so site early-flowering trees away from frost pockets. When planting, keep the graft union well above ground or the value of the rootstock will be lost. Mulch the ground to keep it weed free and moist. Once the tree reaches flowering size, feed it each spring with a balanced fertilizer.

TRAINING AND PRUNING FRUIT TREES

YOU WILL NEED

Tree pruner with a
telescopic handle

Secateurs

SEE ALSO

Tree maintenance
See *Caring for trees,*
pp. 184–185

All kinds of fruit
See *Types of fruit growing,*
pp. 222–223

Cordons and espaliers
See *Growing fruit trees,*
pp. 224–225

The first two to three years after planting, you train and prune in order to form the framework of a fruit tree. After that, the aim of pruning is to stimulate flowering and fruiting. The overall shape of a fruit tree should be like a goblet with branches

This marvellous espalier, laden with ripe fruit, has been trained to form an arch over a path and create an elegant divide between a vegetable plot and flower garden.

growing upwards and outwards from an open centre. This shape allows in maximum sunlight to ripen the wood and fruit. Ideally, correct pruning of a young tree in the early years will have created this goblet shape, so you should not need to cut back the main branches of established trees very much. It is a different matter with the trained forms, which need to be pruned each year in summer to restrict their growth, stimulate fruiting and to maintain their desired shape.

The timing of this summer pruning is usually mid- to late summer: do not cut too early as there will be regrowth, which is a problem in frosty areas. Fruiting spurs may become congested and need thinning out, and this is done in winter. Most apple varieties produce their fruit on fruiting spurs along the stem, and the pruning method is detailed opposite. A few varieties produce fruit at the tips of shoots and these are pruned by having the tips of the leading shoots cut off, and one in three of the old side branches cut back to a young shoot or bud. If you know the variety of apple, you can find out its type by looking it up in a fruit catalogue; otherwise observe where the flowers and fruit are formed.

PRUNING A DIAGONAL CORDON

The first summer after planting a cordon fruit tree (see pp. 224–225), prune the side shoots that arise from the main stem back to three leaves above the basal cluster (the rosette of leaves at the base of a shoot). Prune any young side shoots that arise from the existing side shoots back to one leaf to encourage fruiting spurs to form. Tie the leading shoot to the bamboo cane. When the leading shoot reaches 15 cm (6 in) or so

above the top wire, cut it back in late spring. From now on, you should prune the cordon every year to leave just 1 cm (½ in) of the previous summer's growth.

Once a cordon is established, it will need pruning each summer. Cut back all the side shoots growing directly from the main stem to three leaves above the basal cluster. Cut back shoots arising from side shoots to one leaf.

Ideal for small spaces, cordons give good yields, but need attentive training and pruning.

PRUNING A SPUR-BEARING APPLE TREE

1 Freestanding apple trees are pruned in winter. Cut back the leading shoots on each branch: weak, thin shoots can be cut back by up to half their length; strong shoots by a quarter. Side shoots can also be cut back: weak ones to four buds; strong side shoots to six buds.

2 Overcrowded spurs need to be thinned out to improve fruit quality. Cut out the weakest shoots from each spur; the mass of shoots should be reduced by a third, leaving an open spur. Reduce the total number of spurs on each branch, removing any weak ones.

PRUNING STONE FRUITS

The stone fruits are plum, cherry, peach and apricot. Since these trees are more at risk from diseases such as canker and silver leaf than other fruit trees, they are not pruned in winter. Prune in the summer to remove any dead, diseased or congested wood.

PRUNING A PEAR TREE

Prune a pear tree in winter as you would a spur-bearing apple tree. You may need to take out old branches from the centre of the tree to keep the shape. In summer, prune back any growth with black or scorched foliage to below signs of infection. Disinfect the tools between and after cuts by dipping them in household bleach.

PRUNING AN ESPALIER

The second and third winter after planting an espaliered fruit tree (see pp. 224–225), continue to form tiers for each wire – that is, pruning the leading shoot just above the wire, making the cut just above a good bud. In summer, tie the resulting shoots on to canes and lower them on to the wires at the end of the growing season. The established tiers should now be producing their own vigorous side shoots, and these will need shortening in order to keep the plant's shape. In summer, prune the side shoots as detailed in the first stage of pruning cordons (see box opposite). Once the tree has as many tiers as you want, cut back its vertical leader each year, in late spring. To shorten the length of a tier, cut back its leading shoot, at the same time. From now on prune it each year to leave just 1 cm (½ in) of the previous summer's growth.

An espalier is a decorative and practical way of training fruit trees against a sunny wall.

GROWING SOFT FRUIT

Cane and bush fruit will produce crops for many years if you start with healthy, virus-free plants and give them some good basic care. These are long-term plants, so take some time to choose a suitable site and enrich the soil well before planting. A sunny, sheltered spot is preferred. Some soft fruits

The most popular of the cane fruits, raspberries have a two-year fruiting cycle. However, autumn raspberries, such as 'Heritage' above, will grow and fruit in the same year.

tolerate partial shade, but a frosty, windy site will not produce a large fruit yield unless you give the plants some shelter. The soil should be deep and fertile, moist in spring and summer yet well drained in winter. This can be achieved on most sites by digging in plenty of organic matter before planting, then mulching each year thereafter.

Cane fruit includes raspberries and blackberries, which are vigorous growers and are usually trained against supports. Summer-fruiting raspberries grown on post-and-wire supports take up little ground space and make an attractive screen. If you do not want to put up posts and wires, grow the autumn-fruiting raspberry 'Autumn Bliss'. This can be grown as a freestanding bush in a sheltered site – the fruiting canes do not need tying in to supports, they are simply cut back hard once they have fruited.

Blackberries can tolerate more shade than most fruit, so it is worth trying them against a lightly shaded fence at the bottom of the garden or against a shed. They and their hybrids can soon become unruly, but they can be trained (see Planting blackberries, opposite). The aim of training is to keep new and old canes separate and to prevent plants from rampaging along the ground.

PROTECTING FRUITS

Fruit needs protection from birds, otherwise they will strip the plant. Netting is the most effective way to keep birds off the fruit – you can simply drape bird netting over plants as the fruit ripens, but having a wood or metal framework that keeps the netting off the plants is much better. A temporary framework can be rigged up using bamboo canes propped up against wall or fence-trained fruit. For lower-growing fruit, use rows of wooden stakes or buy a modular metal frame and then drape the netting over it. Cover any sharp parts of the framework, using upturned plant pots and posts. If all your fruit is in one place, it is well worth making a fruit cage, which is like a netted room. It makes it easier to tend to the plants as well as providing shelter and improving cropping. Fruit cage kits with metal frames and plastic netting are available, or you can build your own from timber. It needs to be at least 2 m (6 ft 6 in) high, and designed so that the netting over the roof can be easily removed in winter to prevent snow from buckling the frame.

PLANTING RASPBERRY CANES

1 For a divider or screen, dig a trench 45 cm (18 in) wide, and add well-rotted organic matter to the bottom. Erect a 2-m (6 ft 6-in) post and wire fence with stout horizontal wires at 45-cm (18-in) intervals. Plant the canes in the trench at 45-cm (18-in) intervals. Cover the roots with soil and firm. Cut the canes to 23 cm (9 in). Water if the soil is dry.

2 In spring, sprinkle a general fertilizer, such as blood, fish and bone meal on the surrounding soil, then water it in if the soil is dry. Put down a 5-cm (2-in) layer of mulch, such as well-rotted manure, to keep down weeds and retain moisture in the soil. Water during dry spells.

3 Use garden string to tie in the canes; the canes should be vertical with 10 cm (5 in) between each cane. When the canes reach the top wire, bend them over and tie them in. Remove any suckers that emerge away from the row. You will get fruit the second summer after planting – net the plant to prevent birds eating the fruit (see box opposite).

4 As soon as the fruit has been picked, cut down those canes to ground level. New canes are tied in as replacements, keep them 10 cm (4 in) apart – if there are too many new canes, cut out the weaker ones.

PLANTING BLACKBERRIES

Set up a series of horizontal wires at regular intervals. Allow 3 m (9 ft) between plants, and cut back each plant to 23 cm (9 in), then follow step 2 for raspberries. Tie in new canes as they grow – spread out fruiting canes in a fan, keeping any new ones tied in to the centre. After harvesting, cut out old canes and spread the new ones into a fan.

Helpful hints

There are many varieties of each soft fruit, but most are not widely available from garden centres. Because these are long-term crops, it is worth seeking out a fruit specialist or ordering by mail order to get the best choice. For example, some varieties of blackberry are thornless and there are gooseberry varieties that show some resistance to mildew. Taste is important, so attend tastings and try different varieties. If you have the choice, always buy plants that are certified as virus-free – these will remain healthy for longer than plants that are not certified and which may contain viruses.

BUSH FRUITS

YOU WILL NEED

Secateurs

Spade

Organic matter

Wood for measuring

SEE ALSO

Other berries
See *Growing soft fruit,*
pp. 228–229

All kinds of strawberries
See *Growing strawberries,*
pp. 232–233

Maintaining grapes
See *Growing grapes,*
pp. 234–235

Soft fruit that can be grown as bushes includes all the currants (black, red and white), blueberries and gooseberries. Growing these plants as bushes is similar to growing any other flowering shrub. They will thrive in a sunny border but, for large crops, you need to grow rows of bushes in a

Even a single red currant bush will provide a worthwhile crop. They are such attractive plants that one would not be out of place in a shrub border or an ornamental garden.

dedicated fruit garden. These fruiting shrubs could last for a decade or more, so give them a reasonable amount of space – ideally each should have its own 1.5 x 1.5 m (5 x 5 ft) square, which also makes picking easier, but a space measuring 1.2 x 1.2 m (4 x 4 ft) is adequate. For smaller spaces, training red and white currants or gooseberries as vertical cordons is an option.

A position in full sun is best for all bush fruits, and essential for red and white currants and blueberries. Blackcurrants and gooseberries are worth a try in partial or dappled shade. Although the plants are hardy, avoid frost pockets and windy sites, or yields will be disappointing. A slightly acid soil is preferred by these fruits, but blueberries need a very acid soil – you can grow them in large tubs of peat-based, lime-free compost if your soil is not suitable.

As with all soft fruit, dig plenty of organic matter into the soil, mulch well and scatter a little general fertiliser around the plant each spring. All soft fruit is self-fertile, so only one variety of each type is needed, but several can be grown to spread the cropping period. Blueberries will crop more heavily if two varieties are able to cross-pollinate.

HARVESTING AND STORING FRUIT

During the summer months, soft fruits often crop at the same time and it is hard to keep up with picking and preserving. Grow only the amount of soft fruit you need and include varieties that crop earlier and later than normal to spread out the harvest. Dry evenings are the best time to harvest soft fruit, since the fruit soon rots if picked when wet. Collect it in shallow container

such as clean seed trays so that it doesn't get crushed. It is also worth picking off and disposing of any rotten or mouldy fruit. If it is left on the plants, the spores will probably spread to healthy fruit.

Raspberries should be picked while they are still firm, especially if you want to store them. Gently pull them off, leaving the core and stalk on the plant. Gooseberries can be

tricky to pick and need to be "topped and tailed" before using. You can spread the harvest by using the earliest fruit for cooking and leaving the later fruit to ripen for eating fresh. Blueberries should be picked only when they are really ripe and soft. Currants are best picked by the whole bunch (the strig), since they have skins that break easily if they are handled individually.

PLANTING BLACK CURRANTS

1 Plants can be bought all year round as container-grown plants or ordered as bare-rooted plants for late autumn or winter planting. Here a container-grown plant has been removed from the pot to show its well-formed roots. Any large roots encircling the pot can be trimmed with secateurs.

2 Dig a hole twice the size of the rootball. Mix the soil removed with a bucketful of well-rotted organic matter, then partly refill the hole with the enriched soil mixture. Use a piece of wood across the hole to check that the plant will be planted at the same level it was in its pot or 2.5 cm (1 in) below – bare-rooted plants will have a soil mark.

3 Fill in around the plant roots with the enriched planting mixture. Then firm the ground around the plant with your feet. This ensures that the plant roots make contact with soil rather than resting in an air pocket.

4 After planting, cut back all the shoots to 5 cm (2 in) above soil level. Alternatively, if you have put in a container-grown plant in spring or summer, do this the first autumn or winter after planting.

PLANTING GOOSEBERRIES

1 A gooseberry bush should have a short clear trunk (called a leg) with at least three branches rising from it. Red and white currants also have a leg, and are cultivated in the same way. Dig a large hole and enrich the soil as described for black currants. Plant the bush at the same level it was in its pot. Firm in well.

2 Cut each of the branches back by half their length after planting (or wait until the first dormant season). Cut to an outward-facing bud to encourage an open, goblet shape. The second and third winter, shorten all the new leading shoots by half their length. Remove any suckers or low branches trailing near the ground.

GROWING STRAWBERRIES

YOU WILL NEED

Strawberry planter or large container

Container compost

Garden compost

Garden rake

Fertilizer

Bird netting

Canes and plant pots

Bark chips or straw

Garden shears

Trowel

SEE ALSO

Other berries
See *Growing soft fruit,*
pp. 228–229

Gooseberries and currants
See *Bush fruits,*
pp. 230–231

Maintaining grapes
See *Growing grapes,*
pp. 234–235

Strawberries are a popular fruit that is quick to grow and crop – you can be picking your first fruit within a year of planting. However, they are not without their problems; they are prone to a number of soil pests and diseases. These tend to build up over the years and eventually the plants are affected by viruses. To get around this, strawberries are often grown in a bed for three or four years, which is then cleared and a new bed started somewhere else – such a regime fits in very well with a three- or four-year crop rotation in a vegetable plot.

An alternative is to grow strawberries in pots of compost. While yields are not high, they make good container plants and the fruit is often top quality, since it is held off the ground. Strawberry planters with planting pockets in the sides are available, but if you find these time-consuming to plant up and water try some ordinary pots instead.

Strawberries like a sunny site in a moist but well-drained soil. Most soils are suitable as long as you dig in plenty of well-rotted organic matter a month or so before planting. It is also important to plant in soil that has been thoroughly weeded – strawberry plants

are low growing, so weeding after planting is difficult. Strawberries are one of the few soft fruit that can cope with windy sites, but avoid ground where frost is slow to clear.

Strawberries are the perfect summer fruit and there are varieties to suit all tastes. They make good pot plants, so you can grow them on a patio as well as in a vegetable plot.

STRAWBERRIES IN CONTAINERS

1 Use a special strawberry planter or some pots 25 cm (10 in) in diameter filled with moist compost. Plant up with young pot-grown strawberry plants in the spring or summer. Position the planter or pots in a sunny place on the patio, and keep the compost moist. Rotate the containers every now and again so all the plants get equal amounts of light.

2 After flowering, tiny green fruits will start to form. Cover the containers with bird-netting draped over some canes (put upturned pots over the top for safety) – or put the planter or pots in a greenhouse or on a well-lit porch. Strawberries need to be watered well and fed with a liquid tomato feed once a week throughout the summer.

PLANTING OUT STRAWBERRIES

1 Clear the ground of perennial weeds and dig in garden compost or well-rotted manure a month before planting. A few days before planting, weed again and rake in a general fertilizer. Plant strawberry plants in rows, spacing them 45 cm (18 in) apart and leaving at least 75 cm (30 in) between rows.

2 Mulch the bed with a 5-cm (2-in) layer of bark chips or straw – this keeps the soil moist and the fruit clean. Feed the plants with tomato feed and protect the fruit from slugs and birds. Water the plants as the fruit begins to swell if the ground is dry. After harvesting, cut the foliage back to 10 cm (4 in) from the crown. Destroy the foliage and any straw.

3 Strawberry plants produce runners (horizontal stems with baby plants at the end). It is best to remove these as they grow, especially if space is limited. You can root a few from each plant into a pot – use a trowel to ease it up before cutting – but do not keep propagating from runners, because viruses will build up.

Helpful hints

Strawberries can be planted through a sheet mulch, such as woven polypropylene. This helps prevent weeds growing, keeps the soil moist and the fruit off the ground. When preparing the bed, give it a slight ridge so water will not collect under the fruit. Lay the sheet tightly over it and secure the edges in the ground. Cut crosses in the sheet, peel back the corners, and plant through. For a crop several weeks earlier than normal, cover early varieties with a cloche in late winter or early spring. Ventilate once flowering begins.

TYPES OF STRAWBERRY

It is well worth buying pot-grown plants from garden centres or plants that are grown in modules from mail-order seed companies or fruit specialists, rather than relying on propagating runners year after year (viruses can build up, which reduce cropping and cause the leaves to become streaked and mottled). When it comes to varieties, there is plenty of choice with new types being promoted each year. They are usually one of several standard types. Summer-fruiting strawberries are the largest group and include early and later varieties. For the first fruits under glass, choose a very early variety. This group includes heavy croppers used for making jam.

Perpetuals are so called because they crop over a long period (usually from midsummer to autumn). However, the yields at any one time are not large and these plants will often produce their best crops in the first year. Alpines are strains of the small wild strawberry and are not available in shops because they do not travel well. However, they are pretty and have plenty of flavour and perfume. The plants produce masses of small fruits and small white flowers. They make an attractive edging to a fruit or wild garden and tolerate shade. Alpines are usually grown from seed.

GROWING GRAPES

YOU WILL NEED

Finely pointed scissors

Training wires and posts

Spade

Bamboo canes

Secateurs

Saw

SEE ALSO

Other berries
See *Growing soft fruit,*
pp. 228–229

Gooseberries and
currants
See *Bush fruits,*
pp. 230–231

All kinds of strawberries
See *Growing strawberries,*
pp. 232–233

Grapes were one of the earliest fruits to be cultivated and they remain popular for both their fruits and their ornamental foliage. Before choosing a grape vine, you need to decide whether you want grapes for

Grapes will produce fruit only if they get plenty of warmth over the summer, so it is often worth growing them in a conservatory or a greenhouse if you live in a cold area.

winemaking or as dessert fruit since there are different varieties bred for each use. The training methods vary too. Here we have covered dessert grapes and have chosen just one of the easiest training methods (the rod-and-spur system) of the many available. If you want to grow grapes for winemaking, it is well worth getting a book dedicated to growing grapes in your particular climate so that you can choose an appropriate rootstock and training method.

Training and pruning are necessary to control the growth of the vine and to encourage fruiting. Grape vines are long lived so choose the variety wisely. They need plenty of space so you also need to consider carefully where to put them. Grapes are hardy plants but need a soil that is fertile and well drained, as well as long, warm summers to fruit well. Commercially, grapes are grown on freestanding posts and horizontal wires. This works well in gardens too, but they can also be grown against a warm wall or with the main stem poked through a hole in a greenhouse so the vine can be trained along the inside of the roof. Grapes make good conservatory plants, and can be used to cover a pergola or an arch.

THINNING AND HARVESTING

To improve the quality of grapes, use finely pointed scissors to remove one in every three or four fruits. When harvesting, cut off a section of the main stem using secateurs. Carry the grapes by the stem to preserve their bloom.

THINNING FOLIAGE

For the grapes to ripen, they need as much sun on them as possible. Using secateurs, cut away any leaves that are casting shade on the fruit, and cut the lead stalk where it leaves the stem.

PLANTING AND PRUNING VINES

1 In autumn or early winter, set up three horizontal wires at 45-cm (18-in) intervals, and plant the vine. In winter, cut back the leading shoot to a strong bud near the first wire and remove side shoots to one or two buds. In summer, tie the leader to a cane. Cut back side shoots to five leaves; if any of these shoots have side shoots, pinch back to one leaf.

2 The second winter, cut back the leading shoot to two-thirds of the summer growth. The side shoots will also need cutting back to one bud if growth is strong or to two buds if it is weak. In summer, cut back as in the previous summer and also pinch out any flower trusses.

3 The third winter, prune as you did the second winter. When the leading shoot has ripe wood up to the top wire, shorten it and from then on prune as if it were a side shoot. By spring, shoots will be developing at each spur so (with your finger and thumb) pinch out all but the strongest two. Later, the weaker one can be shortened.

4 Established vines have a vertical leading shoot and side shoots that spread horizontally along the wires. In summer, prune side shoots from the stem back to five leaves if they have no flower trusses, and those with trusses to two leaves beyond the last truss. Pinch out trusses to leave one per side shoot, and any shoots arising from side shoots.

5 In winter, cut back the leader on an established vine to a bud below the top wire. Untie the leader and lower on to one of the horizontal wires. Return to position and tie in when the buds break in spring. Also, prune side shoots arising from the main stem to one or two buds. Thin out any congested spurs by sawing off old sections.

ROUTINE CARE

Grape vines are pruned only in midwinter. At other times sap can bleed out of cuts. The summer "pruning" described above is actually pinching out very young growth between finger and thumb.

Grapes grown under glass need to be kept humid and well ventilated, and also may need to be hand-pollinated. Powdery mildew can be a problem for grapes grown both in- and outdoors. Keeping the vine watered well will help prevent the disease but, once it strikes, you may need to spray with a suitable systemic fungicide. Mulch the plant each spring with well-rotted manure.

GROWING CULINARY HERBS

YOU WILL NEED

String and pegs

Sharp sand

Organic matter

Slabs or bricks

Garden fork

Trowel

Old tin bucket for mint

SEE ALSO

All sorts of herbs
See *Herb gardens,*
pp. 238–39

Long-term use of herbs
See *Harvesting and storing*
herbs, pp. 240–241

Herbs were probably among the first plants to be cultivated. A herb bed has a long and honourable history from medieval monasteries to the modern window box.

Traditionally, herbs were grown in formal beds devoted exclusively to such plants. This is still a charming way to grow them, but they can also be planted in the flower garden as many have attractive flowers and foliage.

Many herbs, such as purple sage (*Salvia officinalis* 'Purpurascens'), variegated thyme (*Thymus vulgaris* 'Silver Posie') and frilly

purple basil (*Ocimum basilicum* 'Purple Ruffles'), have unusually coloured leaves. Although the flavours are slightly different, you can use these hybrids in the same way as the common types.

Generally a herb garden should be in full sun. Many herbs originated in the dry climate of the Mediterranean and they grow well in raised beds with good drainage. Parsley, mint and sorrel are the exceptions, preferring full shade, and marjoram, which likes semi-shade. To contain their roots, plant mint and lemon balm in a bucket with the bottom removed.

Most herbs are perennial, but some, such as dill, basil and coriander, are annuals and have to be sown each year. Parsley is difficult to germinate, so it is worth buying small plants from a garden centre. Often many seedlings are sown together in one pot; if so, divide them carefully and replant. It is a biennial, so sow each year to keep up the supply. August is the best time for this.

Chives increase rapidly; simply divide up the clump of bulbs, and plant each bulb in its new position.

Herbs are pretty plants in their own right and look good when mixed with other perennials such as lady's mantle and delphinium, as in this large bed of herbs and flowers.

HERB BOXES AND POTS

Although most herbs need dry, sunny conditions, parsley, sorrel and mint prefer some shade and moisture. A bright north-facing window box is ideal for them. It also has the advantage that you can keep an eye on the wandering roots of the mint, which can be very invasive. Alternatively, grow parsley in strawberry pots.

KEEPING IN TRIM

Herbs repay frequent use! Cut back thyme and sage in spring and rosemary after it flowers, as well as trimming them for use throughout the year. They do not grow from old wood. Marjoram, dill, fennel, parsley, basil, mint and bay can be pinched out as needed. Cut chives down to 2.5 cm (1 in) when using, to encourage new growth.

MAKING AN HERB BED

1 Dig over the plot carefully, removing weeds, and allow the soil to settle for a week or two. Mark out the bed with string, and set out the paths with paving slabs or bricks, laying these in on a bed of sand. Add compost to the planting squares and, for heavy soils, roughly rake in a spadeful of sharp sand per metre (yard).

2 In the least sunny part of your herb bed, position the parsley, mint and sorrel. They prefer shade and do not like dry soil. Incorporate some extra organic matter in this segment if necessary. Plant the mint in an old tin bucket with the bottom knocked out to curb its invasiveness, and then complete the planting of this square.

3 In the other segments, position the larger plants such as rosemary, sage and fennel. Give them plenty of room to spread out. Plant them, and then fill the spaces in between with smaller herbs such as tarragon, thyme and savoury.

4 A nice finishing touch is to edge the beds with chives. Carefully divide up a clump and plant each bulb in position.

5 When the rest of the planting is completed, plant the bay in the centre bed. The soil here should be deeply dug and well prepared, since a bay tree will grow happily for many years. You can keep it clipped to the size you want, and it makes a beautiful centrepiece. In cold regions, grow the bay in a container and move it indoors in winter.

Helpful hints

Work out what herbs you are likely to use most, and make sure you have good supplies of these, then experiment with other, more unusual ones. Try to grow them as near to the kitchen door as possible to make harvesting quicker and easier. Make a bed of culinary herbs and keep them separate, so that other plants are not accidentally used for cooking.

Many other plants have edible leaves that are fun to use in cooking. Nasturtium flowers, for example, can be used in salads and nettles for soup (but remember to use gloves when harvesting them).

HERB GARDENS

PLANTING SUGGESTIONS

Keep the culinary herbs separate from those with medicinal uses so that if you send someone out to pick a bunch of herbs, they cannot come back with anything inedible. Some of the medicinal herbs have very powerful effects and can be harmful if misused. Remember that a herb garden follows the principles of general garden layout, with structural plants such as bay or rosemary forming the backbone of the design, followed by permanent smaller shrubs such as sage. Keep a good balance of evergreen and deciduous herbs so that your herb garden looks good in winter too.

▶ SEED PRODUCERS
Blue-flowered borage and tall yellow fennel are two herbs to watch since they seed prolifically. Fennel is easy to pull out and remove, but the leaves of borage have tiny hairs which can irritate the skin.

Many people grow herbs for their poetic and historical associations, rather than for culinary and medicinal uses. They suit a variety of garden styles, ranging from a *potager*, or kitchen garden, to a rose garden. Plantings of herbs conjure up pictures of romantic meetings, of star-crossed lovers and maidens sighing over their baskets, gathering petals and herbs for nosegays or potpourri. Each plant had its own message: rosemary or forget-me-not for remembrance, and of course, the rose as a symbol of true love. This imaginative aspect can be emphasized in your design for a herb bed, using traditional, symmetrical patterns or a simple cartwheel layout. The design can be highlighted with box hedging and completed with a statue or standard bay tree as its focal point. Even a small herb garden, intended strictly for kitchen use and laid out in four squares, follows a centuries-old tradition and could be seen in monastery gardens during the early Middle Ages.

▲ HUES OF BLUE AND PURPLE
Here is a collection of herbs that includes purple sage, fennel and angelica, with the accent on blue tones. The colours of *Allium* and *Lavandula stoechas* are accentuated by a bright blue pot in the background.

▲ BOXED BEDS
These box-edged beds contain medicinal and culinary herbs. The yellow flowers of rue can be cut back hard to encourage the production of more blue-grey leaves.

◀ TRADITIONAL
This mass planting is reminiscent of an old-fashioned garden of "simples", which would have been cut down to preserve for winter and medicinal use.

▼ FORMAL USE
This highly stylized garden uses clipped box hedging and herbs such as French lavender and purple sage to contrast with its formal layout.

HARVESTING AND STORING HERBS

YOU WILL NEED

Metal racks, cardboard boxes, or brown paper

Assorted herbs

Fine muslin

Clear, airtight jars

Freezer bags or boxes (for freezing herbs)

Wine vinegar

Wax paper

Rose petals

Optional additions: pinks, acacia, jasmine, bay, lemon verbena, lemon balm, lavender

Potpourri spices

SEE ALSO

Herbs for cooking
See *Growing culinary herbs, pp. 236–237*

All kinds of herbs
See *Herb gardens, pp. 238–239*

Our ancestors used herbs every day for many household purposes – some for cooking, some for medicinal use, and others for strewing on the floor. Herbs also were used for posies, carried to ward off germs. Nowadays herbs are used mainly for cooking, although herbal remedies and cosmetics are increasingly popular again. Harvest lavender to use in small cushions and sachets to place among clothes and in airing cupboards. When you are trimming your herbs, use the

cuttings, especially those of strong aromatics like rosemary and cotton lavender (*Santolina*), to hang up or place in a bowl to scent a room. You can also make potpourri from rose petals, with added scent from herbs, flowers and spices.

Some herbs, such as bay, sage and thyme, can be used directly from the plant throughout the year. Others are more aromatic and flavourful before they set flowers. Most have to be harvested and stored if you are to enjoy herbs from your garden all year round.

Harvesting methods for herbs are based on drying or freezing; see opposite for simple instructions on how to preserve your herbs for use in the kitchen.

Herbs can also be used for making teas. The classic herbal tea is chamomile, but lemon balm, fennel, hyssop, sage, marjoram and mint are also good ingredients. Mints make refreshing teas either on their own, or added to a lemon tea and drunk ice cold. Balm and mint are best used fresh, but other teas can be made from dried herbs.

In this large, formal herb and kitchen garden, dainty white-flowered feverfew will seed itself and grow well even in dry, shady conditions; they also like an open, sunny aspect.

SAVING ROSE PETALS

Dry the flowers and herbs in a warm place, then mix the rose petals with a little salt and place in a jar. Screw the lid on tightly and leave for five days, stirring twice a day. After this, add the other dried flowers and herbs and the potpourri spices. Leave for three to four weeks, mixing occasionally.

HERBAL VINEGAR

Most herbs can be used for vinegar. You will need 90 ml (5 tbsp) of chopped herbs to 500 ml (1 pt) of vinegar (wine vinegar gives the best results). Put the herbs in a glass jar and pour warmed vinegar over them. Cover with wax paper and screw the lid on tightly. It will be ready after three weeks; strain out the herbs before use.

DRYING HERBS

1 Harvest leafy herbs, such as sage, thyme and tarragon, before they flower. Choose a dry, sunny day when their aromatic qualities are at their strongest, keep away from the sun or it will disperse their volatile oils. Pick them carefully, but don't mix them, or their perfumes will blend with each other. Sort the herbs, removing any bruised or yellowing leaves.

2 Lay herbs on metal racks (or brown paper or flat cardboard boxes), covered with a fine muslin, to allow the air to circulate. You will need a separate tray for each herb. Set it in a warm, dry place. (You may use the oven; keep the door open and see that the temperature doesn't rise above 32°C/90°F). If herbs are dried in the sun, they lose their flavour.

3 Turn the herbs daily, but avoid handling them as much as possible. They are ready when they are brittle but still green. Don't leave them until they are brown or the flavour will be much weaker.

4 Turn each bunch of herbs lightly between your fingers to separate out their stems and any unwanted pieces. Store the remaining herbs in clean, airtight jars.

FREEZING

One of the best ways to preserve the freshness of softer-leaved herbs such as basil, dill leaves, parsley, sorrel and mint is to freeze them – the flavour is far better than when these herbs are dried. Pack small bunches directly into freezer bags or boxes, and freeze them immediately after picking. They will last for up to six months.

Helpful hints

Pick lavender before the flower buds have fully opened. Tie up the stems with soft garden twine and hang them from a hook in a warm place to dry. Alternatively, they can be dried on trays in an airing cupboard or other warm area. When they are dry, remove the flowers from the stems and put them into lavender bags for scenting your clothes, in a bowl to add fragrance to your home, or gather about 10 shoots together and braid the stems with a purple satin ribbon. In cooking, lavender can be used with chicken, or to flavour fruit dishes. It tastes like rosemary, but is a little more aromatic.

SEASONAL TASKS FOR EARLY TO MID-SPRING

SEE ALSO

Routine care: late spring
See *Seasonal tasks for late spring, pp. 244–245*

Routine care: summer
See *Seasonal tasks for summer, pp. 246–247*

Routine care: autumn and winter
See *Seasonal tasks for autumn and winter, pp. 248–249*

Every season brings with it a new display of plants to enjoy – and a new group of tasks to carry out. Below are some reminders of the most crucial tasks you need to be doing in early and mid-spring. This is when the garden starts into growth, and you need to clear away the debris of winter and get ready for the year ahead. But do not be tempted to do too much too soon – most pruning, planting and sowing should be done once growth has gathered pace. Take account, too, of the local climate; gardeners in cold areas may have to delay tasks for a few weeks, while those in warmer areas may be able to start them earlier.

You know it is spring when the bulbs yield up their flowers and the trees burst into blossom, signalling that it is time to tackle any outdoor sowing, pruning and planting tasks.

TASKS AROUND THE GARDEN IN EARLY TO MID-SPRING

DECORATIVE PLANTINGS	LAWNS	EDIBLE GARDEN	UNDERCOVER	MAINTENANCE
• Clear the borders of dead foliage.	• Keep off the lawn when the grass is wet or frozen.	• Prune any fruit not yet tackled.	• Start off dahlias, begonias, and other tubers in pots.	• Clean the patio before the containers are put out. Use a water-pressure sprayer to remove stains from the patio effectively without using chemicals.
• Weed borders and remove insulation around borderline hardy plants.	• Repair any broken lawn edges during mild dry spells.	• Tie in new growth, especially on wall-trained fruit.	• Start overwintered tender perennials, such as fuchsias, into growth. Remove any dead or diseased foliage, then place the plants in a light, warm place (about 10°C/50°F) and water them gently.	
• In mid-spring, apply a 5–cm (2–in) layer of mulch to areas of bare earth. This will keep down weeds and help to conserve moisture.	• In mid-spring, re-seed bare patches. Protect seed from birds by netting it securely.	• Mulch fruit trees and soft fruit with well-rotted manure or garden compost.		• Check long-term container plants. If they have roots coming out of the drainage holes, transplant them into a bigger pot.
• Renovate old flower beds by lifting and dividing mature perennials.	• Mow the lawn, setting the blades high for the first couple of cuts.	• Remove weeds from vegetable areas and dig in manure.	• Move young plants into bigger pots as they grow.	• As container plants start into growth, increase watering and start feeding four weeks after repotting.
• Apply fertilizer if garden soil is poor. Use organic feeds, such as well-rotted manure, to improve the soil.	• Inspect the lawn for weeds and moss, small patches can be dealt with by hand or with a spot weeder.	• Start sowing vegetable seed indoors and outdoors.	• Ventilate the greenhouse during warm spells but remember to close windows and vents on cold nights.	
		• Start off seed potatoes indoors; plant out early varieties when they start to sprout.		

Give some attention to the lawn in spring, reseeding bare patches and repairing any damaged edges. This is also the time for the first mowing of the year.

TECHNIQUES FOR EARLY TO MID-SPRING

PRUNING	WEEDING AND WATERING	CONTROLLING SLUGS	SEED SOWING	PLANTING
• Many shrubs and climbers are pruned in early spring, including clematis plants that flower in late summer or in autumn. • Check plants for damage – young growth often catches the frost – and cut back to healthy wood. • Cut out any all-green shoots on variegated plants. • Cut back shrubs, such as *Buddleja davidii*, that flower on shoots produced in the current year.	• Remove weeds as soon as they appear. Tiny annual seedlings can be removed by hand. Hoe over large areas – choose a warm, windy day and the seedlings will quickly shrivel up. Dig out dandelions and other perennials, removing as much root as you can. • Automatic watering systems and water butts are useful if you have a lot of containers to water, but they need setting up in advance.	• When new shoots emerge or young plants are put into the ground, slugs will become a problem. Use a barrier to keep them away, or apply a slug control.	• Check that seeds saved from last year are still viable: line a plastic box with a double layer of damp kitchen paper; add a pinch of seed, put a lid on the box and keep in a warm room. Check after two weeks; if the seeds have not germinated, throw them away. • From mid-spring sow outdoors, sowing in rows at least a hoe's width apart to make weeding easier.	• Any hardy plant can be planted now if the soil is workable. • If you want to plant a flower border, buy your herbaceous perennials now when they are sold in small pots; they will cost more later on.

SEASONAL TASKS FOR LATE SPRING

SEE ALSO

Routine care: early to mid-spring
See *Seasonal tasks for early to mid-spring,* pp. 242–243

Routine care: summer
See *Seasonal tasks for summer,* pp. 246–247

Routine care: autumn and winter
See *Seasonal tasks for autumn and winter,* pp. 248–249

This is a busy time in the garden, and the hours you spend now will be amply rewarded later in the year. There is plenty of general maintenance that needs doing on flower beds. Spring bedding comes to an end and summer bedding needs planting out, while lawns require regular mowing from now on. This is an important time in the greenhouse, and cold frames come in handy for helping tender plants grown under cover to get used to outdoor conditions. All new plants and cuttings need particular attention if the majority of them are to survive – and you need to watch out for pests. Hardy plants should be planted out as soon as possible, so they can start establishing their root systems. As the weather is warming up, and many plants are producing growth, this is a critical time for watering.

It is difficult to keep away from the garden in late spring – not only are there plenty of jobs that keep you busy, but borders are filled with some of the most appealing displays.

TASKS AROUND THE GARDEN IN LATE SPRING

DECORATIVE PLANTINGS	LAWNS	EDIBLE GARDEN	UNDERCOVER	MAINTENANCE
• Discard most spring bedding after flowering.	• Mow the lawn each week, reducing the cutting height to 2 cm (¾ in).	• Make sure all fruit plants are mulched and watered well.	• Harden off seedlings started indoors. Place them outside in a shady, sheltered area for 20 minutes the first day, then increase the time daily over a 10-to-14-day period before transferring outdoors.	• Newly planted subjects and plants in containers need regular watering.
• For tulips, pinch off the top of the flower stems; leave the foliage to feed the plants for good flowers next year.	• Mix grass clippings with drier material before composting.	• Net strawberries before they ripen.		• Water newly sown lawns or new turf with a sprinkler until the roots have established. Existing lawns should not need watering.
• Keep polyanthus flowering well by lifting, dividing and replanting healthy sections every two years.	• Apply a lawn feed, or a lawn "weed and feed" if there are too many weeds to take out by hand.	• To reduce maggots in apples in autumn, hang pheromone traps in apple trees.	• Indoor tomatoes should be planted now if you have not yet done so; plant out outdoor tomatoes as soon as any danger of frost has passed.	
• Fork in fertilizer before planting summer bedding.	• Do not mow lawns with naturalized bulbs until six weeks after the bulbs have flowered.	• Continue to sow vegetables. Sow salads little and often for a constant supply.		• Watch out for pests on young growth and act promptly. Alternatives to chemical sprays include picking pests off by hand or directing a jet of water at them.
• Spray roses which are prone to fungal diseases with a fungicide.		• Protect carrots and brassicas, which are prone to flying pests, with a crop cover of fine plastic mesh.		

Late spring flowerers, including small violas and charming bleeding heart (Dicentra), bring a delicate touch to this subtle border.

TECHNIQUES FOR LATE SPRING

SOWING	PRUNING	SUPPORT AND TYING IN	PLANTING	PLANTING AQUATICS
• Finish sowing any hardy annuals; most will still flower this year. • Check the packets of half-hardy annuals, since many can be sown outside now. • Once the seedlings have emerged, keep weeds down by hand weeding or hoeing. • Thin out seedlings to their final spacings; it is easier to do this in moist soil.	• From mid- or late spring, prune young specimens of grey or silver-leaved shrubs like cotton lavender, wormwood and lavender so that they keep their foliage colour and shape. • Cut out one stem in three from spring-flowering shrubs, choosing any stems that look misshapen, diseased or old.	• Border flowers that flop over in summer should have their supports put in place well before they are needed, when the foliage is only 30 cm (12 in) high. • Cover the tops of canes or sticks with upturned flowerpots to protect your eyes from injury. • As climbers and wall shrubs grow, tie them to the supports with raffia in a loose figure of eight.	• Plant up container plants early and keep them in a frost-free place. They may be too small for the container now, but the extra space will give them room to grow, and large containers are easier to water than lots of small pots. • Spring weather can be unpredictable; if it turns cold, give tender plants a liquid feed to avoid a check to their growth.	• Early summer is a good time to buy aquatic plants, such as water lilies. Check that the variety is hardy if you want to leave it out all year and make sure that it is not too vigorous for your size of pond. • Inspect aquatic plants for blanket weed and pests before adding them to the pond.

SEASONAL TASKS FOR SUMMER

SEE ALSO

Routine care: early to mid-spring
See *Seasonal tasks for early to mid-spring,* pp. 242–243

Routine care: late spring
See *Seasonal tasks for late spring,* pp. 244–245

Routine care: autumn and winter
See *Seasonal tasks for autumn and winter,* pp. 248–249

This is the season to enjoy all the hard work you have put into the garden through the year. As well as sitting and admiring the garden, now is the time to reap the harvest from crops, since fruits and vegetables will be approaching their peak. Harvest repeat croppers, such as beans, tomatoes and soft fruit, frequently to keep them producing well. Watering is one of the most crucial tasks at this time of year, particularly for container, flowering and cropping plants. Other key jobs include regular feeding, checking plants closely for pests and diseases, and taking cuttings. As always, the work put in now will pay you dividends in the seasons that follow.

Few things beat the pleasure of eating crops you have grown and nurtured yourself. Here, an informal planting of herbs, onions, beans and lettuces combines practicality and beauty.

TASKS AROUND THE GARDEN IN SUMMER

DECORATIVE PLANTINGS	LAWNS	EDIBLE GARDEN	UNDERCOVER	MAINTENANCE
• In early summer, plant out any remaining tender plants. Water well. • Sow biennials in early to midsummer for colour next spring. • Pinch out the growing tips of young wall flowers to make the plants bushy. • Give container-grown, acid-loving evergreens, such as azaleas and camellias, plenty of water to fatten up flower buds for next spring.	• Continue to cut the grass if it is growing. If growth slows because of a dry spell, take less off by adjusting the cutting height of the mower. • Water newly laid or sown lawns. Established lawns should not be watered even if they turn brown. • Late summer to early autumn is a good time to sow grass seed, so prepare the ground well a few weeks before.	• Net fruit and pick when ripe. • Fruit cordons can be summer pruned in midsummer. • After strawberries have cropped, cut the foliage back. Plants more than three years old may need to be replaced. • Water tender crops that have been planted out. • Water leafy crops or they will be tough. Water peas and beans when they start to swell.	• Ventilate and damp down the greenhouse regularly. • Pinch out side shoots from cordon tomatoes but not from bush types. • Feed tomatoes as soon as fruits form and continue every week or two as directed on the fertilizer packet. • Move houseplants outside during the day; put them in a shaded spot for increasing amounts of time each day.	• Give plants in containers a liquid feed every week or so; use a balanced feed for foliage plants and a tomato feed for flowering or fruiting plants. • Watch out for fungal diseases. Some, such as powdery mildew, take hold after dry spells; others, such as grey mould, spread after heavy rain. • It is worth spraying tomato and potato crops against blight.

There is no need for the vegetable garden to look drab – liven it up with a few flowering plants such as colourful dahlias.

TECHNIQUES FOR SUMMER

HARVESTING	TAKING CUTTINGS	DEADHEADING	PRUNING	LATE SOWING
• As well as summer vegetable and fruit picking, pick herbs for preserving while they are still at their peak.	• Cuttings of many types of plant can be taken over the summer, for example, pelargonium, hebe, and escallonia.	• Most flowering plants are worth deadheading to encourage additional flower production.	• If you see suckers, trace them back to where they emerge from the plant and remove them.	• Sow hardy flowers and some vegetables outdoors in late summer to early autumn. They will crop earlier than the same variety sown in the spring.
• Harvest seeds from plants when ripe.	• Pot up cuttings individually once they have rooted.	• Deadhead repeat-flowering roses to keep more flowers coming, but leave alone any varieties grown for their hips.	• Prune spring-flowering shrubs that bloom on one-year-old wood, such as lilacs and azaleas, within a month after the end of flowering.	• In cold or wet areas, protect the seedlings with a cloche.
• Some seed can be sown fresh in late summer to early autumn, or seed can be dried and stored in a cool, dry place until the following spring.			• Prune plants that flower in late spring, such as brooms, in early summer, and early-summer shrubs, such as mock orange and rock roses, in mid- to late summer.	• Seed can also be sown in small pots and kept in a cold frame, porch or cold greenhouse.

SEASONAL TASKS FOR AUTUMN

SEE ALSO

Routine care: early to mid-spring
See *Seasonal tasks for early to mid-spring,* pp. 242–243

Routine care: late spring
See *Seasonal tasks for late spring,* pp. 244–245

Routine care: summer
See *Seasonal tasks for summer,* pp. 246–247

This is when crops yield up the remaining harvest, and shrubs and trees give late colour as the garden starts to slow down. The soil is still warm, so this is a good time to plant large hardy subjects, such as trees, shrubs and perennials, giving them a chance to establish themselves before spring. Spring-flowering bulbs can also be planted now. Most maintenance is concerned with tidying up fallen leaves and plant debris, clearing out summer pots (and filling them with winter bedding) and repairing and relaying lawns.

The vibrant colours of foliage in autumn more than make up for the colder nights. Fallen leaves can be used for leaf mould. Leave some piles as hibernation sites.

TASKS AROUND THE GARDEN IN AUTUMN

DECORATIVE PLANTINGS	LAWNS	EDIBLE GARDEN	UNDERCOVER	MAINTENANCE
• Clear bedding, and leave or cut back perennials. • Plant out bulbs for next spring. • Insulate borderline hardy plants.	• Create a new lawn using grass seed or turf in early autumn. • Repair or renovate existing lawns if they have suffered over the summer.	• Harvest remaining crops, and clear beds. • Plant and prune fruit trees and bushes. • Lift potatoes and store in a cool, dark, frost-free place.	• Clear the greenhouse of tomatoes and clean thoroughly. • Bring in tender plants before the first frosts. • Cover cold frames with carpet at night.	• Before storms, check that ties on trees, wall shrubs and standard roses are secure but not tight.

TECHNIQUES FOR AUTUMN

PLANTING	TAKING CUTTINGS	SHREDDING	PROTECTING ROOTS	PLANTING CONTAINERS
• Plant evergreens by early autumn or wait until spring. • Deciduous plants can be planted after leaf fall. • Firm new plantings if they have lifted out after frost.	• Take cuttings of deciduous shrubs, using pencil-thick stems that have grown this year. • Root cuttings in a sheltered garden or use a growing bag or pot of damp sand.	• Use a shredder to chop up prunings; this will speed up composting. Let prunings dry out first; sappy growth may jam the machine.	• Bring small pots under cover when the weather is bad. • Insulate larger containers with bubble wrap, hessian or garden fleece; even hardy plants may die if their roots freeze up.	• Reuse empty summer pots by filling them with mixtures of ivy, winter-flowering heather and ornamental cabbage. • Plant bulbs, such as tulips, small daffodil varieties and bulbous irises, in pots for spring colour.

SEASONAL TASKS FOR WINTER

SEE ALSO

The edible garden
See *Training and pruning fruit trees, pp. 226–227*

Looking after the garden
See *Weather protection, pp. 174–175*
See *Pruning, cutting and harvesting, pp. 180–181*
See *Pruning shrubs, pp. 182–183*

Once the garden has been put to bed, very little regular plant care has to take place, although fruit trees need to be pruned, and you need to protect plants from strong winds, heavy snowfall or icy conditions. Make the most of any dry warm days to get maintenance jobs, such as cleaning your tools and digging over the vegetable plot, out of the way before the advent of spring. In wet or cold weather, you can use the extra time you have to plan ahead for the coming year.

The cold weather signals rest time for most plants – and for the gardener – but it is worth creating a winter border that can be seen from within the warm confines of the house.

TASKS AROUND THE GARDEN IN WINTER

DECORATIVE PLANTINGS	LAWNS	EDIBLE GARDEN	UNDERCOVER	MAINTENANCE
• Move pots of winter-hardy bedding to shelter in high winds or very cold spells.	• Keep off the grass when the ground is very wet or frozen. Clean and service the lawn mower.	• Prune fruit trees and bushes. • Dig over the vegetable plot.	• If the temperature dips below –5°C (23°F), place a cloche or a double layer of garden fleece over vulnerable plants.	• Clean tools, pots and storage areas. Make repairs to walls now because climbers are dormant and access is easier.

TECHNIQUES FOR WINTER

PLANTING	COMPOSTING	PRUNING	WEATHER PROTECTION	FORCING AND STORING
• Unpack bare-rooted plants straight away. Plant if the weather is mild, but if the soil is frozen or very wet, pot them up or heel them in temporarily. • Use your foot to firm in plantings that have been lifted out of the ground by frost.	• Turn over the compost heap on a sunny winter day.	• Prune wisteria and other vines in midwinter. • In late winter to early spring, prune summer-flowering deciduous shrubs, such as lilac and buddleja.	• Brush snow off tops of hedges and ornamental conifers promptly; otherwise the weight of the snow may cause the branches to break. • If ice forms on the pond, place a pan of hot water on the ice to melt a hole in it.	• Blanch rhubarb for an early crop. • Check stored produce regularly for signs of rotting.

INDEX

ACKNOWLEDGMENTS

If the publishers have unwittingly infringed copyright in any illustration reproduced, they would pay an appropriate fee on being satisfied to the owner's title.

Photographic credits
t=top; b=bottom; r=right; l=left; c=center

All photographs by Steven Wooster except pages 22 David Jordan, 46/47 Graham Rae, 48 br Ron Sutherland, 49 Steve Gorton, 51 Chas Wilder, 52/53 Graham Rae, 54 bl & br Steve Gorton, 55 Steve Gorton, 56/57 Alistair Hughes, 63 Steve Gorton, 64 cr Liz Eddison, 65 Chas Wilder, 101 tr Liz Eddison, 137 tr Liz Eddison, 137 bl Brigitte Thomas/The Garden Picture Library, 140 JS Sira/The Garden Picture Library, 141 tr Clive Nichols/The Garden Picture Library, 141 bl Joanne Pavia/The Garden Picture Library, 154 bc Chas Wilder, 155 tc Chas Wilder, 170 br Andrew Lawson, 172/173 David Jordan, 175 Steve Gorton, 178 bl Harry Smith, 178 br Peter McHoy, 179 tl Harry Smith, 179 tr & tc Peter McHoy, 179 cl Jane Legate/The Garden Picture Library, 179 bl David Askham/The Garden Picture Library, 182 bl & br Steve Gorton, 183 Steve Gorton, 201 tl, tr, ml & mr Adrian Weinbrecht, 202 Howard Rice/The Garden Picture Library, 204 c Jerry Harpur, 214 Liz Dobbs, 215 cr Liz Dobbs, 216 c Jerry Harpur, 216 bl & br Steve Gorton, 217 tl & tr Liz Dobbs, 217 cl & cr Steve Gorton, 217 br David Jordan, 218 cr & bl Steve Gorton, 219 cl,cr & bl Steve Gorton, 220 cr John Glover/The Garden Picture Library, 220 br & bl Steve Gorton, 221 tr Harry Smith, 221 cl, cr & bl Steve Gorton, 221 br John Glover/The Garden Picture Library,
222 bl Clive Nichols, 223 tl & br John Glover, 223 bl Mayer/Le Scanff/The Garden Picture Library, 224 bl & br Steve Gorton, 225 Steve Gorton, 226 br Harry Smith, 227 tl, tr, cl & cr Steve Gorton, 227 br Harry Smith, 228 Harry Smith, 229 tl,tr,cl & cr Steve Gorton, 229 bl Peter McHoy, 230 Harry Smith, 231 tr, tl, cl & cr Peter McHoy, 231 bl & br Harry Smith, 232 bl & br Chris Linton, 233 tl & tr Chris Linton, 234 c Clive Nichols, 234 bl & br Steve Gorton, 235 Steve Gorton, 242 Sunniva Harte/The Garden Picture Library, 243 Nigel Francis/The Garden Picture Library, 244 Mark Bolton/The Garden Picture Library, 245 Ron Evans/The Garden Picture Library, 246 Juliette Wade/The Garden Picture Library, 247 Ron Sutherland/The Garden Picture Library, 248 Brigitte Thomas/The Garden Picture Library, 249 Howard Rice/The Garden Picture Library.

Illustration credits
Karen Gavin pp. 24/25
Vanessa Luss pp. 100/101

Acknowledgments
Equipment: Compost bin supplied by The Recycle Works Ltd p. 97; Porta-kneel supplied by NBS Sports & Leisure p. 143; lawnmowers supplied by Atco-Qualcast Ltd, Suffolk; DekBlok and LokPost supplied by Supreme Concrete Ltd pp. 34–35; and NeverBend range of garden tools supplied by Spear and Jackson.

Thanks to Country Gardens, Tring, Herts; Oliver Blacklock; Joe Gordon; John Kelly; Rob Law; Michael Spilling; Tim Stansfield; Suzanne Tuhrim; Paul Watson; and Sally Wilton.